CHAMPION CATS OF THE WORLD

Contributors

A. A. DAMSTEEG
International Cat Judge, Netherlands

E. VON EYTZINGER
International Cat Judge, Fédération
Internationale Féline d'Europe

EDNA FIELD
Cat Fanciers' Assoc. Inc. Board of Directors, United States of America.
Official, Long-Hair Cat Club of Canada. All-breed Judge, United States and Canada.

RICHARD H. GEBHARDT
Cat Fanciers' Assoc. Inc. President, United States of America.
International All-breed Judge

ÅSE HAUGEN
International Cat Judge, Norway. Official, Rasekattclubben, Norway

P. HOLLENSTEIN
President, Féline Fédération Suisse. Senior Official, Fédération Internationale Féline d'Europe.
International Cat Judge

BESS HIGUCHI
Liaison Officer, Tokyo, Japan, to the Cat Fanciers' Assoc. Inc., United States.
Cat Judge in Japan

M. RAVEL
Founder President, Fédération Internationale Féline d'Europe.
Secretary, Fédération Féline Française. Secretary-General, Cat Club de Paris

Assistance received from

L. DEKESEL
Secretary/Treasurer, De Vrienden der Kat, Belgium

B. KASTEGREN-REMBORN
Secretary-General, Fédération Internationale Féline d'Europe. Official, Swedish Cat Club

M. LOCHET
President, Union des Associations Félines de France

LA BARONNE DE SAINT PALAIS
President, Cercle Félin de Paris

M. SANDIKÇIOĞLU
Professor of Zoology, Ankara University, Turkey

CHAMPION
CATS
OF THE WORLD

CATHERINE ING
MA DPhil

GRACE POND
FZS

photographs by

SALLY ANNE
THOMPSON

GEORGE G. HARRAP
& CO. LTD

London   Toronto   Wellington   Sydney

ACKNOWLEDGMENTS

The authors would like to express their thanks and appreciation to their friends throughout the Cat Fancy for all the help and encouragement they received, and particularly to Mrs E. Aitken, Prof. C.-A. Bodalsen, Miss D. Collins, Mrs A. E. Davies, Mr N. C. Dexter, Mrs K. K. Dyson, Mrs N. Hardy, Mrs D. Hindley, Mrs P. Hughes, Miss S. Hussain, Miss N. O'Faolain, the Rev. L. M. Styler, Mrs E. Towe, and Mrs E. Watson. Grateful thanks are also due to Liberty and Co. Ltd and Sanderson Fabrics for generously providing furnishings and other material used as backgrounds in a number of the photographs

First published in Great Britain 1972
by GEORGE G. HARRAP & CO. LTD
182–184 High Holborn, London, W.C.1
Text © *Catherine Ing and Grace Pond* 1972
Photographs © *Sally Anne Thompson* 1972
ISBN 0 245 50623 3

Composed in Bembo type
Made and printed in Great Britain by
William Clowes & Sons, Limited, London, Beccles and Colchester

CONTENTS

LIST OF BREEDS

References to pages in the text are given in roman type.
Numbers of illustrations are given in italics.

6

FOREIGN SHORT-HAIRED VARIETIES *(excluding Siamese)*

SIAMESE VARIETIES

GLOSSARY OF TERMS

Blaze. Contrasting coloured stripe or mark running from forehead to nose.

Brindling. Wrongly coloured hairs mixed in with those of correct colour.

British. Certain varieties of short-haired cats with roundish heads.

Brush. The short, full tail of a long-haired cat.

Butterfly Markings. Pattern of markings forming the shape of a butterfly on the shoulders of Tabbies.

Calling. The sounds or noise made by a female cat when in season.

Challenge Certificate. A card given to the winner of an adult open breed class. Three such wins given by three different judges at three shows entitle a cat to be called a Champion.

Characteristics. Distinguishing traits as in the standard of points.

Cobby. Short, sturdy, and compact body shape.

Coarse. Harsh and thickish coat texture.

Cross-bred. A cat produced by crossing one pedigree variety with another.

Dense. Thick, close coat.

Frill. Longer hair around the neck, usually brushed up to form a frame to the face. Also referred to as a ruff.

Foreign. Certain varieties of short-haired cats with long, lithe lines.

Gestation. The period of time that cats carry kittens from conception to birth, approximately 63–65 days.

Hot. Used to describe the incorrect reddish tinge seen in the coats of some Cream cats.

Inter-breeding. The mating of cats closely related—*e.g.*, brother to sister.

Intermingled. A coat of two coloured hairs mingled together—*e.g.*, Blue-Cream in Britain.

Kink. A bend in or thickening of a joint in the tail.

Kitten. A cat before the age of nine months in Britain, eight months in the United States.

Mask. Dark colouring on the face, as in Siamese cats.

Neutering. The castrating of a male kitten or cat.

Oriental. The almond eye shape of Foreign short-haired cats.

Outcross. The mating of one cat with another of an entirely different strain to introduce new blood.

Patched. A coat with a patched effect, as in the Tortoiseshells and Whites.

Pedigree. Having at least three generations of pure breeding.

Pencillings. Delicate markings on the faces of Tabbies.

Points. The darker colour seen on the face, paws, and tail of some cats. Also the marks given for the required characteristics in the set standard.

Prefix. Registered cattery name preceding the name of cats bred in that cattery.

Queen. A female cat used for breeding.

Ruff—see *Frill.*

Self-coloured. A cat with a coat of the same colour all over, without markings.

Spaying. The removing of the ovaries of a female cat.

Standard. The set pattern of characteristics required for each variety and for which one hundred points are given.

Snub. The short, flat noses seen in some long-haired varieties.

Stud. A male cat used for breeding.

Ticking. Contrasting colouring appearing on the tip or in the form of a band on each hair of the coat.

Tufts. Hair growing from the ears or from between the toes.

Type. Characteristic.

Wedge. The shape of head found in the Foreign varieties.

Whip. A long, thin, and tapering tail.

1 ORANGE-EYED WHITE LONGHAIR

2   ORANGE-EYED WHITE LONGHAIR

3   BLUE-EYED WHITE LONGHAIR

4   ORANGE-EYED WHITE LONGHAIR

5   ORANGE-EYED WHITE LONGHAIR

THE CAT

INTRODUCTION

The cat is, in many countries, at once the commonest and the most mysterious of all domestic animals.

It is certainly common. Wherever cats are kept, either as pets or as hunters to keep down rats and mice, there also they swarm. As a licence is not required to keep a cat in any modern country, no census can be attempted. Any observant person, however, must have noted the enormous numbers that haunt farms and alleys, houses and gardens, factories and ships. Though many, and in some countries most, of these are strays or 'gone wild', still, if they are of the same species, they remain technically 'domestic cats'. The millions in the world are beyond human computation, and there is no lack of material for observation and study.

Nevertheless, cats remain mysterious. This is partly because their history is obscure. We should not be surprised by this, since early recorders lacked the means of scientific examination; and if they had had these means, they might still not have told us much of what we should like to know. Even modern scientific observation has failed to discover the relationship between the domestic cat (late Latin *felis*, from *feles* or *faeles, domesticus*) and the indigenous British wild cat (*felis catus*) still to be found in the Highlands of Scotland. Physiologically they are very similar, though *felis catus* is usually slightly larger, and they can mate together, but nobody has ever been able to tame *felis catus*, one of the most ferocious of animals, and he is certainly not *domesticus*. If such uncertainty can prevail today, the obscurity of early records and references in various countries is natural. Attempts at distinguishing breeds were hardly made before the first cat show at the Crystal Palace in 1871, and breeders still face difficulties. As we shall see, obscurity is typical of the lore of the cat. To uncertainty about its true history, moreover, we have to add the fact that, from the earliest to the latest times, the history has been encrusted with myth, legend, and superstition.

This last fact is probably a result of the more fundamental reason for the mysteriousness of the cat: qualities apparently discrepant and contradictory inherent in the animal itself, and to some degree present in all members of the race, whatever the variations between breeds and individuals. They are qualities which arouse endless interest in this beautiful

9

and intelligent animal, and cause it to be at once among the most deeply loved, and certainly the most deeply disliked, of domestic animals. It has one very strange and sad distinction: alone among domestic animals it can cause a peculiar horror. Sufferers from aileurophobia experience in the presence of a cat, even when they cannot see it, feelings of distress quite distinct from the symptoms of allergy, and from simple fear and dislike. They may even like a cat at a distance!

The cat is loving and ferocious. It is a tender and careful parent and an implacable enemy. It is usually hardy, but fastidious about its comforts. It loves routine, but will suddenly completely change its habits. It is cautious and courageous, indolent and athletic. It may play like a kitten throughout a life of twenty years, but it is always capable of stern concentration on a job of hunting. It is a carnivore with a wide-ranging taste for vegetables, and nobody can tell how it acquired its liking for fish and milk. It can be an exhibitionist, and it has a strong feeling for privacy. It is prepared to sponge on human beings, and also to 'go wild'. It is highly intelligent and often obstinate. However physically dependent it may be, it retains always some independence of character. It will sometimes let itself die (of starvation) on the onset of illness, but it is singularly tenacious of life under the most unpromising conditions.

To sympathetic and hostile observers alike, the cat's tenacity in living is its most obvious characteristic, giving rise to the proverbial idea of its 'nine lives'. Some of its 'lives' it certainly owes to its marvellous muscular and nervous organization. While it is untrue that a cat "always falls on its feet", it is true that it can achieve astonishing leaps, involving twists and landings that would make the fortune of a human acrobat. It can thus save itself from many dangers. Because of the shape and direction of its claws, it finds it easier to climb up than down, and one may see it marooned twenty feet up in the boughs of a tree rocked by a high wind. Just when one has decided that the only hope is to call the fire brigade, the cat wriggles, takes off from an impossible position, turns in the air, and lands on the top of a wall three inches wide. This muscular control and judgment save it as prey, and serve it as hunter. Being small, the cat has depended for survival on speed and caution, as well as on skill and claws. It uses its speed and skill to escape enemies, to fight them, and to hunt. The so-called cruelty of a cat with a mouse or a bird is probably the result, not only of its joy and pride in play, but of its need to exercise its finer skills. Its consummate muscular prowess, curiously enough, seems to make it unnecessary for it to keep in training, except perhaps by stretching; a cat that has lounged away most of the winter months in front of a fire will run out in the spring and deal with walls and trees with untroubled mastery. This muscular mastery gives it part of its wonderful beauty, the dancer's grace and power that survive torn ears, a bitten tail, and attacks of eczema and mange.

Sheer endurance, however, provides most of the 'nine lives'. Many of us have wondered how, for example, uncontrolled and unfed farm cats, wild with famine, survive at all. (Dogs used for ratting are fed, whereas cats are expected to live on mice which are not nearly sufficient.) Once, during the Second World War, a cat was accidentally cased up in England with some machinery destined for the Near East. After a long-lasting and dangerous voyage the machinery was uncrated in Egypt. Out walked a very thin cat, followed in line astern by a whole family of thin kittens. She had evidently kittened soon after the voyage began, and had kept herself alive, and suckled her family, by licking the grease used to protect the machinery. Such determination to live and give life shows us something of the central tenacity which must be the secret of, for example, those scrawny creatures one may see in Provençal towns, desperately licking the waste water in the drain from a little restaurant with what Dickens calls "the sickly eagerness of starvation".[1]

The story shows also another source of racial strength for survival—the highly developed maternal, and sometimes paternal, feelings in cats. In spite of a few cases of killing and eating kittens (by toms, very rarely by too-young mothers), "the beast", as Herodotus observed in the fifth century B.C., "is fond of offspring". This *might* mean that the beast likes having numerous offspring and, indeed, some cats kitten as often as is physically possible, and free-ranging toms work hard. In the context, however, the statement clearly refers to the absorbing love and care that mother cats give to their kittens. There are few sights more expressive of whole-hearted delight than that of a cat suckling and washing her kittens, purring and crooning all the time; but her motherhood goes beyond this simple pleasure. She is on guard, and if she suspects pursuit, hostility, or even undue curiosity, she will move her kittens from their birthplace to a hidden shelter. If an enemy appears, she will face it, tail swelled, fur puffed, claws ready; the writer has seen a mother cat drive off a dog at least six times her size and weight, and *ride* it away down the path from her kittens.

She also teaches her young. Cleanliness and various skills are not the result merely of instinct in kittens. The mother gives demonstration lessons in play, hunting, and so on— and she will smack a disobedient or inattentive kitten. However poor and harried she may be, she educates her young. One night I watched a tiny, emaciated cat in a back street of a town in Provence conduct her starveling, mouse-sized kittens through a hole in a gate behind which she hid them during the daylight hours, look anxiously up and down the street for danger, exercise the children in running and some kinds of play, and then take them back into hiding.

Finally, the mother cat gives the last necessary touch to education: she insists that her grown kittens shall live independent of her. Cats are not guilty of the human maternal vice of trying to possess and dominate their grown-up offspring. Yet their maternal feelings are so strong that they will on occasion mother other animals. A cat of mine successfully fostered papillon puppies left motherless at a day old.

Small wonder that cats grow up courageous, cautious, and independent. Even a small kitten when startled will turn to face a suspected enemy, spitting in its miniature way. Mature toms engaged in serious battle—over hierarchy, or territory, or a female—are a terrifying sight. Locked together with muscles and claws, they seem to lose consciousness of their surroundings, and will batter themselves against walls and ground unaware of blows and bruises while they engage the enemy. Serious wounds are inflicted, and a tom's first spring can be a dangerous time for him. Yet even fighting toms can be tender, visiting their mates during and after kittening, and playing with their young.

Males and females alike are capable of love and friendship, with each other, sometimes with other animals, and with human beings. It is quite untrue that cats are lacking in

[1] Describing "a most wretched cat" in Chapter XXXVI of *The Old Curiosity Shop*.

affection for human beings. *Given the chance* (and this is very important) they often develop deep devotion for their owners (or slaves). There are innumerable instances of cats pining in the absence of their human friends, and changing all their habits till they find them again. They often seem to know when their owners are in any kind of trouble, and to offer special evidences of affection as comfort. A tom setting out for his night's work will keep running back to explain that he *must* go, though he would like to stay with you. A mother will welcome a trusted human friend at her kittening, or bring her kittens to be admired. But the human friend must earn trust. Cats will not tolerate mockery, contempt, or domination.

Thus, they will not pander to any human desire to display mastery. 'Performing cats' are almost unheard of. Highly intelligent, they will not be 'trained' to do the unreasonable. At their own whim, in moments of exhilaration, they will give startling performances of dancing, acrobatics, or clowning. They will invent their own 'tricks', or imitate with contemptuous ease the tricks of other animals, such as 'begging', which they have seen secure treats; but nothing will induce them to show off to order. They will not stoop to make a public display of obedience or affection, and it is the experience of all cat-lovers that their cats more often than not reserve their strongest demonstrations of affection for occasions when they are alone with the object of their love. There are, of course, signs other than physical condition of whether or not cats are on terms of confidence with human beings. If they are, they will engage your gaze, look *at* you, when you look at them; otherwise, they look through you or past you.

Of all domestic animals, cats are the most immediate indicators of men's economic condition. When times are bad the animals that provide meat and milk will obviously be

CARVING ON THE LOUTH CROSS, MONASTERBOICE, IRELAND.
TENTH CENTURY

cared for as long as possible; but the cat, partly because of its apparent independence and pride, is left to fend for itself. When times are good men begin to care for the cat again, taking pleasure in its grace and intelligence.

Cats must have some privacy. In illness, they often go into hiding. Despite the far-heard operatic overtures and accompaniments to courtship and mating, free cats will rarely copulate under human eyes, though the runner-up in the competition for a female in season is sometimes allowed to be present, as a kind of groomstom, and to join in singing the epithalamium.

The arias and recitatives of courting or fighting cats are never silenced for long by human objurgations or showers of missiles. Clearly, this form of self-expression is important to the cat. Purring and talking too are important. Cats vary from taciturnity to volubility, but all talk to some extent, and they evidently convey clear meanings to each other. Even human beings learn to recognize definite meanings in certain cries of cats: there is no mistaking the note with which a mother weaning her kittens calls them to some titbit.

Being individualists, cats vary in the proportions in which they combine their characteristics. There are feline as well as human fools, rogues, and freaks. But the characteristics are there, perceived even by the unsympathetic, recognized by Kipling in "The Cat that Walked by Himself" in the *Just So Stories*. Here, the earliest man and woman come to terms with some of the animals. The Woman easily tricks the Dog, the Horse, and the Cow into doing what she wants of them; they acquiesce completely, and accept without a murmur the humanly-orientated names she bestows on them of First Friend, First Servant, and so on. But the Cat, secretly watching everything that happens, comes to make his own terms. By his cleverness with the baby, and with a mouse, he strikes successful bargains with the Woman for a place by the hearth and a share of the warm milk. At the close of each bargain he insists, "'But still I am the Cat that walks by himself, and all places are alike to me,'" and when bargains are to be made with the Man and the Dog, he reaffirms, "'But *still* I am the Cat that walks by himself.'" Man and Dog are enraged and, though the bargains are kept on both sides, "from that day to this," says Kipling, "three proper men out of five will always throw things at a Cat". Here, and even more clearly in the poem belonging to the story, Kipling shows a preference for the totally subdued animals; but he can observe imaginatively. At the end of the story we are told that the Cat is pleasant and useful in the house, but "between times, and when the moon gets up and night comes, he is the Cat that walks by himself, and all places are alike to him. Then he goes out to the Wet Wild Woods or up the Wet Wild Trees or on the Wet Wild Roofs, waving his wild tail and walking by his wild lone."

Here is the secret. Men and women who insist on total domination over uncritically submissive animals never care much for a cat. Others, who are prepared for the uncertainties of a more complex and variable relationship, love the cat not only for the beauty of eyes and fur and endlessly graceful movement, not merely for cleverness, not even just for the cat's love of them, but precisely *because* the cat can wave his wild tail and walk by his wild lone. Here is something demanding respect and wonder, as well as protective care. "Who knows," says Montaigne, "when I play with my cat, whether she makes sport for me or I for her?"

From the cat who climbed the Matterhorn to those who protest that they cannot bear to go out when there is snow on the ground: from the Van cats of Turkey who are said to go swimming for pleasure to "the poor cat i' the adage" who "amat pisces, sed non vult tingere plantas" (loves fish, but doesn't want to get his paws wet): from the cats 'on the strength' of official establishments like Harwell who earn a wage for keeping pests down to the pampered Persian pet who never does a paw's turn: from the cats of Ancient Egypt who received divine honours to the cats tortured to death because they were supposed to be devils: from the heart-breaking strays who struggle with dustbin lids to get at a fish-bone to family pets who develop fads for beetroot, cauliflower, green peas, asparagus, cake, chocolate, or rum: they all have it, this inner, mysterious core of independent personality. This is what Eliot means when he says that each cat has, in addition to two exoteric names, a third

> that no human research can discover . . .
> His ineffable effable
> Effanineffable
> Deep and inscrutable singular Name.

THE CAT IN HISTORY

The history of cats, like all great histories, has prehistoric origins. Zoogeographers tell us (and who but other zoogeographers can answer them?) that the distribution of animal genera was determined by the shifting and settling of the land masses of the world hundreds of millions of years ago. Some animal kinds occur, in various species, all over the world, others are limited to certain continents. In Australasia there are no indigenous small felines, and no signs (in fossils or elsewhere) that there ever were small felines there. In the Americas there are small native felines, but none closely related to our familiar domestic cat. He developed and had his progeny entirely in Asia, Africa, and Europe, and the domestic cats now common in the Americas and Australasia are all emigrants from Asia, Africa, or Europe, or such emigrants' descendants; and most of them emigrated from Europe with human explorers or settlers, or travelled proudly as prize specimens of the European breeders' skill.

The ancient evidence of geology and the like is as solid as rocks can make it, but the early historical periods have to be filled in (with all cat-like caution!) by deduction. Some apparent references to cats in historical sources are, as we shall see, probably not references to cats at all; and we can only deduce long familiarity with cats when we suddenly meet an unmistakable reference which, by its detailed knowledge, suggests that cats must have been known and observed *as such* for generations. Even in the centuries after such references, we often have to draw conclusions about the distribution, treatment, and status of cats in most countries from the tone or attitude suggested in proverbs, folk-lore, and artistic presentations. To divide the historically valid from the artistically impressive or the anthropologically 'interesting' requires cat's-whisker delicacy, but the blundering human attempt must be made.

The European domestic cat's cradle was probably North Africa (though Africa itself may have been a reception area for Asiatic cats). All evidence unites to deny that the indigenous European wild cat ever became domesticated. His cousin, apt for domestication, came from elsewhere, and it seems increasingly likely that he came from the only country that has certainly treated the cat as divine (some hints of divinity elsewhere cannot be confirmed). The goddess Bast (or Oubasted—she is named in several ways) was Egyptian. In the *History* of Herodotus, a Greek born in the fifth century B.C. in Asia Minor, we have the first unmistakable reference to cats in European literature; and it may be that the interest Herodotus showed in cats in Egypt was precisely the interest that a traveller feels in facts and customs different from those of his own country. Certainly, Herodotus had an interest in Egyptian cats beyond any that he revealed in their other domestic animals, and he is worth quoting in full. In Section 66 of Book Two, he says:

> The number of domestic animals in Egypt is very great, and would be still greater were it not for what befalls the cats. As the females, when they have kittened, no longer seek the company of the males, these last, eager but unable to mate with them again, practise a curious artifice. They seize the kittens, carry them off, and kill them, but do not eat them afterward. Upon this, the females, being deprived of their young, and longing to supply their place, seek the males once more, since they are particularly fond of offspring. On every occasion of a fire in Egypt the strangest prodigy occurs with the cats. The inhabitants allow the fire to rage as it pleases, while they stand about at intervals and watch these animals, which, slipping by the men or else leaping over them, rush headlong into the flames. When this happens, the Egyptians are in deep affliction. If a cat dies in a private house by a natural death, all the inmates of the house shave their eyebrows. . . .
>
> The cats on their decease are taken to the city of Bubastis, where they are embalmed, after which they are buried in certain sacred repositories.

There are obscurities in this paragraph; for example, it is possible that the "men" mentioned were guards actually placed to save the animals from their apparent attempts at suicide. But the passage is clearly important for several reasons. Wherever it gives details, it may be supposed to be accurate, for those which are testable are verified by other evidence: the principal cats' cemetery was indeed at Bubastis, as archaeology and kindred studies have shown. Archaeology has shown also that Herodotus is right in stating that the cat is only one among many animals worshipped (often in cults varying from district to district) by the Egyptians; mummified shrews, ibises, ichneumons, and so on have been found, as well as cemeteries for divine, or consecrated, cattle. Where the details are vague, we may suppose that they represent a practice misunderstood by Herodotus, or deliberately concealed.

It is likely that the explanation of the Egyptian cats' supposed attraction to a fire is hinted in the paragraph preceding the description of cats, where Herodotus states that he shrinks from discussing religious matters. In ancient religions divine animals are often (for complex reasons) also sacrificial animals, and the need for sacrifice is satisfied at intervals (usually annual). This certainly occurred in connection with Apis, the divine bull, in Egypt. There may well have been a yearly sacrifice by fire of a cat or cats among the worshippers of Bast, to which they all assented on religious principle; but—each family would find it intolerable that its own hearth companion should be sacrificed. So, at the season of sacrificial fires, they would mount guard to try to ensure their own pets' safety—and an alien inquirer like Herodotus might easily hear some tale of cats and fires that he did not understand, and was perhaps not even meant to understand.

Certainly, the Egyptians made their cats companions as well as incarnate gods. A wall-painting from a tomb of about 1400 B.C. shows a family fowling-party with a cat flushing the birds. (Incidentally, this is the only example of a cat working *in this way*; later working cats have different jobs.) As divine manifestations of Bast, or as animals sacred to Ra, their cats were highly cared for, even bedecked with ear-rings and amulet necklaces (which they presumably doffed when they went fowling). Herodotus simply gives us verbal confirmation of what is suggested by art and funerary practices. The great Bubastis necropolis for cats has yielded up bodies of kittens as well as full-grown cats carefully mummified. The process was less elaborate than that used for important human bodies, but the bandaging is neat and skilful, and when the bandages are unwrapped, there is the fur and the little body. Mummy-cases were often elaborate. Wooden cases were shaped like cats and painted. Box-shaped cases were decorated. A very beautiful bronze case in the British Museum has on the lid two effigies, one sitting, one crouching, both, no doubt, portrait models of the dead cat. The mingling of domestic affection with reverent devotion in the Egyptian feeling for cats is perhaps best shown in a bronze figure of the cat goddess Bast with her children: the goddess (like zoomorphic deities in many ages and many places) is shown as part-human, part-feline, and she stands in dignity; but her four children are all naturalistic kittens. From at least the second millennium B.C. to the second century A.D. cats appear in Egyptian painting (sometimes lurking among lotuses), modelling, and sculpture, and their appearances vary from the supremely dignified bronze statuettes, through faience groups that balance reverence with amused affection, to little wooden dolls with painted eyes and movable jaws. Many an Egyptian leaving the "warm precincts of the cheerful day" must have felt comforted by the prospect of meeting again those respectfully buried animals that he had both loved and honoured.

In one way, Egyptian cats were certainly very like present-day European cats. The hieroglyphs representing their name are among the few to which sound values have been tentatively assigned. The name was probably pronounced MIAOW.

This fact of language is the first of several pieces of linguistic evidence that can hint to us, through misty ages, the cat's movement into increased recognition. There were languages in which cats seem to have had to share a word with other small mammals such as weasels, and when such a word is used we cannot be sure without other evidence that a cat is in mind. For instance, the two words used in Sanskrit for *cat* were also used for other small animals, but one of them (*mārjāra, mārjārī*) was, I suspect, usually employed for cats as it seems to be connected with the verb *mṛj-*, meaning 'to lick, to clean', and, as we shall see, the cat's passion for washing was sometimes recognized as strongly characteristic. The languages of the Eastern Mediterranean also failed in early days to distinguish between cats and martens, weasels, stoats, and so on. The linguistic evidence is one of the main reasons for concluding,

6-7   BLACK LONGHAIR

8   ODD-EYED WHITE LONGHAIR

however reluctantly, that in the Bible cats have no part—not even a share of the bits of Jezebel that the dogs left.

In the strange passages in Isaiah xiii, 21, and xxxiv, 14, where the Authorized Version says that "the satyr shall cry to his fellow", some more modern translations have substituted "wild cat" for "satyr"; but the word which has been variously translated may itself be a misreading of a Hebrew word for 'kite'. Indeed, any supposed Biblical cat turns out, on pursuit, to be quite as elusive as a Cheshire cat, and to leave not even a grin behind—only a kite! The only other possible reference occurs in the Epistle of Jeremy (Baruch vi, 22), where idols are proved not to be gods by the fact that "upon their bodies and heads sit bats, swallows, birds, and the cats also". These cats, of course, do not appear in the Authorized Version at all, as Baruch was regarded as apocryphal; in any case, the Greek word here did not necessarily mean 'cat', and the Syriac version gives us weasels! The latest translation of all, the New English Bible, keeps cats in Baruch, but turns the satyr/wild cat of Isaiah into a he-goat! Perhaps, after all, there *is* a grin! In all seriousness, however, it seems likely that an animal deified by the Egyptians might well be ostentatiously ignored by the Children of Israel after the Egyptian captivity.

It is not only in the Old Testament that the confusion of words conceals cats from us. The Greeks do not seem to have been affected by the interest of Herodotus in cats, and when Aristotle uses the word αἴλουρος in the *Historia Animalium* he may be referring to martens, civets, and so on. Certainly, Aristophanes in *The Acharnians* has used it simply of one of a medley of small animals.

So long as *feles* remained the commonest name for a cat in Rome, there was no sign of any great interest in it. Cats are not mentioned as popular pets. It is, no doubt, unlikely that maidens who chirruped with sparrows or cooed with doves, or more sophisticated ladies who displayed their charms while fondling snakes or monkeys, would have had much use for cats. Nevertheless, it seems strange that among the many small mosaics of Rome, we do not find cats; perhaps we may account for it by the great love (in various senses) for doves and fish that these mosaics display. The Tabby cat catching a bird in a mosaic at Pompeii may or may not have belonged to a family; there is nothing to show.

Before the destruction of Pompeii in A.D. 79, however, the history of language was showing a change of consciousness that is very important in the history of cats. According to that great philologist, Dr Onions, our word for 'cat' probably came from North Africa; he cites as a parallel the Nubian *kadīs*. In the early centuries of the Christian era a word related to this appeared in and travelled through nearly all European countries, Mediterranean, Atlantic, Baltic, Slavic. It supplanted αἴλουρος in Greece and *feles* in Italy; and all over Europe we find increasingly *catt, kottr, katte, kat, kazza, katze, kat, chat, gat, gato, gatto, cath, kattos, cat(t)us, kotu, kot, kate, cait*. The word seems to have moved north from Africa, as we might expect, when trading with Africa was developing under the Roman Empire, and to have come into use among the Romans along with their domestic acceptance of the cat we know. It is therefore not surprising that the elder Pliny, writing in the first century A.D., describes, in the zoological sections of his *Natural History*, an animal that we can clearly recognize as our domestic cat. Pliny filled notebooks with his own observations for this work, as well as drawing on Greek sources, and his descriptions may be based on first-hand knowledge. He knew, for example, how cats deal with excreta. As Pliny drew some of his zoological information from Greek sources, so, for centuries to come, compilers of encyclopaedias and bestiaries drew their information from Pliny. From him, however, they drew material that really did concern cats. Wherever we find a word etymologically connected with *cat*, we find information about a cat; he may be a wild cat or a domestic cat, but at least he will not be a weasel. In fact, the domestic cat accepted by the Romans probably came from Africa, and the word travelled with the thing. Both may have been among the "novelties" that Africa was said to produce. The Greek proverb to the effect that "Africa is always producing some novelty" referred to a belief that Africa was full of monsters. By the time Pliny rendered it as *Africa semper aliquid novi affert*, some of the monsters may have lost their monstrosity through being domiciled with the Romans.

After leaving imperial Rome, we find for some time no record of the cat in the Western world. The earliest Christian art ignores them—unless we may count as Christian 'art', as distinct from Christian teaching, a mysterious apocryphal gospel known as the Gospel of the (Holy) Twelve. Unfortunately, M. R. James did not translate this in his New Testament Apocrypha of 1924, so that I have been unable to confirm what I am told of material in it: that there was a cat with her kittens underneath the manger in which Jesus was laid, and that on two occasions during the earthly ministry Jesus was represented as protecting a friendless cat, and using a cat as an example of those smaller and weaker creatures that a good man should treat with gentle kindness. This highly attractive material probably indicates an attitude of non-Jewish Semitic peoples to which we shall return.

Meanwhile, however, the historical cat was attaining recognition in Western Europe. As soon as the storage of grain is seen as profoundly important, the value of the cat begins to be understood. Therefore, when Western European peoples settled down to cultivation of grain, they found that they had to protect the animal that protected the grain from rats and mice. "The house that Jack built" might almost be taken in part as a child's potted history of human settlement with its reference to "the cat that killed the rat that ate the malt". Parts of an accumulative rhyme of this kind may go back many hundreds of years. Certainly, by the time of the tenth century in Wales, the cost of kittens was controlled by law—and the cost increased after the kitten had caught its first mouse, and so proved its value. (Guernsey immediately after the Second World War provides a gloss on this. For unhappy reasons, cats had become scarce, and a common kitten commanded a very high price.) Very much earlier than this, possibly as early as the fourth century, there was an Irish saying that seems to refer to a law: "The immunity of a cat is a kitchen." This means that if a cat scratches you or knocks something over, you may only punish him if he is not in the kitchen; in the kitchen, he must go unpunished. At first sight, this may seem odd: surely, it is where the cat may steal the joint or put his nose in the bowl of milk that we may wish to punish him. But if we regard the kitchen as representing the place where food-supplies were kept, we can see that there was a point in granting its freedom to the animal which could keep down the rodents that were the most serious threat to grain and fats. The kitchen would, indeed, be the cat's domain.

It is Ireland too that gives us our first clear indications of cats used in Christian contexts. The stories of the Navigations of St Brendan (fifth century) include references to cats, and the Book of Kells (an illuminated MS of the Gospels of, probably, the eighth century) has enough cats among the illuminations to show familiarity. Most remarkable of all, however, are the cats on a Celtic High Cross in Louth, of uncertain date, but certainly not later than 935. On one side, beneath the feet of Christ, are two cats, formalized in their relation to each other and in the strict patterning of the sweep of the tail over the haunch (the two cats are seen from the side, but formally opposed head to head), but otherwise treated with a naturalism proving long and close knowledge of cats and their ways. One of these cats is washing a tiny kitten, held in her forepaws; the thrust of her tongue over the little head, her hold on the body, even the minute tail of the kitten, are clear in stone after a thousand years. The other cat is holding a bird in exactly the same way as the first one holds the kitten (that is, with gentle, motherly care), and I suspect that the correct interpretation of this fact might add something to our knowledge of the Christian iconography of the early Middle Ages. (On another side of the cross are two toms, both formalized and distorted to make them fit into a twisting pattern.) These are the first cats to appear in important relation to a Christian monument and, I believe, the only ones to occur on a cross. The double fact of the close natural observation of the female cats, and of their acceptance into a Christian context, shows how thoroughly the cat had been accepted into the Irish world of good things. It is not surprising that many Irish folk tales are concerned with cats.

In the far north of Europe the cat had not yet settled into anything like this gentle form of acceptance. It is true that he sometimes appears in what one expects to be a Christian

WALL-PAINTING OF FREYA RIDING A CAT, SCHLESWIG CATHEDRAL.
TWELFTH CENTURY

19

setting, but in a very startling way. In Schleswig cathedral there is a twelfth-century wall-painting of Freya, chief of the Valkyrie and a goddess, riding (bareback, but with bit and bridle) a cat so heavily striped that he reminds one of Tiger Tim. There is certainly nothing here of affectionate, or even close, naturalistic observation; either the cat is as big as a horse, or the goddess is remarkably small for a Valkyrie, Chooser of the Slain. Sometimes, cats drew her chariot. Freya has sometimes been identified with Frija (Frigg, Frigga), queen of Odin, king of the gods, but they have separate origins, and Frija seems to have no necessary connection with any kind of cat. There is a painting of her in the same cathedral riding what is, no doubt, a tree, but looks remarkably like a broomstick. She was sometimes identified with the Roman Diana or Hecate. (Diana performed many functions, and had different names for different functions; as Queen of the Underworld she was known as Hecate.)

These identifications may help to account for a pernicious and persistent misapprehension that has constantly falsified accounts of cats in the Middle Ages and early Renaissance. It is often assumed that for several centuries the cat lost his place as grain-guardian and hearth-companion to men because he was always distrusted as a witch, or a witch's companion, throughout the ages of the strongest belief in, fear of, and attacks against witches. This is nonsense. Cats certainly often incurred suspicion as witches' friends, but they did so *only along with other animals*, and they hardly ever achieved a particular kind of beastly prominence in the annals of witchcraft usually reserved for horned animals. We shall soon see what is the cat's place among the witches. Meanwhile, we should consider the evidence for their everyday position among men during the witch-hunting ages.

Middle English writings are full of references to cats and proverbs concerning them. These show, invariably, both a simple acceptance of the cat's presence and an awareness of his nature that reveals unfrightened observation. One of the commonest proverbs, current for several centuries, concerned cleanliness: anything very clean was described by saying that it was "as clean as if a cat had licked it"—and the implication is never derogatory. Another chooses the cat to sum up a natural observation: "As the kitten is, so will the cat be," or "The cat shows what the kitten becomes." References in literature confirm these impressions. The *Ancrene Wisse* (or *Ancren Riwle*), an early thirteenth-century manual of behaviour for anchoresses, taught that, while it would be foolish for an anchoress to keep a cow, which might involve her in embarrassment if it strayed and were impounded, she might keep a cat (apparently for company—there is no reference to a cat's possible usefulness). The late Middle Ages show the cat equally comfortably settled. Several of the *Canterbury Tales* show that Chaucer expected his fourteenth-century audience to recognize the cat's place. In "The Miller's Tale" there is a reference to the kind of hole in a door that lets the family cat go freely in and out (the modern cat-door, specially fitted, was then more simply supplied). The Wife of Bath, full of fellow-feeling, points out that a cat, when her fur is sleek and handsome, goes off at dusk about her social and sexual occasions. Chaucer even seems to use treatment of a cat as a hint about human character; the Friar who is the villain of "The Summoner's Tale" is shown, near the beginning, pushing a cat off a bench so that he may sit down in comfort—and we feel something of heartless self-indulgence in the Friar's casual act. We shall find treatment of cats used for similar purposes centuries after this. In the same century Langland, in *Piers Plowman*, refers casually to the political allegory about belling the cat—when small people wished to find a means of protecting themselves against a dangerous, powerful man, they could not carry their ideas into practice. Skelton, writing at the end of the fifteenth and the beginning of the sixteenth century, refers in *Philip Sparrow* to the cat as an enemy, but this is simply because the poem is a dirge on the death of a young girl's pet sparrow, who has fallen victim to the household "Gib, our cat". Nowhere, in any of these references, is there any sign of any superstitious horror of cats.

In the sixteenth and seventeenth centuries, we have not only Montaigne's musing consideration of his pet cat, and Topsell's careful description in his *Historie of Four-footed Beasts*, but, most important, Shakespeare's view. Shakespeare, above all men, could represent both the common and the great-minded view of any matter; and the nearest he ever comes to condemning a cat is in the easy contempt of Hotspur's

> I had rather be a kitten and cry mew
> Than one of these same metre ballad-mongers

—which is hardly an expression of serious horror. Perhaps the most famous and most characteristic of Shakespeare's references is to "the *harmless, necessary* cat"—a sufficiently clear indication of his age's attitude. His other most famous reference is to "Letting 'I dare not' wait upon 'I would', Like the poor cat i' the adage." Now, the "adage" in question goes back through several centuries of English forms of the proverb to medieval Latin. The pernickety cat, longing to eat fish but reluctant to wet his paws, has been accepted with affectionate laughter for generations, and has certainly not been regarded with horror during those generations.

The centuries we have just briefly outlined were the centuries of the great witch horrors. The first great British witchcraft trial was of Dame Alice Kyteler. This took place in the fourteenth century, the century in which Chaucer wrote so pleasantly about cats. The only animal referred to in her trial is a cock. In the following generations the accounts of trials in England, Scotland, France, Germany, and the Channel Islands often refer to animals as the companions of witches. These companions, in the strands of history that follow the perpetuation of ancient religious cults, overlaid by official Christianity, were divisible into divining familiars and domestic familiars. The first were believed to reveal truths, sometimes of the future, to the witch; the second were believed to obey her commands. In many trials, cats are certainly mentioned among both kinds of familiars; but so were hedgehogs, dogs, weasels, and many other small animals. The familiar of the Witch of Edmonton was a dog. The simple fact is that many witches (whether we think of them as followers of an ancient cult, as self-deceived believers in their own magic powers, or as misunderstood, solitary neurotics) were lonely women (sometimes lonely men) who, then as now, valued domestic animals for giving them the companionship they urgently needed. Such animals had to be small—the witch could not afford to maintain a large animal—and it had to be capable of showing some signs of attachment. So, of course, a cat often appeared; and if its master or mistress came under suspicion, so did the cat—but then, so did the hedgehog, dog, or any other small animal in like case.

The other, supremely important, appearance of animals in cases of witchcraft is as the divine being. This, for anthropological reasons we cannot here pursue, was almost invariably a horned beast—bull, ram, buck, or, most frequently of all in Western Europe, he-goat. The cat hardly ever appears as the dark Satanic god; his appearances as such in Guernsey in the sixteenth century, France in the seventeenth century, and, as late as the eighteenth century, in Lapland, are quite abnormal. We must repeat, the cat's part in witchcraft, whether in divining or in casting spells (as in the attempt of the Berwick witches to kill King James VI and I by drowning) is no greater, and often less, than the part played by other animals. Why, then, does the modern imagination persist in regarding the cat as peculiarly the animal of witchcraft?

We have already hinted at one reason. The identification of Frija with Diana/Hecate would lead to mixing their characteristics; and Diana/Hecate's night-riding would be mixed with Frija's riding through the air, and that in its turn with Freya's riding on some form of cat. Not only was Diana/Hecate associated by Christians with witchcraft—she was said to have created the cat. The amateur 'Comparative Religion' of earlier days might well too readily bring the cat into special association with witchcraft. Further, hindsight is apt to pick out of earlier beliefs and practices what suits the taste of later ages; and the decorative possibilities of a cat with arched back and looped tail, accompanying a witch on a broomstick, were too good to be ignored. Finally, any imaginative person may feel a cat to be uncanny—the shining of the eyes in the dark, the silent movements, the skill and perception of the creature, might easily seem preternatural to the inventive fancy. We must not be led by these tendencies into forgetting the clear fact that, during the witch-hunting centuries, the cat continued to be a valued household friend. At the very moment in English writings when North European beliefs were equated with witchcraft—that is, when Freya and her cat might be referred to—there is no reference to cats. Wulfstan, in his eleventh-century *Sermo Lupi ad Anglos* ("Wulfstan's Address to the English"), delivers stern warnings against superstitious practices, against trust and belief in "wiccan and wælcerian", that is, sorcerers and choosers-of-the-slain, witches and Valkyries. Here, if anywhere, we might find the cat, as the mount of Freya, chief of the Valkyries, to be mentioned as dangerous and abominable. There is no reference to him at all.

This is not to suggest that cats did not suffer as witches or witches' companions, but simply to point out that they were not unique in their sufferings. Frazer, in *The Golden Bough*, gives us several examples of cats suffering for reasons that seem to us superstitious but which, no doubt, seemed in earlier centuries religious or moral. He tells us of cats burnt during Lent in the villages of the Ardennes, and again at midsummer at Paris, at Metz, and in the Vosges. In some cases the sufferings were prolonged, on the grounds that evil must be thoroughly driven out. On the other hand, the manner in which these cats were sacrificed sometimes suggests that they were taking the place of sanctified human beings in much earlier rites, so that the cruelty does not necessarily always indicate the horror of moral condemnation. Even where it does, the cats may have been carrying the terrible but ultimately honourable burden of scapegoats. Cocks and other living creatures sometimes, indeed often, suffered similarly. What is important is that we should maintain a balanced view of our forefathers' activities—as, indeed, they could do themselves. The last century of the greatest witchcraft persecutions, the seventeenth century, was also the worst. From this century there comes to us a painting of an old woman and a cat, who are both seen with compassionate affection. Now in the Louvre, the picture, by Nicolas Maes (1632–93), is called *Le Bénédicité*; it shows an old lady sitting at her frugal supper-table. She has not yet begun her supper, for she is still saying grace. Beside her on the floor, however, is her cat, already tucking into his supper. He is clearly an honoured companion for, though the old lady is evidently poor, the cat is wearing a smart yellow collar. Now, this is exactly the kind of couple that would have been seen by hysterical crowds, over-excited by witchcraft scares, as a witch and her familiar. At this very period such couples were being seen in this way by some crowds; but here is this beautifully humane picture to prove to us that the superstitious horror was far from universal.

In fact, as we have already seen, the centuries of danger were also centuries of acceptance. The *Ancrene Wisse*, which recommends an anchoress to keep a cat, refers to the Devil as "the cat of hell" but only, it seems, because he will catch sinners. This *may* be the function of a cat in a strange painting by Met de Bles, now in the Museo Correr in Venice. In a *Temptation of St Antony*, there is the usual horrid corner of surrealist beastlinesses showing some of the temptations; but in the middle of this sits a perfectly naturalistic cat watching a perfectly realistic gridiron with a fish cooking on it. The cat may represent the Devil waiting for a lost soul (fish) to finish cooking himself. Again, the cat as Devil appears to be functioning in a highly moral way.

The medieval and early Renaissance centuries are those in which the cat established himself not only as a recognized domestic kind, but as an individual. The common English names occur with increasing frequency: Gib, Tib, Tibbald, Grimalkin, Grizel. It will be noted that many of these seem to refer to grey as the commonest colour among cats at this time. Common-places about the cat have descended through the encyclopaedic knowledge of Isidore of Seville and Albertus Magnus from Pliny. The cat is there, established in nearly all homes, and, of course, stories begin to gather round him. The historical Richard Whittington lived from *c.* 1358 till 1423, and his continuing fame (into modern panto-mimes) certainly depends more on his cat than on himself. Now, various attempts have been made to explain away Dick Whittington's cat. He (Dick, not the cat) certainly made his fortune through trade, and we have been told that this was shown by the statement that he prospered through "*achat*" (French, "dealing for money"); or through coastal trade with a "*cat(t)*" (a Norwegian word for a kind of ship). Either of these explanations is plausible, but the trouble is that neither is more plausible than the other, and they cannot both be true. More likely than either is the explanation that Whittington, being the kind of real person who turns very rapidly into a popular hero (like Robin Hood or El Cid), attracted to himself any pleasing story that happened to be going the rounds. This happened with all heroes of the kind—King Arthur, Charlemagne, Sir Francis Drake, any who could be felt warmly by the people, became heroes, or at least characters, in stories that the people loved. King Arthur attracted to him the story of the Grail and, at a lower social and literary level, Dick Whittington attracted to himself the story of a valuable cat. The cat in this story is clearly the cat in the stories that lie behind the tale of Puss in Boots, and that tale we shall deal with in another section. What matters is that we have here almost certain evidence of cat stories being part of a widespread, happy folk-culture.

No wonder, then, that Shakespeare so readily accepted the cat, and no wonder that in the seventeenth century we begin to find some of the earliest stories of individual men and their individual cats. One of the most charming tales concerns Newton, arguably the greatest scientist the world has seen, certainly one of the two greatest physicists, and a major mathematician. He had a cat who, like all the cats we have all known, was always on the wrong side of the door; so, that he might not be interrupted in his studies, he made a hole in the door for the cat (like the door in the Carpenter's house in "The Miller's Tale"). The cat, however, kittened, and the great mathematician, recognizing the difference in size between a full-grown cat and a kitten, made another hole in the door, for the kittens to pass through. It is comforting to find that one of the greatest of all known human minds could (literally) lose its normal sense of proportion where cats were concerned.

In the eighteenth century, the cat is clearly established both as an important member of a self-consciously civilized society and as a being worth close observation. The observing naturalists of the century (usually amateurs) began again to watch for themselves the animal that Pliny had observed, and who had rarely been studied at all scientifically in the intervening sixteen centuries. So, White of Selborne watches the quick cat as well as the slow tortoise; Cowper notices how his Tortoiseshell cat investigates a snake; and Bewick, recorder *par excellence* of birds, does some beautiful engravings of cats, in particular, one of a cat crossing a stream by a plank bridge. Naturally, the cat finds its way into much of the literature of the period; this is the century when Perrault brings *Le Chat Botté* out of the folk-tale into literature. Smart, Cowper, Gray, and many others use the cat artistically. But one of the greatest of all literary figures never uses the cat for this purpose, but accepts him as a necessary part of human living. Dr Johnson and his cats are well known, but his treatment of them is worth recalling. We know the name of only one of them, Hodge. What we are told of Hodge reveals not only much of Johnson, but something of the casual attitude to cats in every generation. Boswell, an aileurophobe, says that he must not, in describing Johnson's character,

omit the fondness which he shewed for animals which he had taken under his protection. I never shall forget the indulgence with which he treated Hodge, his cat; for whom he himself used to go out and buy oysters, lest the servants, having that trouble, should take a dislike to the poor creature. I am, unluckily, one of those who have an antipathy to a cat, so that I am uneasy when in the room with one; and I own, I frequently suffered a good deal from the presence of this same Hodge. I recollect him one day scrambling up Dr. Johnson's breast, apparently with much satisfaction, while my friend, smiling and half-whistling, rubbed down his back, and pulled him by the tail; and when I observed he was a fine cat, saying 'why, yes, Sir, but I have had cats whom I liked better than this;' and then, as if perceiving Hodge to be out of countenance, adding, 'but he is a very fine cat, a very fine cat indeed.'

This reminds me of the ludicrous account which he gave Mr. Langton, of the despicable state of a young gentleman of good family. 'Sir, when I heard of him last, he was running about town shooting cats.' And then in a sort of kindly reverie, he bethought himself of his own favourite cat, and said, 'But Hodge shan't be shot: no, no, Hodge shall not be shot.'

9   BLUE LONGHAIR

10–11   BLUE LONGHAIR

12   RED SELF LONGHAIR

13   RED TABBY LONGHAIR

Here we have not only the price that Boswell sometimes had to pay for his devotion to Johnson (though he loved him, he could not love his cat, though he was prepared to be polite about him), but signs of Johnson's strong justice and delicate sensibility. Servants and cat alike are to be happy; and Johnson, like all sensitive companions of cats, cannot quite help feeling that the cat may understand very well what is said, and can suffer from wounded feelings. We see also the immediate leap to the defence of the pet in an imagined danger. Hodge shan't be shot—our cats shan't be burnt. The young man who shoots cats is in a "despicable state", because he is living casually and mindlessly. Pope, Thomson, Gray, Cowper, and many others show us that one of the great growths of eighteenth-century civilization was the conviction that man's inhumanity to man was unlikely to be cured among men who were not merciful to their beasts.

So highly developed was Johnson's feeling for cats that I suspect it may have been the cause of his notorious failure to appreciate Gray's comic *Ode on the Death of a Favourite Cat drowned in a Tub of Goldfishes*. Johnson savaged this delightful mock-heroic piece, though we know that he loved comedy and could appreciate the mock-heroic. It seems that he could not bear the death of a cat to be treated as a joke, even in a graceful *jeu d'esprit*.

We may note in passing that the oysters for Hodge are not a parallel to the expensive fine bread squandered by Chaucer's Prioress on her little dogs. Over half a century later, Dickens's Sam Weller could still say that there seemed to be an association between oysters and poverty, without in the least implying that the connection is one of cause and effect. Oysters were cheap, and it was love rather than money that Johnson lavished on his cat.

The steady acceptance of the cat that we have seen in England during several centuries had its parallels elsewhere. We shall see in another section how important the cat had become in some European painting, and that its appearances there indicate its acceptance into human homes.

In the Near and Middle East, though the references are few, we may believe that the cat had his recognized place. We have seen that cats are mentioned in an apocryphal Gospel, which probably originated east of the Mediterranean, and this indicates acceptance. There is a proverbial saying about a cat, "The cat is the lion's aunt", based on an early story which has spread throughout Islam and which we shall find in the section dealing with legends about cats. Muhammad is the first great figure to whom a characteristic cat story is attached. The tale goes that a cat had gone to sleep lying on the sleeve of his garment; when the time came that he must go away, he could not bear to disturb that beautiful, relaxed sleep, so he cut off the sleeve and went away without it. The tale has also been told of Richelieu.

In the Far East the cat had been well known for centuries. By the time of the increased communication between East and West that the expansion of trade brought about, many servants of the East India Company and others must have felt some familiarity in the remote countries where they worked when they found a recognizable domestic animal there. Confucius is said to have had a cat, and his contemporary in the sixth century B.C., Lao-Tze, taught a universal kindness to living creatures. The cat does not seem to have been regarded as either godlike or devilish by the Chinese, though at one stage, when the central kingdoms indicated their contempt of outsiders by giving them animal designations, one people was indicated by MIEW. As the art of China came to include domestic scenes, the cat appeared

25

there, as it did also in Japan. Up to the present day, the delicate drawing of some Japanese artists has often been exercised on cats.

In India, the story of the cat in the part of the false yogi (recounted in the section devoted to myths and legends) certainly existed as far back as the seventh century A.D., for there is a picture of this hypocrite of that date—and to this day in Bengal one of the terms used for a hypocrite, which also means "cat-yogi", shows the continued existence of the story. It is impossible to generalize about the attitude to cats in an area so large as the Indian sub-continent. There are districts in which it was held dangerous to touch a cat, for by so doing you would contract leprosy. On the other hand, there is a small sect in the north which demands that anyone who injures a cat shall present a golden image of a cat to the temple. It is notable that no cat appears in pictures of the Buddha, and there is a tale that when the Buddha called the animals to be blessed the cat failed to respond, and so alone remained unblessed among the animals; but nobody seems to know whether this story accounts for the cat's absence from the pictures, or whether its non-appearance in the pictures gave rise to the story.

More homely is the cat's place among the Hindus, who associated the cat with the female divinity specially concerned with children and their welfare and celebrations. This is probably the reason for a nursery rhyme which is widespread among Hindus:

> Putu will go to her father-in-law's home; who will escort her?
> The tom-cat is at home; he has tightened up his Kamarband.

The reference, of course, is to child-marriages; and when the question is asked as to what company the child will have in her strange new home, the brave and loyal cat is represented as girding himself up to go and give familiar protection to the child.

Certainly, a country where cats appeared in nursery rhymes could not be quite strange to Westerners, for the nursery rhymes of Europe very often concerned kittens who lost their mittens, or three tom-cats knocking at the door, or, indeed, any age and variety of the domestic cat. In the late nineteenth century, moreover, a Bengali writer, Bankimchandra Chatterjee, was the first to use a cat for deliberate social comment; as a highly articulate representative of the starving, outcast millions of the world, the cat makes a detailed, argued plea for social justice.

European writers sometimes seem almost to use the cat as a test-case for judging men, and we find this several times in the nineteenth century (we have seen Chaucer hinting it earlier). In *Shirley*, Charlotte Brontë makes Caroline Helstone describe the man she loves: "'I know somebody to whose knee that black cat loves to climb, against whose shoulder and cheek it likes to purr . . .' 'And what does that somebody do?' 'He quietly strokes the cat, and lets her sit while he conveniently can, and when he must disturb her by rising, he puts her softly down, and never flings her from him roughly.'" How different from the Friar! All the Brontë sisters loved animals, and Anne as well as Charlotte uses love for a cat in her fiction.

Dickens's attitude was more ambiguous. He sometimes sees the cat as something of a moral barometer; the starved cat in the kitchen is a sign of the hardness and meanness of the Brass household in *The Old Curiosity Shop*. On the other hand, a well-fed cat sometimes seems to him to belong to the undeserved comforts of the smug hypocrite, like the Matron in *Oliver Twist*. The terrible Carker, in *Dombey and Son*, is likened to a cat, and Diogenes the dog barks at him as though somebody had said, 'Cats, boy! Cats!' Dickens's only detailed picture of a cat is itself ambiguous. Lady Jane, a beautiful long-haired grey, lives with the terrible old Krook in *Bleak House*. He has saved her from being killed for her skin, and she brings some touch of sympathy to the old drunkard. Yet neither he nor she is really approachable, and when Krook comes to his horrible end, Lady Jane runs out wild upon the roofs. As so often in Dickens, something ancient and fundamental is suddenly glimpsed through the cracks he makes in the Victorian surface. Lady Jane is at once Krook's nearest approach to kindly humanity, and a creature ready to go wild when her world breaks up. In general, Dickens, while hating the ill-treatment of cats, had no specially warm feeling for them, and his attitude probably represents the commonest feeling of the mid-nineteenth century—decent people don't ill-treat cats.

A majority of Englishmen at that time probably shared Dickens's feelings. Cats were useful animals in a house, because they kept down the mice. The women-folk seemed to like making pets of them, and, of course, it was nice for the children to have so many little verses written for them about furry pussies, and cats and kits were familiar in old rhymes. Kittens were sweetly pretty things, and one would not be cruel to them for the world. Indeed, it was distressing to see that people in other countries were sometimes rather harsh to cats as well as to other animals. The cats of comfortable households were almost certainly very comfortable themselves.

Other cats, however, scraped a mere existence in their myriads. Whenever Cruikshank draws a cat it is a lean and angular creature. It is true that Cruikshank tends to lean and angular effects, but, even so, his cats give the impression that he had seen very many that

"THE DOMESTIC CAT"
WOOD ENGRAVING BY THOMAS BEWICK, 1753–1828

27

were far from well fed. Dinah and her kitten in the *Alice* books, Edward Lear's portly Foss, the lovely "Pussy, O, Pussy my Love" so adored by the owl, must have been outnumbered by those of lean and hungry look. Even superficial fashion, however, could raise an animal's status, and when socially ambitious women followed those of higher rank in taking pride in fine cats, they were to some extent preparing the way for the 'Fancy'. The first cat shows could have been successful only in a world ready for them, and they in their turn fostered interest and pride in the breeding and care of fine animals. Soon this led to interest in particular breeds, to investigation of exotic breeds, and to the establishment of professional breeders who worked hard to secure true breeding from certain strains. Even these specialized interests, however, helped to create a climate of respectful interest in all domestic cats. An attractive feature of some recent cat shows, in Britain and other countries, has been the necessity for creating classes in which the ordinary pets of children and common cat-lovers can be shown. Care for the pet makes it possible for the cat fancy to come to birth, but the flourishing of the fancy in itself intensifies care for the common cat. It is noticeable that as clubs and societies and shows have spread from country to country, so, on the whole, has the good treatment of the common cat. There remain hideous exceptions, but these are decreasing. One of the most heartening sights I ever saw was in Rome. Here, though the cats that haunt the Colosseum and the Pantheon and other famous ruins are fed by visitors, there are still some wretched waifs. Yet, a few years ago when a cat show was being held there at which proud beauties of international fame were appearing, there was one exhibit of a few flourishing cats which had been rescued from starvation by a society formed for their protection; and a long queue was waiting to make donations to the society's funds.

Danger and thoroughly bad economic conditions may, of course, at short notice bring cats low. The cat has never been regarded as an animal desirable as food, but at all times of severe famine, and particularly at times of siege, cats have been eaten. (After all, shipwrecked sailors have sometimes been reduced to eating each other!) There is also a long-standing joke, hovering always just on the borders of belief, to the effect that cats have often been eaten by those who thought that they were dining on something else. The joke is made in perhaps its purest form by Sam Weller, in *The Pickwick Papers*:

> "Wery good thing is weal pie, when you know the lady as made it, and is quite sure it an't kittens; and arter all though, where's the odds, when they're so like weal that the wery piemen themselves don't know the difference?"
>
> "Don't they, Sam?" said Mr. Pickwick.
>
> "Not they, sir," replied Mr. Weller, touching his hat. "I lodged in the same house with a pieman once, sir, and a wery nice man he was—reg'lar clever chap, too—make pies out o' anything, he could. 'What a number o' cats you keep, Mr. Brooks,' says I, when I'd got intimate with him. 'Ah,' says he, 'I do—a good many,' says he. 'You must be wery fond o' cats,' says I. 'Other people is,' says he, a winkin' at me; 'they an't in season till the winter though,' says he. 'Not in season!' says I. 'No,' says he, 'fruits is in, cats is out.' 'Why, what do you mean?' says I. 'Mean?' says he. 'That I'll never be a party to the combination o' the butchers, to keep up the prices o' meat,' says he. 'Mr. Weller,' says he, a squeezing my hand wery hard, and vispering in my ear—'don't mention this here agin—but it's the seasonin' as does it. They're all made o' them noble animals,' says he, a pointin' to a wery nice little tabby kitten, 'and I seasons 'em for beef-

steak, weal, or kidney, 'cordin' to the demand. And more than that,' says he, 'I can make a weal a beefsteak, or a beefsteak a kidney, or any on 'em a mutton, at a minute's notice, just as the market changes, and appetites wary!'"

Even here, it is "with a slight shudder" that Mr Pickwick replies, "'He must have been a very ingenious young man, that, Sam.'"

It is usually rabbits that are supposed to be replaced by cats. That great dictionary of food, *Larousse Gastronomique*, refers to the belief as a mere story, but it takes the story sufficiently seriously to provide the reader with diagrams of the bones of a cat and a rabbit so that he may, if he feels suspicious in a cheap restaurant, decide for himself what he is eating. In some villages in Spain it is said that, when the local tavern offers free snacks, the gift co-incides with the disappearance of somebody's cat. An admirable restaurant in Florence, which is prepared to make jokes about its own excellent food, has cartoons on the walls, of which one shows "our own rabbit farm" with smug cats licking their lips over the fish-bones they have stripped, and another shows a mixed spitful of fowl, chop, cat, and so on. Where the joke declares itself on the surface like this the client and the cat are probably both safe.

There is no legal prohibition in Britain on a butcher or a restaurateur selling cat flesh so long as he does not claim that it is something else. Otherwise, however, cats now have protection in law, along with other animals, from cruelty or from neglect where ownership has been established. Severe penalties may be imposed, in several countries, on people found guilty of cruelty to cats; recently, a Frenchman in Paris was severely punished for throwing out of the window a cat which had angered him by stealing part of his dinner. Many human beings are quick to assist the police and inspectors from the Royal Society for the Prevention of Cruelty to Animals; a small girl has been known to join battle with three boys bigger than herself in order to rescue a cat they were tormenting. The owner-ship of cats presents something of a legal problem. As they do not require licences, owner-ship, where there is any question about it, often needs to be demonstrated by records of purchase, as with any chattel. If one has acquired one's cat by any other means than purchase (as most people have), custom and habits have to be brought into evidence; it would be interesting to know the ideas on this subject of those cats who firmly take human beings into their possession, and claim ownership of houses they walk into.

It would be difficult for our laws totally to ignore animals recognized by laws many centuries ago, and so firmly entrenched in our consciousness as the innumerable traditional and proverbial phrases in many languages show. Pussy-willows, catkins, cat-tails, and other plants and flowers are named for their likeness to cats or their fur in many languages. Silence, slyness, speed, boldness, and other qualities are named from cats in French, Italian, German, Spanish, and other languages. In French and German a pig in a poke is already named a cat in a bag; it is in English that the animal is named for what it truly is only *after* it is let out of the bag. In some countries it is sleeping cats rather than sleeping dogs that one is advised to leave lying. A cat may look at a king, but may be killed by curiosity or care. Something sufficiently ridiculous may make a cat laugh, and in Cheshire cats grinned when their heads were shown on cheeses. They may be swung where there is enough room, per-haps for the same reasons as they were hung in a bottle to provide human sport, or fought

29

like Kilkenny cats. Cat-lap is a very weak soft drink, but very strong liquor is enough to make a cat speak. A cat and dog life seems always to mean quarrelling, but cats and dogs come down together in heavy rain. Cat and Fiddle and Cat and Kittens appear on inn signs (and stealing pewter pots of various sizes is "cat and kitten sneaking"); and in parts of Cheshire and Lancashire, the Lion Rampant has been domesticized into the "rompin' kitlin'". To live under the cat's foot is to bow to petticoat government, and it is only when the cat is away that the mice can play. They have no hope of belling the cat. If you can almost see in the dark, you are cat-eyed; on the other hand, you may wish to take a short cat-nap during the day. Fashion models slink or strut along the cat-walk, and hope that they will not be received with cat-calls, like unsuccessful actors. Some modern girls wear cat-suits. Cats on hot bricks and cats who have swallowed the cream are alike all grey in the dark. There are few parts of our life that have not been expressed in cat terms.

The great popularity of the cat has been shown in every imaginable way (and in ways at which the imagination boggles) in the last few generations. Almost as soon as chocolates and other confectionery (including *langues-de-chat*) were packed in decorative boxes, cats and kittens appeared on the lids. Kittens peered out of flower-pots, old boots, watering-cans, and laundry-baskets on dozens of calendars and greetings cards. Grammatical kittens and analytical kittens have been pressed into service to endear parsing and analysis to school-children. Nightdress-cases, sherry-decanters, pepper-pots, door-stops, and lamps have all tried to look like cats. One may sneeze into a cambric cat or sport on one's lapel a cat made of anything from base metal to diamonds. Cats will receive your cigarette ash or hump their concrete backs on your rockery. They appear in pottery, glass, stone, platinum, and plastic. Fortunately, among the many vulgar falsifications of cats' beauty and dignity, there are some beautiful presentations. Many cats on cards and calendars have been accurately and imaginatively drawn, painted, or photographed. News stories of cats up trees, finding their way home cross-country, making friends with other beasts and birds, acting as fire alarms, or otherwise making good copy, do not always vulgarize the creature. Several Eastern European countries, and one Middle Eastern, have produced beautiful issues of postage stamps showing different breeds of cats. The real cat will survive any amount of misrepresentation, as he survives in the living world.

He has rarely been deliberately contemptuously mocked with any success. He has had his place in cartoons of animals since the late days of the Egyptian dynasties, and Krazy Kats have pranced and postured and tricked and been tricked through miles of cartoon strips and films. Tom and Jerry are not allowed to be long absent from television screens. In such farce and comedy, however, the cat is nearly always seen pleasurably, and both his victories and his defeats call out our affection. There is every hope that Felix of (naturally) happy memory will keep on walking, keep on walking still.

THE CAT IN MODERN SCIENCE

Animal-lovers who let their hearts overrule their heads are apt to bridle and bristle when science is mentioned in relation to animals, and think at once of secret horrors committed in the name of 'vivisection'. Fortunately, however, such horrors are the exception, not the rule. Inevitably, there are a few cruel men among scientists as there are among the rest of men, but, these exceptions apart, modern scientists are largely compelled to treat cats (and other animals) better than many laymen often do.

Although it is vital that we should be constantly vigilant against cruelty, we must—in fairness to scientists, to ourselves, and above all to cats—look at the facts objectively.

In the first place, cats in Britain and many other countries are protected by the laws which control all scientific work involving animals. For example, no animal that has undergone a major operation which could involve acute post-operational suffering is legally allowed to emerge from the general anaesthesia under which the operation has had to be performed if the operation was performed purely for purposes of scientific inquiry; the animal *must not* wake into the consciousness of acute pain. Only cats suffering for veterinary purposes, when their pain may be reasonably regarded, as with human patients, as a prelude to the enjoyment of restored health, are allowed to have such pain inflicted on them. In fact, scientists holding licences for experiments on animals are subject to penalties for infringement of the regulations even more severe than the penalties which may be imposed on the louts or fools who torment animals thoughtlessly.

In the second place, it is now well recognized that experiments with drugs or in psychological training lose all or some of their validity if they are performed on unhealthy animals; and an unhappy animal is never entirely healthy. It is therefore scientifically necessary that experimental animals should be kept under conditions ensuring their maximum possible happiness.

It is under such lights that we should view 'cats in science', and so recognize something of the interest and wonder of what is revealed to us. Certainly, cats have already benefited from scientific work. X-ray photographs taken for general interest in the early stages of X-ray experiments have led to X-ray studies which enable veterinary surgeons to judge their work with extreme accuracy. Being small, cats can be examined by X-rays with almost perfect completeness, whereas a horse still has to be treated by vets who cannot, as yet, have a true picture of parts of the horse's body. Thus, any necessary operation on a cat can be approached with wonderful certainty of information.

Similarly, experiments with drugs on cats have led to great extensions among the medicines available for treating cats. Because parts of the nervous system are highly developed in cats they have often been used for both qualitative and quantitative experiments with drugs. The results sometimes show marked similarities between human and feline reactions, sometimes startling contrasts. For instance, morphine seems never to induce a pleasurable calm in cats, but to produce at once the frantic and apparently distressing over-excitement which occurs only exceptionally in human beings. Whatever the results of such experiments, they produce information leading to improved treatment of cats as well as of human beings.

All such studies produce some enlightenment, even where definite solutions to problems still escape us. How does a cat produce its purr? We do not yet know for certain, but when we do we shall add a possibly helpful understanding to our pleasure in the comfortable sound. Are the movements of a cat's tail voluntary or involuntary? It seems that they are sometimes the one, sometimes the other; and when we know more, we may be better fitted to receive some of the communications that cats make.

When we know why blue-eyed white cats are nearly always deaf we shall understand something of the connection between pigmentation and the senses; and then we shall probably also know more about human albinism. Tortoiseshell cats are almost invariably female. The very rare Tortoiseshell male is not normal, being sexually impotent. Again, pigmentation seems to be an indicator to other factors.

Much that we do know reveals the marvellous complexity of physiology in cats which can lead to a better knowledge of the even greater complexity of human physiology. A distinguished pharmacologist has used the cat to exemplify the activities of the sympathetic nervous system. In *Drugs, Medicines and Man* (Allen and Unwin, 1962), Professor J. H. Burn says:

> The nerves of the sympathetic system are active under the influence of the emotions of anger and fear. If a cat is suddenly confronted with a dog, a discharge of impulses along all the sympathetic nerves of the cat takes place. The discharge is not confined to the sympathetic nerves supplying one area or one organ, but it occurs throughout the sympathetic nerves. A series of changes occurs which would assist the cat if it had to fight, or if it decided to run away. For fight or for flight the greatest possible supply of blood is needed for the muscles of the limbs and trunk. The first change is that the sympathetic nerves to the heart cause it to beat at a faster rate and with a greater force. Then the blood, which normally is distributed along three main routes, to the skin, to the intestines and to the muscles of the limbs, is cut off from two of them. Sympathetic nerves reduce the supply of blood to the skin and the intestines in order that a greater supply may go to the muscles. Then sympathetic impulses pass to the liver to cause a more rapid breakdown of the store of glycogen, so that more glucose may enter the blood to provide energy for muscle contractions. Then sympathetic nerves arrest the movements of the intestines. To compensate for the reduction in blood flow to the skin, the hair is erected to allow a greater heat loss. To enable the cat to follow the movements of the dog with greater ease, the pupils of the eyes dilate. To enable the cat to have the maximum supply of air to its lungs, the small tubes or bronchioles, into which the trachea (or wind-pipe) divides, are dilated and the airway is thus increased.

Even this complex activity is far from being the whole story. The erection of hair is caused partly by the secretion of adrenalin from the adrenal glands, stimulated by the situation; and the fur, thus puffed out, increases the cat's apparent size and so increases also its threatening aspect. Fear, anger, hostile action; cause, effect, result; need, purpose, activity; all work to and for each other in almost simultaneous operation to psychosomatic effect.

A cat that has kittened at once cleans up. She cannot afford to leave lying about anything which might lead an enemy by smell to her lying-in place. But in eating the placenta she also gains essential nourishment when she is first feeding her young. Again, the activity seems to be multi-purposed and multi-effective.

32

14   CREAM LONGHAIR

15 BLUE-CREAM LONGHAIR

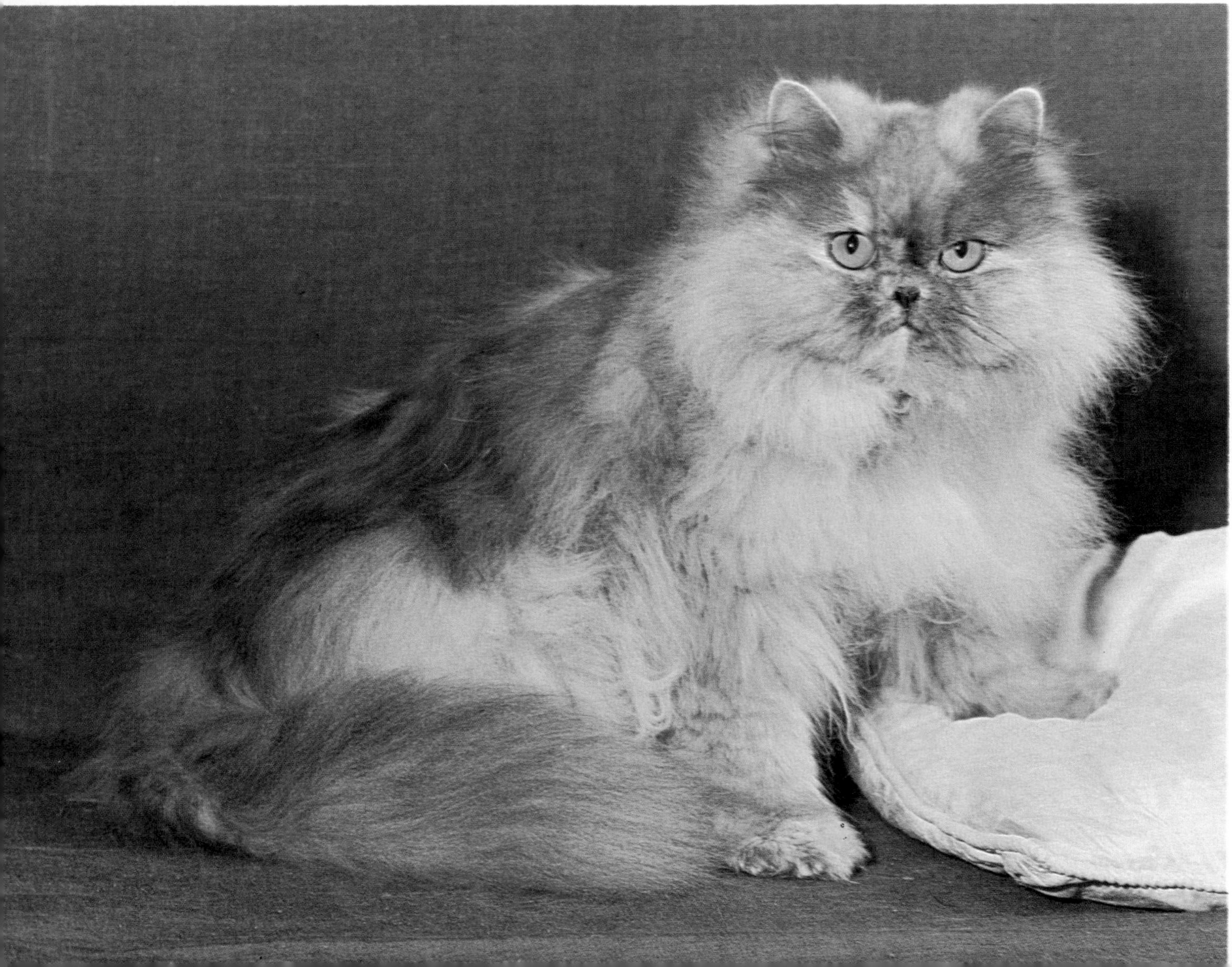

16   SMOKE LONGHAIR

17   CREAM LONGHAIR

After generations of careful breeding, cats of certain kinds now breed true, but they have, on the whole, proved resistant to the specialized breeding from near-freaks that has wrecked the health of some dogs. We may hope that the unhappy hairless cat will not breed, or at least not produce offspring suffering from this unlovely and dangerous deprivation.

One of the most significant physical facts about the cat is so obvious as often to escape attention. A cat's face is flat between the eyes; the eyes can therefore work together, and therefore a cat has stereoscopic vision. Now, this is remarkably rare among animals. The majority of animals familiar to us have facial structures that divide the two eyes so that they cannot focus together. The results of this difference are far-reaching. Stereoscopic vision gives the power of judging distances, and focusing sharply on objects at varying distances. To this, as well as to muscular endowment, much of a cat's sheer physical cleverness, its speed and accuracy, must be due. But stereoscopic vision gives the power of judging distances because it enables its possessor to see three-dimensionally. Thus, a flat-faced animal (such as a human being) literally sees a world different from the world seen by, say, a dromedary. According to some major philosophers, the way we see affects the way we think. It may be that any animal with binocular vision *begins its thinking* as a human being begins his thinking, in a way fundamentally different from the way the brain can ever operate in animals in which the eyes have to work separately. The relations between thought and sense-experience are still obscure, but such relations exist; and our recognition of cats' cleverness may be a recognition of an activity passing beyond sense-experience, but taking rise in one kind of sense-experience similar to our own. There are, of course, ways in which a cat's vision differs from ours. We do not know whether it sees colour as we do. It seems to follow rapid movement more readily than we can. Its adjustment to degrees of light through its astonishing range of contraction and expansion of the pupil is far beyond ours; it cannot literally 'see in the dark', but it can make use of light so faint that the human eye is aware only of darkness.

Cats are known to rank high among animals for intelligence. By intelligence we mean here not 'trainability' but a capacity for finding things out, or working them out. In tests with puzzle-cages, cats come immediately after monkeys. (They are followed by rats, whose intelligence is a main cause of man's inability ever to clear them out completely from markets and food-stores. It is fortunate for us that, in other contexts, cats are prepared to follow rats—fast!) In these tests, an animal is placed in a cage from which it can easily get out *if* it can discover how to work the simple gadget that opens the door. Most animals prowl or scurry or fumble round the cage until they accidentally (at any rate, for the first time) move the gadget. Some cats behave like this, but others sit quietly, looking about them and, it seems, thinking; for then they raise a paw, work the opener, and walk calmly out. Perhaps the observers then feel as silly as some of us do when we are left in a ridiculous position by a cat that has suddenly, in the middle of a game, decided to stop playing and return to a serious occupation like washing. It was a sad day for cats when knobs replaced lever-latches on nearly all doors, for they can turn only very loose knobs, whereas they could, and often did, work a lever, even when they had to stretch high or jump from the ground to do so.

33

We may remark in passing that cat-owners who bore each other with tales of their pets' cleverness in opening doors or striking typewriter keys are, in their amateur way, beginning that process of observing and recording which was the method of the first great naturalists. Amateurs' tales are often exaggerated, and therefore inaccurate, but their suggestions sometimes inspire the professionals to their strict observation; and observation in its turn suggests some of the experiments which can solve problems.

Some of the most interesting scientific work on animals today in fact depends more on observation than on experiment. The comparatively new science of animal behaviour needs for its success to watch animals as nearly as possible under their natural conditions. Most of the work has been done on animals which live and move in flocks or herds, because it is their behaviour that throws light most immediately on obviously 'social' problems; and we know how fascinating the books of Konrad Lorenz and Robert Ardrey can make these studies of hierarchy, aggression, and territorial sense among animals. Cats are not flocking animals, but they have been shown to share some of the herd animals' behaviour over territory, as it is described by Robert Ardrey:

A territory is an area of space, whether of water or earth or air, which an animal or group of animals defends as an exclusive preserve. The word is also used to describe the inward compulsion in animate beings to possess and defend such a space. A territorial species of animals, therefore, is one in which all males, and sometimes females too, bear an inherent drive to gain and defend an exclusive property. . . . We may also say that in all territorial species, without exception, possession of a territory lends enhanced energy to the proprietor. Students of animal behaviour cannot agree as to why this should be, but the challenger is almost invariably defeated, the intruder expelled. In part, there seems some mysterious flow of energy and resolve which invests a proprietor on his home grounds. But likewise, so marked is the inhibition lying on the intruder, so evident his sense of trespass, we may be permitted to wonder if in all territorial species there does not exist, more profound than simple learning, some universal recognition of territorial rights.

We all know that this is true of cats. They also show, however, signs in this connection of a slightly unusual form of the sense of hierarchy. In thickly-felinated suburban areas, where every cat usually preserves easily its own territory against invaders, there is sometimes an incredibly tough wandering tom whose mere appearance on a wall is enough to send otherwise proud and confident land-owning cats back into their families' houses. He is, presumably, a kind of Robber Baron who has proved himself in many great fights and so wrung from his more respectable neighbours a right, *de facto* if not *de jure*, to stalk their lands.

Such a right may occasionally override another arrangement that cats use in their territories. As Lorenz, in *On Aggression* (Methuen, 1966), puts it,

Leyhausen and Wolf have demonstrated that, in domestic cats living free in open country, several individuals could make use of the same hunting-ground without ever coming into conflict, by using it according to a definite timetable, in the same way as our See-wiesen housewives use our communal wash-house. An additional safeguard against undesirable encounters is the scent marks which these animals—the cats, not the housewives—deposit at regular intervals wherever they go. These act like railway signals whose aim is to prevent collision between two trains. A cat finding another cat's signal on its hunting-path assesses its age, and if it is very fresh it hesitates, or chooses another path; if it is a few hours old it proceeds calmly on its way.

The practice described here brings us to some of the most remarkable facts recently discovered about cats. Clearly, they have some of the feelings for territory and for hierarchy that flocking and herding animals have; equally clearly, their respect for a timetable in their use of hunting territory shows recognition of individual rights. In fact, the cat is not a herd animal, and his behaviour has sometimes gone unobserved by those seeking only for obvious social structures among animals, on the assumption that, except in breeding relationships, he is entirely a solitary, almost an Ishmael. It is true that he spends much time alone, and that in some places and at some times he seems to meet his kind only to fight or to mate; but Dr Paul Leyhausen has offered, on the basis of prolonged observations by himself and his assistants, the remarkable suggestion that cats are neither pure solitaries nor herders, but animals fully capable of living alone who nevertheless *deliberately cultivate society when they feel like it*. In a large farming area of Germany, where the cats have homes with human families but are also free to range, there are places where, during two or three hours of the night, cats gather apparently purely for companionship and, perhaps, conversation. They are neither mating nor fighting. A few cats remain for the whole of the time, the others come and go, remaining with the company for varying lengths of time; some sit still, some change their places from time to time. For what an amateur's observation is worth, I can confirm these findings from my own experience. On several occasions, when searching for lost cats, I have, at about midnight, come upon groups of cats of anything up to a dozen, sitting quietly in an old barn or in a corner of a great pasture. Their mood was clearly neither sexual nor warlike. The impression was for all the world like that of a quiet and friendly club. Dr Leyhausen states that the groups under his observation behaved as though they had come together like people dropping into a club when they felt like it.

The inferences Dr Leyhausen has drawn from these facts are remarkable—and, I believe, inescapable. Studies of herd animals have sometimes been carelessly used to suggest that human society may, or ought to, be considered as simply a great ant-heap or rabbit-warren in which neither privacy nor individual choice is of any importance; seen in this light, humanity might be expected to flourish when all its members are thrust willy-nilly into great tenements, living, working, and travelling in masses. The cats who can live and work alone, yet enjoy each other's company when they seek it from choice, perhaps offer a more profitable field for human study. Clearly, they flourish under conditions allowing them both privacy and company, both space and shelter. Cats run home when light is come, but they probably run home more readily when they have been free to go abroad. Men perhaps are more happily gregarious animals when they are not compelled to be gregarious. If they spend some time alone, they may be happy to seek companionship. If they are compelled into herds, they either seek privacy in holidays or lose their capacity for self-reliance. If they cannot find a balance between space and privacy on one hand, and close quarters and company on the other, they either fall contentedly below their potential for development or

35

suffer the nervous and psychic ailments increasingly common in our great cities. Cats, highly intelligent, highly developed organisms, flourish under conditions that may offer us a better model than an ant-heap. Defoe showed even Robinson Crusoe's cats approaching a greater dignity than their owner recognized, in their willingness to be friendly and their refusal to be mere slaves.

It may be that a less-than-conscious sense that cats choose their company makes some of us highly value their affection when they give it.

THE CAT IN MYTH, LEGEND, AND FOLK-LORE

The great number of phrases and proverbs in which cats appear is a sign of the cat's importance in legend. Such phrases occur throughout Asia, Africa, and Europe. Most of them are quite impossible to date; at the time when they are first recorded, they appear in familiar reference, as proverbial phrases that are evidently long-established, and so first recording is no evidence of date of origin. Some first references are themselves so old that the phrases they record are probably of very great antiquity. A few such phrases may have originated simply as obvious metaphors or similes, of which the aptness was so immediately evident that they soon passed into common use. Others, however, certainly represent memories of tales involving cats, and such memorial phrases probably constitute a majority of the verbal references. Even today there are one or two cat-terms in common use which are derived from cat tales many centuries old. They are often used by speakers ignorant of the originating story but, once the story is known, its connections with the surviving phrase are so evident as to be quite unquestionable. Though these terms are few, they indicate something of the kind of history that may lie behind such phrases, at once common and puzzling, as "like a cat on hot bricks"; perhaps there was once a story of a cat jumping and landing unexpectedly on hot bricks. Perhaps there was once a tale of Puss in Gloves, which gave rise to the Italian proverb, *Gatta guantata non piglia sorce.* When Dickens's Dorrit family are in Italy, Fanny Dorrit warns her sister Amy "'that Mrs. General, if I may reverse a common proverb and adapt it to her, is a cat in gloves who *will* catch mice'."

Though we can only occasionally trace the legends of cats into surviving phrases, we may try to find another kind of order among the confusing plenty of cat myth, cat legend, and cat folk-lore by roughly classifying the material. The old anonymous stories (often the sign and the origin of folk-beliefs) may be divided into two main classes. The first (small) class may properly be termed myths, in that they embody beliefs about creation, and about the connection between natural phenomena and a god or gods. The second class is that of the legends which, though they may contain much of the mysterious or even the magical, do not directly concern the divine. Each of these two classes may be sub-divided into two sections. In each, the first section is concerned with cats simply because they are animals, not specially because they are cats; the second section is concerned with cats because they *are* cats, characterized by some attribute or attributes which distinguish them from other animals. The same divisions and sub-divisions may at times be detected among many folk-beliefs.

Clearly, the dividing lines cannot always be observed. Myth shades into legend, and general animal activity becomes specialized through variant versions of a story into typically feline activity. The divisions must be fluid, and they are sometimes very uncertain indeed, but at least they give us a clue, however fragile, to hold as we enter the labyrinth.

One early mythological appearance showing the cat as divine is, at first, the clearest possible evidence that the cat was divine as *one* among other animals, not as the *only* possibly divine animal. The Egyptian goddess Bast takes her place beside Anubis (jackal), Thoth (ibis), Hathor (cow), Khepri (scarab-beetle), and many other zoomorphic deities; she cannot claim precedence over jackals or cows. When not actually divine, the cat was sometimes held sacred to Ra (Re) and, later, to Isis—but then, so were other animals and birds. Very soon, however, there are hints that the cat's special nature is beginning to be recognized. It becomes impossible to confuse the cat with the cow. Bast(et) was increasingly regarded as a benignant deity, and this, coupled with her femininity, may have given rise to the appearance of cats among toys, suggesting a special relation with children. We may remember how Kipling recognized a cat's special skill with, and attraction for, children. Again, the cat's association with the male Ra tends to give way to the association with the female Isis.

In Hindu belief, it is a goddess who is connected with cats, and she is the goddess concerned with children's play and welfare. It is evidently impossible in a case like this to be quite sure whether we have an arbitrary association between a divinity and an animal, or whether there is some special reason for the association. On balance, however, it seems as though some special connection between the cat on one hand and ideas of the female and of children's happiness on the other hand is indicated by some old mythologies.

Among the Romans there grew up a story that the cat was created by Diana. Apollo (her brother, according to late identifications) had created the lion, and, in order to mock him, Diana created a miniature lion, the cat. This is one of the few entirely light-hearted mythical stories, and we may receive it as such with gratitude. The other Roman attempt to mythicize the cat hardly leaves the ground, for it belongs to that least impressive activity of the Roman genius, the endeavour to bring divine life into abstractions by personifying abstract nouns. *Libertas*, deified liberty, was represented in statuary with a cat. True, liberty may be worshipped; true, a cat acts out some of the central ideas of liberty—but myths, like poets, are born, not made.

Another near-myth regards the cat as older than the lion in the order of creation. Islamic belief was that the lion, new-created in all his strength and beauty, was yet lacking in skill and wisdom. Accordingly, he was sent for education to the cat. She taught him nearly everything she knew—to stalk, to wait, to pounce, to kill. One day, the lion thought to exercise these skills on his preceptress, so much smaller than himself. He prepared to spring and kill; but there was just one art that the cat had not yet taught him. She ran up a tree, and so saved herself by exercising that one art. To this day, the cat is known in Islamic lands as the lion's aunt, even by people who do not know that she is so called because she was, though smaller and weaker, a little older and wiser than the lion. This is evidently a mythical

37

tale depending on a quality characteristic of the cat, its sheer cleverness, and therefore not suitable for relating of other animals.

The cat's cleverness gives it, perhaps after generations of experimental tale-telling, a very special place in what became the most popular version of an extremely ancient legend. All over the world the oldest stories of heroes send the heroes travelling through adventures (sometimes in the underworld) which are both mysterious and dangerous. Some of these stories are very ancient in origin, and concern those heroes whom the story-tellers regard as the direct links between their respective races and the gods who made the earth and first lived in it. Old as they are, however, these stories reappear, in however changed a form, late in historical periods and, in fact, provide the model for a large majority of heroic adventure stories. In the old stories the hero is often accompanied, sometimes helped, through his adventures by a guide who may be a human friend but who is very often some not-quite-human being, a ghost, or an animal of a definite kind. Probably the earliest example is Enkidu, the 'wild man' who accompanies the hero Gilgamesh in the Babylonian epic of some time early in the second millennium B.C. At first sight it seems an impossibly far cry from the Epic of Gilgamesh to Perrault's *Contes de ma Mère l'Oye* of A.D. 1697. Mother Goose stories are not epic. But the simple fact is that Perrault was giving artistic form to old folk-tales, themselves possibly the remnants of ancient heroic stories; and le Maistre Chat, Puss in Boots, is the example of the animal guide which finally retained the widest currency in the popular imagination. Andrew Lang in 1888 went exploring as far as he could for the sources of Perrault's tales. Many of them he found to be very old, and versions of the clever cat guide were widespread centuries before Perrault. There had, in different parts of the world, been different animal companions—horse, dog, fox, and so on. The cat at first simply takes its place among these. In one of the two main sub-divisions of the tale, however, it comes to be pre-eminent. In some of the oldest stories, the hero who needs guiding is (like Gilgamesh) already a king or a prince. In another group, possibly later in origin, the hero is a lad of humble birth who is brought to rank and power as a result of his successful passing through his adventures; and in this group of tales, he often owes his success to his animal guide. It is here that the cat becomes important. It is his cleverness that brings success to the hero. Whittington's fortunes are built upon his pet's skill in ridding Barbary of its plague of rats and mice. *Le Chat Botté*, late and 'literary' as it is, retains the very essence of the clever-cat-guide story of centuries of popular telling:

> The youngest son of a poor miller was disappointed to find that his sole inheritance was a cat. When, however, he set out to improve his poor fortune the cat persuaded him to follow his (the cat's) advice. As a result of a series of clever plans and tricks by the cat, the young man (who was himself not at all intelligent) found himself accepted as the Marquis of Carabbas, with a fine wife and a fortune.

Partly because of Perrault's skill, partly because of the ideal conjunction of a hero in every sense simple and a *very* clever guide, this version of the old legend of a hero accompanied into fortune by a faithful animal is the only one which is still widespread today. It is amusing that two of the pantomimes which are still (in however debased a form) on the stage handle developments of what was originally the same story: *Dick Whittington* and *Puss in Boots*. Nowadays, of course, Puss's boots are often skating-boots.

There is a conviction among most readers of stories where the heroes achieve success only through the skill of their cat friends, that such heroes will never be capable of looking after their own fortunes. The cat watches his 'master' with anxiety, unable to trust the 'hero' to behave properly, yet the talented animal, whatever the mysterious sources of his wisdom, never does throw over the human fool whom some obscure destiny has set him to guard and assist. There is a pathos in the mystery of these creatures, serving so well the men who at times seem not only more foolish but also less magnanimous than the beasts. It is not surprising that in some of the stories the clever cat shows not only devotion but irritation. Disney gave the trait to the kitten in *Pinocchio*.

Where the cat continuously plays a central role in a traditional tale it is nearly always in right of his cleverness. This is evidently a main source of his importance in stories of the 'Whittington' kind, though it is here mingled with more complex and mysterious elements. When the cleverness is separated out it seems to make a story that is a cross between a fable and a *fabliau*, where proverbial wisdom is accompanied by laughing admiration for a clever trick. The mixture is complete in the very old Indian tale of the False Yogi. A rat and a bird had pounced simultaneously on a titbit of food. Neither was strong enough to wrest the prize from the other, and neither could defeat the other in argument. Accordingly, they decided to take the case to arbitration. Near at hand sat a contemplative cat, still, quiet, thoughtful—apparently meditating upon the eternal verities. They begged the cat for a righteous decision and the cat, sure enough, told them that such a decision must depend on a proper interpretation of the teachings of holy scripture. He embarked on a long exposition of texts and their theological and moral implications, so that at length both rat and bird, lacking a Scottish congregation's appetite for sermons, were nodding off to sleep. At this point, the cat, watchful behind his air of holy detachment from this world, pounced—and cleared the board. The story is many hundreds of years old, and still referred to by present-day Bengalis.

A more modern Indian story seems almost to assume that the cat accepts his reputation for cleverness, and will go to any lengths to preserve it. A cat who had defeated men in contests of cleverness strolled off into the jungle, and was there accepted by a family of tigers as a sage and hunter, because he had so cleverly presented his claims. The time came, however, when hunting was needed, and the tigers proposed that the cat should join them. He, however, said that he could not waste time on ordinary hunting, and would wait till the tigers had beaten up the game before him, when he would dispatch the game. The tigers duly beat towards the cat many beasts far too large and strong for the cat to tackle, and, indeed, the cat was attacked and wounded to death by the other beasts. When the tigers returned the cat was dying, and he told them, "I was so amused by the absurd little animals you drove up for game that I have laughed myself to death!"—and died.

Naturally, the cat has a place among folk-beliefs, including those that regard an animal as a totem of family or tribe, and therefore peculiarly sacred to that family or tribe. This belief sometimes takes the form of regarding the animal as the repository of the family's soul or spirit, or at any rate of a secondary soul of the family. Perhaps the most remarkable example of such a belief is told by Frazer in *The Golden Bough*:

39

A tale told by the Ba-Ronga of South Africa sets forth how the lives of a whole family were contained in one cat. When a girl of the family, named Titishan, married a husband, she begged her parents to let her take the precious cat with her to her new home. But they refused, saying, 'You know that our life is attached to it'; and they offered to give her an antelope or even an elephant instead of it. But nothing would satisfy her but the cat. So at last she carried it off with her and shut it up in a place where nobody saw it; even her husband knew nothing about it. One day, when she went to work in the fields, the cat escaped from its place of concealment, entered the hut, put on the warlike trappings of the husband, and danced and sang. Some children, attracted by the noise, discovered the cat at its antics, and when they expressed their astonishment, the animal only capered the more and insulted them besides. So they went to the owner and said, 'There is somebody dancing in your house, and he insulted us.' 'Hold your tongues,' said he, 'I'll soon put a stop to your lies.' So he went and hid behind the door and peeped in, and there sure enough was the cat prancing about and singing. He fired at it, and the animal dropped down dead. At the same moment his wife fell to the ground in the field where she was at work; said she, 'I have been killed at home.' But she had strength enough left to ask her husband to go with her to her parents' village, taking with him the dead cat wrapt up in a mat. All her relatives assembled, and bitterly they reproached her for having insisted on taking the animal with her to her husband's village. As soon as the mat was unrolled and they saw the dead cat, they all fell down lifeless one after the other. So the Clan of the Cat was destroyed; and the bereaved husband closed the gate of the village with a branch, and returned home, and told his friends how in killing the cat he had killed the whole clan, because their lives depended on the life of the cat.

The Bataks of Sumatra sometimes have one of their external souls (of which they may have up to seven) in a cat, and therefore treat the cat with great care and respect, for if the holder of an external soul is killed, the man with the inner soul will die. This is not the place to go into the origin of such beliefs. Perhaps the most important thing about them for our interests is that they show a ground for the care of animals in the conviction that human and animal life may be integrally connected. Such beliefs, of ancient origin, are concerned with the cat only in those parts of the world where the cat is indigenous. It may be that self-preservation is always the first motive behind human desires to preserve the safety of other beings.

The stories told so far have been collected from times and places millennia and miles apart. This is unavoidable, but it is also important. For all the differences of detail, stories about animals in general and about cats in particular show, if they are the true signs of deep and wide belief among peoples, some features in common. The relation of cats to divinity, the long and august descent of a Principal Boy's stage companion, the almost identical beliefs of peoples separated by thousands of miles of land and sea, reveal both a profound sense of a link between human and animal life that it may be unwise, even dangerous, to sunder, and very often a respectful, even delighted, appreciation of some of the cat-ness of cats. The belief in the links, the appreciation of cat nature, may not always have led to love and kindness, but they accept the cat as a living fact that may not be disregarded. In most places and times where the domestic cat existed, he was noticed. At times, no doubt, he acted the human performers off the stage as readily as a Principal Boy may be acted off by The Cat.

18-19   BROWN TABBY LONGHAIR

21   SILVER TABBY LONGHAIR

22–23   TORTOISESHELL LONGHAIR

It is therefore natural that many lands should have popular stories and superstitions about cats which cannot be immediately related to the world of myth and symbolical legend, but which show an established popular interest. As we might expect from their early recognition of the rights of cats in law, the Irish have many old stories of cats. Some are magical. In the tenth-century *Voyage of Mael Duin* there is a cat guarding a treasure. It is a playful creature, but none the less alert. When the villain attempts to steal the treasure, the cat (playful as ever) jumps right through him and burns him to death.

There was a King of the Cats, who had his home at Knowth (a necropolis now being excavated). According to a thirteenth-century story a man satirized this king, Irusan Mac Arusan—and terrible consequences befell the man.

One Irish story uncannily forecasts a modern topic of discussion:

Now Miach, son of Diancecht, was a better hand at healing than his father, and had done many things. He met a young man, who had lost one eye, at Teamh Air one time, and the young man said: 'If you are a good physician you will put an eye in the place of the eye I lost.' 'I could put the eye of that cat in your lap in its place,' said Miach. 'I would like that well,' said the young man. So Miach put the cat's eye in his head; but he would as soon have been without it after, for when he wanted to sleep and take his rest, it is then the eye would start at the squeaking of the mice, or the flight of the birds, or the movement of the rushes; and when he was wanting to watch an army or a gathering, it is then it was sure to be in a deep sleep.

So much for the possible dangers of transplants! Both cat habits and cat indomitability are clear here—and we applaud them.

FROM THE EIGHTH-CENTURY BOOK OF KELLS, TRINITY COLLEGE, DUBLIN

41

Oddly enough, there seem to be no common superstitions about cats among the Irish. It is in superstitions that in other countries we find traces of old stories that may or may not be still extant. Some superstitions, no doubt, descend from beliefs and practices of ages deeply committed to magic, lawful or forbidden. The beliefs and practices are no longer understood, or deeply felt, but they leave traces in popular ideas about luck, good or bad.

Cats appeared among other animals in the rites and activities of those known as witches. Animals provided some of the disguises and concealments of officiating 'devils', and were sometimes companions of witches, either to carry out their commands or to bring them their 'devil's' commands, or purely for company's sake. They were also occasionally used simply as part of a spell-casting process.

It was only very rarely indeed that the 'devil' took a cat's form. In Guernsey in 1563, however, one Martin Tulouff confessed that, in the house of Collenette Gascoing, "there were five or six cats, of which there was one that was black, which led the dance . . . that he kissed the said Cat and said that it was on all fours . . . and that they all went on their knees before the Cat and worshipped it, pledging their faith to it, and the said Vieillesse [Collenette] told him that the said Cat was the devil". In 1652 a French witch said that the devil "entered her room in the form of a cat and changed into the shape of a man clothed in red", who took her to the Witches' Sabbath.

Cats appear more frequently as diviners or messengers. At Edinburgh in 1630 Alexander Hamilton confessed that he used to seek information from a devil that "was in use sumtymes to appeir to the said Alexr in the liknes of ane corbie at uther tymes in the schape of ane katt and at uther tymes in the schape of ane dog and thereby the said Alexr did ressave reponsis frome him". Once, Hamilton cured one Thomas Homes of a sickness; on the Devil's instructions, he threw at him a cat "quha therewt vanischet away". Among horses, toads, weasels, "mouses", and other animals, cats often brought messages and carried out errands. The innumerable references to animals in the trials are often so worded as to suggest that either the witches themselves or their enemies were reluctant to think of these animals as ordinary domestic creatures. There is a particularly interesting account of a trial at Chelmsford in 1556. Elizabeth Francis

learned this arte of witchcraft of hyr grandmother whose name [was] mother Eue. Item when shee taughte it her, she counsiled her to renounce GOD and his worde and to geue of her bloudde to Sathan (as she termed it) whyche she delyuered her in the lykenesse of a whyte spotted Catte, and taughte her to feede the sayde Catte with breade and mylke, and she dyd so, also she taughte her to cal it by the name of Sathan and to kepe it in a basket. Item that euery tyme that he did any thynge for her, she sayde that he required a drop of bloude, which she gaue him by prycking herselfe, sometime in one place and then in an other. When she had kept this Cat by the space of XV or XVI yeare, and as some saye (though vntruly) beinge wery of it, she came to one mother Waterhouse her neyghbour, she brought her this cat in her apron and taught her as she was instructed by her grandmother Eue, telling her that she must cal him Sathan and geue him of her bloude and breade and milke as before.—Mother Waterhouse receyued this cat of this Frances wife in the order as is before sayde. She (to trye him what he coulde do) wyld him to kyll a hog of her owne, which he dyd, and she gaue him for his labour a chicken, which he fyrste required of her and a drop of her blod. And thys she gaue him at all times when he dyd anythynge for her, by pricking her hand or face and puttinge the bloud to hys mouth whyche he sucked, and forthwith wold lye downe in hys pot againe, wherein she kepte him. Another tym she rewarded hym as before, wyth a chicken and a droppe of her bloud, which chicken he eate vp cleane as he didde al the rest, and she cold fynde remaining neyther bones nor fethers. Also she said that when she wolde wyl him to do any thinge for her, she wolde say her Pater noster in laten. Item, this mother Waterhouse confessed that shee fyrst turned this Cat into a tode by this meanes, she kept the cat a great while in woll in a pot, and at length being moued by pouertie to occupie [use] the woll, she praied in the name of the father and of the sonne, and of the holy ghost that it wold turne into a tode, and forthwith it was turned into a tode, and so kept it in the pot without woll.

This passage is remarkable for its mixture of everyday domesticity and an apparent faith in the marvellous. The cat is carried in an apron and, like most ordinary cats, it likes chicken. We are not told how it dealt with the hog, and there seems nothing very strange about it until it is turned into a toad. It could hardly have helped being named Sathan. It seems to have flourished, for it is said to have had a long life. Here, however, we meet one of the difficulties in accepting any of these accounts. Other witches claimed to have had cats for impossibly long periods of time, and it is clear that either they or their accusers hardly distinguished between one pet and its successor. It was just that they had to have some small companion, and a succession of cats may for each witch have borne the same name—Sathan, or Gille, or Ginnie, or Tyttey, or Tissey, and so on. Sometimes the cats were gifts, sometimes they were inherited. A pot lined with wool was the usual bed for such a domestic familiar. Everything about the cat seems normal, and it is only the way the facts are adorned that makes them seem strange. It is quite probable that when Mother Waterhouse became poorer she simply changed her cat for a pet that would be even cheaper to keep, and the fact is so narrated as to make it seem marvellous. A word or two can turn the commonplace into the mysterious, and when we are told that witches had familiars "like" or "in the likeness" of dogs or toads or weasels or cats, it is simply a wording that adds wonder to the too-prosaic fact that they really had dogs or toads or weasels or cats. In the accounts of English witch-trials there is never any indication that the animals were legally punished with their owners. Indeed, they so often 'vanished' or were magically changed that they probably made their escape or were taken over by friends. As soon as we pick away the accretions that fear has added to these accounts, we find cats living with witches much the lives that they lived with their neighbours, and their neighbours probably thought little about them except at times of accusation and trial.

The occasions when cats sometimes suffered were those when they were used in making spells. When the Berwick witches tried to raise a storm to drown King James they threw a cat into the sea. King James had some reason to distrust witches, and *Macbeth*, which is said to cater for the King's shuddering interest, gives us in the witch scenes a pretty gallimaufry of the creatures associated with witchcraft. At one point, sure enough, we are told, "Thrice the brinded cat hath mewed." Some horrible old customs lingered long in backward districts, and in *North and South* Mrs Gaskell uses the ill-treatment of a cat in a superstitious practice to make the heroine, Margaret Hale, realize that the lovely-seeming agricultural South of England is not in all ways superior to the industrial North.

43

Nowadays, fortunately, superstitions about cats linger mainly in the mental area of casual half-beliefs about luck. Little figures of cats are often worn as 'charms', and many people believe that particular kinds of cats are lucky or unlucky. What is curious is that beliefs of different areas contradict each other. In most parts of England a black cat is regarded as lucky, and it is a good omen if a black cat crosses your path when you are setting out on some important project. In some of the eastern counties, however, the black cat is unlucky. Now, these are the counties in which Matthew Hopkins, the most inveterate and 'successful' witch-finder of the seventeenth century, was most active. Witches' cats are recorded as being white, grey, brindled, yellow-dun, as well as black; but it is not impossible that a black cat was regarded as specially likely to be witch-like. Certainly, the very rare appearances of the master-devil as a cat are in the form of a black cat. The black cat is also regarded as *un*lucky in most parts of the United States; and we need only look at the place-names of Boston, Lincolnshire, and Boston, Massachusetts, to remember that some of the seventeenth-century English settlers in America came from the eastern counties of England. New England suffered, a generation later than East Anglia, from an even more virulent form of the witch-panic roused by Matthew Hopkins. Is this the historical reason for a superstition which joins the United States with East Anglia against the rest of England?

One persistent superstition seems to have confused the cat with yet another creature. It is sometimes believed to 'suck the breath' of a sleeping baby. The Romans ascribed this practice to the screech-owl!

It is pleasant to close this sometimes distressing section with a modern superstition that brings us full circle back to some of the earliest beliefs about cats, and keeps alive the most loving and happy elements in the early beliefs. In Northern Egypt to this day the soul of a sleeping child is believed to go into a cat. So, at the times when children are sleeping, one must be very careful to do no harm to cats, for any one of them may be giving temporary shelter to a child's soul. Bast is no longer invoked; but the link between her and happy children, between cats and love and protection, is not yet broken.

THE CAT IN THE FINE ARTS

The myriads of cats in the living world are almost adequately represented by their millions of appearances in the visual and plastic fine arts. Even to list these appearances would be impossible without the aid of a computer Puss in seven-leagued Boots. All we can hope to do is point to some of the times and places where cats have appeared in modelling, painting, or drawing, and consider the most significant treatments of feline nature in these modes.

The early connection of all arts with religion, education, and play holds with cats as with other subjects. Such connections are clear in the wall-paintings of Egyptian tombs or of Mycenean shaft-graves, or in figurines of creatures obviously held sacred; such presentations clearly have purposes not quite identical with the purely 'aesthetic'. This fact, however, does not preclude them from consideration as works of 'art' in every sense, any more than the piety of, for example, Fra Angelico has precluded his paintings from the appreciation and judgments of the historians and critics of art. Whatever the original or avowed purpose of a statue or a painting may be, we may respond to it as an example of a 'fine art' wherever its execution is of such quality as to demand respect even from those who are not, perhaps cannot be, responsive to its original purpose.

In fact, the cat, by the very nature of its physical being, has presented difficulties in representation of the kind that often call out the highest artistic gifts in the mere solution of the technical problems. There are two main facts about a cat's body that seem to ask for opposite solutions to the problems of representing it. The first fact is that this body is of a finely-articulated bony structure made active through complex, firm, but delicate muscles and nerves. The second fact is that this structure is (except in rare sad freaks) always covered by a silky-soft fur; the fur varies, from cat to cat and on the same cat, in length and in colour; sometimes the fur follows and emphasizes the lines of muscle, sometimes it goes contrary to them; when every separate hair is as fine as gossamer the hairs sometimes grow together so thickly that it is difficult to catch a glimpse of the skin. The first, structural, fact about a cat seems to demand a treatment in art that will emphasize clear, firm, strong modelling; best provided, perhaps, by sculptural modes. The second, furry, fact about a cat seems to demand a treatment that will suggest or imply flow, and movement, and shadow colours; best provided, perhaps, by fine brushwork. Either treatment, in fact, emphasized to the exclusion of the other, excludes something essentially feline. It is as though the cat presented eternally the problems of the nude and of the clothed figure at one and the same time; it is never, when fully itself, either dressed or naked. Perhaps it asks always for that mysteriously intimate fusion of structure and 'drapery' that we find in the Three Graces in Botticelli's *Primavera*. Such fusion alone could embody both its stillness and its movement. It has, therefore, offered both a seductive invitation and a daunting challenge to artists; invitation and challenge have both been accepted, sometimes with profoundly interesting results.

If we have to choose between emphases, and put either structure or surface first, we shall, no doubt, on the whole choose artistic treatments of the cat that emphasize its structure. The supple firmness, elegant strength, poise, and movement distinguish it from other beasts more certainly than the lovely, silky clothing which it shares with rabbits and squirrels. It is therefore not surprising that we should find our admiration for cats in art directed first to modelled representations. It is the statuettes produced by the Egyptians, rather than their paintings, which can still hold us entranced by the sheer beauty of the thing-in-itself and not simply by the reminder of something we know and love.

The great statuettes (there are no major big statues of cats) are all in bronze, which the Egyptians came to handle with great mastery. No doubt many have been lost, but those that remain reach occasionally heights of mastered feeling and craft which can hardly be surpassed in this kind. Several of the best are in the Egyptian Collection of the British Museum, but there are also fine examples at the Hague, in New York, and in Cairo. The first purely physical characteristic of these statuettes to strike us is, perhaps, the perfect containment of the structure. Though the tail-end is often allowed to curve outward from the main mass, it never distracts from the satisfied sense that the mass is self-sufficient, self-

45

supporting: that the three dimensions of the modelling concur in pointing to a centre of gravity—and this, as we shall see, has great importance. There is no fussy detail in the modelling. The separation of toes is indicated, shoulder-blades and arch of back are clear, the tail is tapered, the ears are shaped and angled with certainty; but no detail distracts from the poise of the whole. No attempt, doomed to failure, has been made to model whiskers or fur, except where it can be felt accenting the line down the back or above the eyes. It is perhaps a measure of the achievement of these figures that where the amulet of a necklace rests on the chest, or the ears show the holes made for ear-rings, these details suggest neither frivolity nor irrelevance. Everything is relevant to the seeing of a creature embodying the dignity of the divine in life, a dignity seen with both reverence and love.

The 'centre of gravity' we have referred to is not merely physical. It involves also the 'gravity', in an extended sense, of any living creature so fully *recognized* in its right to its own nature that something of the essence of that nature appears in the presentation of the individual. It shows Schweitzer's generalized "reverence for life" particularized into veneration for the specific forms of life. *Haeccitas*, quiddity, this-ness, have come into full cognition; and this is why generations who do not share Egyptian religious beliefs can nevertheless recognize something of the 'holy' in these statuettes of cats. The cat shown—whether Bast herself, or one of her kin, or a cat sacred to Ra—is always lean (though not emaciated). The limbs are long. The pose in these religious statuettes is always a sitting one, with the paws placed neatly together. The head is held high on the neck.

This last is the detail in which these figures differ most sharply from the figures, often colossal, of Pharaohs or anthropomorphic deities. The human-shaped figures in their stillness seem often to be held by an invisible weight above them (there are, of course, famous exceptions). The cat figures retain always an air of 'lift', of possible upward movement. Their stillness, therefore, impresses the observer with a feeling of a willed acceptance, of power and movement held in check by self-control, not by control from outside. It is partly this that gives the figures their loneliness, their inescapable dignity, their kinship with a sadness which one would not dare to pity. Religious and atheist alike can recognize the right to veneration of such presentations.

Bronze, now so firm, once so malleable, has been the perfect substance for such modelling. The particular miracle of statuary, that the profoundly still can hold the profoundly living, is caught in this medium. In these cats the flowing bronze settles into an embodiment of the quiet which only a sense of life can make profound. The central excitement of many great works of art is here. Arts which move through time can suggest rest and stasis. Deeply still objects, like these figures, can suggest all the moving possibilities of life.

After these astonishing performances, there is nothing comparable in the sculptural treatment of cats. The Egyptians themselves relaxed outside their creation of these religious symbols; and then they created some of the first in a long line of cats modelled in lesser modes. True, some may have been religious in intention; naïve faience Basts may have been in some households the early equivalents of oleographs of the Madonna or the Christ in thousands of European cottages. But some faience and wooden cats were clearly made for fun—whether the fun of the maker or the fun of the recipient hardly matters. Some little doll-cats must have given fun to both maker and child. Of course, serious feelings

46

remained in some of the modelling of mummy-cases, but when we move away from exquisite bronze-work we do not always know what to make of, for example, some wooden mummy-cases. Lumpish, clumsy, roughly-painted—were these cases perfunctory performances of a duty, cynical law-keeping evasions of the real duty, or innocent failures to express the spirit of the duty in the letter? Most of them were, almost certainly, the last. Somebody once said that nowhere in the world will you find more sincere feeling and more bad art than in a graveyard, and the queer, clumsy mummy-cases of some Egyptian cats demand humane consideration. Their absurdity is as funny and as pathetic as Petrouchka.

The little faience figures, however, which attempt no dignity, are the measure of most later modelling of cats. Very rarely a cat appears in the church carvings executed by the anonymous carvers of fruit and dogs and foliage and demons. With a few exceptions, however, one notable, cats disappear from major sculpture but after many centuries re-appear, persistently, in ceramics. Some of the most famous houses producing pottery and porcelain have had nothing to do with cats. Others have turned out cats for generations. Quite often, "turned out" seems to be the appropriate term for the production; the results are so obvious, so undistinguished, that we simply feel that a demand is being automatically supplied. But this fact should make us think. There was and still is a demand for cats modelled and fired into pottery and porcelain. The houses and factories satisfying this demand have been working in close connection with a real desire of 'the people'. They have, therefore, produced the kind of 'folk art' which brings together mastery of a technique (sometimes involving trade secrets) on the one hand and the simple desire of 'people' on the other hand. Such art often brings together also social classes usually regarded as separated. A fine lady and her waiting-woman may equally wish for a modelling of a pet, and they will find the satisfaction of their wishes in the modelling of different clay, by different workmen, on the designs of different artists. A Chelsea china scent-bottle which has in recent years passed through the sale-rooms, showing a cat and a mouse, was probably bought (perhaps even commissioned) by a lady of some standing in about 1755. Before and after that, however, the Staffordshire works were producing cats, spotted, veined, brindled, in an assortment of colours and sizes that probably satisfied the lady's woman and her kin. Certainly, from as early as about 1745 till the nineteenth century, Staffordshire ware showed cats of various kinds, and used them for demonstrating skill in different materials and techniques—stoneware, salt-glaze solid agate-ware, and so on. Sometimes a cat offered a chance for sharp observation translated into pottery, as in a figure, of about 1800, of a cat standing over a mousehole with a mouse in its mouth. During this period Ralph Wood modelled ceramic cats. In all this work there is an interesting wedding of a largely naturalistic, sometimes sharply observant, treatment of shape and attitude with a debonair, to-hell-with-it gaiety in colours—any colours. When a refined company like Rockingham turns to cats in the early nineteenth century, with, for example, a pair of cats sitting side by side on a green base, its refinement goes into gentleness rather than into naturalism in colouring. Rockingham, Staffordshire, and Chelsea came together to pro-duce versions of a favourite animal for every level of society that could afford a china model of its pet. Both cats and craftsmen might now be startled by the craze for Stafford-shire figures—and wish that the craze had come in time to benefit them directly.

Before and after this period the Chinese had been making ceramic cats. The cats never reached the peak of interest of some other animals in Chinese ceramics, but it was used as a means of showing off some of the wonderful colours—aubergine, strange rich yellows, and so on—of Chinese work in porcelain.

Some of the European houses most famed for 'fine' work, such as those of Meissen and Dresden, seem to have shown little interest in the cat. This, one feels, must mean a lack of interest in either designers or customers, or both, as the challenge of the cat figure must have been exciting to craftsmen. Where, however, the pottery and porcelain houses had a close connection with popular taste and desire, we find cats. The old potteries of Delft, with their ups-and-downs (down almost to extinction in the late nineteenth century, recently up again), made some enchanting cats, with a merry mingling of naturalism and fantasy that must entrance all but the most curmudgeonly. The modelling caught, even when proportions were non-naturalistic, the *point* of cats' attitudes; the colouring was the usual blue and white—but it was deployed gaily in blue floral sprays over the white, firmly-modelled bones and muscles of the cat.

In recent generations the Royal Copenhagen Porcelain Works have made several cats. As might be expected from the house that made the great 'Flora Danica' table service, the interest here has been naturalistic. Sitting and lying cats have been faithfully reproduced, and the soft grey-blues used by the works for this kind of production may have emphasized their interest in Blue Persians and Blue-point Siamese. They have made some beautiful cats—with never a sign of claw or tooth.

During the last decade or two a few, mainly anonymous, workers in ceramics and glass have picked up the popular cat figure, and used it to express something of their sense of deep-lying form. In Venice, where the glass-blowers will blow you any kind of cat to suit your sentimental fancy, you may, nevertheless, find glass cats exemplifying simplified form to the point where only a single, intense mood is felt. Even little bronze figures intended for the (not too poverty-stricken) tourist market often show a clear sense of essentially *cat* anatomy in the modelling underneath whatever joke or sentimentality may be appealing to a purchaser.

Some of the ceramic and glass work has been beautiful and imaginative. It is difficult, however, to find in it the depth of understanding and the height of craftsmanship which make the Egyptian figurines great. In all the centuries between the Egyptians and ourselves only one plastic treatment of cats reaches the Egyptian level. The astounding cats on the Louth cross show, in the sensitive carving of a stone hard enough to keep its lines through a thousand years of weathering, a familiar knowledge combined with reverence adequate to be balanced with Egyptian statuettes.

The sculptural forms did, then, show at times a wonderful appreciation of cat structure and even what feels like cat nature. Outside the moments of great apprehension, there have been modellings showing humour and affection. It was hardly within the power of sculpture and modelling, however, to show, except by implication, the flowing softness manifested in some parts of cats' lives, nor the place they take among other living beings in the world. If we want the colour and softness and speed of cats, and the part they play in human and animal affairs in general, we have to move away from sculpture. There are, of course,

24　TORTOISESHELL AND WHITE LONGHAIR

25   CHINCHILLA

26–27   CHINCHILLA

28   BI-COLOURED LONGHAIR

exceptions, but the figures presented by sculpture and modelling are often isolated and, however living, deliberately stilled. Various kinds of two-dimensional pictures try to present the cat's fur, colour, and movement, and they bring it into relationships with other beings, relationships which often give it a place in human history or fable not hinted in other ways of presenting the stories.

Painting has been the greatest medium for presenting the cat under these lights, but before we look at painting proper we may see what other two-dimensional modes have to offer. Mosaic and tapestry have both presented pictures. Both give us glimpses of the cat, but these are rare. The mosaic cat of Pompeii is not only almost unique in his kind, but good in any terms. The sharp edges provided by the tesserae give immediacy to tabby marking, claws, eyes, and muscular tension as the cat holds down the bird he has caught. The whole thing is sharply sinewy and direct, neither softened by sentiment nor distanced by reverence. It asks for neither love nor hate in the viewer's response, simply for recognition of a fact that he may also observe in the world about him. It is remarkable that the recording of the fact selects a situation and a physical attitude of the cat selected frequently by still-life painters in the Low Countries and France many centuries later.

Tapestry, or arras, which entered upon the great period of its career early in the fourteenth century, also shows us cats, but not in the presentations which most of us think of first when we think of tapestry. The tapestries of the late Middle Ages, in which scenes and subjects are presented in a way that seems to belong essentially to the medium, not merely imitating pictures better executed in another medium, have no truck with cats. Here, the scene is often the garden-shifting-into-woodland-back-into-garden, and the cat was not an inhabitant of that world of woods and walls. Nor was the world of moral teachings, the other region of tapestries of this period, any more his *milieu*. In fact, he comes

DETAIL FROM A ROMAN MOSAIC, POMPEII

49

into tapestry when the weavers are at work, either in the great workshops of Flanders or France, or in Italy itself, on the cartoons of Italian draughtsmen accustomed also to designing with or for paint. Such tapestries have really been thought of as paintings, only the picture happens to be woven instead of painted. There is nothing essentially *woven* in them, and the pictures may be concerned with any of the scenes or topics of other kinds of pictures. There is an interior scene in a tapestry woven by Flemish weavers from an Italian cartoon in which a common-sensical cat crouches as close as he can to a brazier. There is a *Last Supper* in a series of tapestries, now in the Uffizi in Florence, showing the last days of Christ, in which one of the disciples is bending down to offer a roll to a cat. Most charming of all, there is a *Naming of the Animals by Adam* in a series in the Accademia in Florence in which a pair of Tabby cats walk with demure calm behind a pair of rats. They form part of a beautifully imagined presentation of an unfallen world in which kindness and courtesy reigned. The animals approach and pass Adam in several lines, grouped according to their kinds. The reptiles and their kin form a line whose pace is set by the leader—a snail! None seeks to hurry the slow creature. Similarly, the cats, for all their lithe strength, show no signs of a desire to pounce on the rats in front of them.

It will be clear that, in these last examples, pictorial cats are finding their way into stories in which they are not mentioned in the first telling. In painting cats appear all over the place, in likely and unlikely places. That they were bound to do so becomes clear when we look at early miniature painting in illuminations. Cats crop up, evidently not because a subject required them but simply because the artist could not keep them out. In the MS of the *Geographiae libri octo* of Ptolomaeus Claudius in the Old Library at Venice, there are cats (formalized) worked with birds and other animals into the illumination at the foot of a page; they are not illustrating the text! Again, in a Service Book now in the Museo dell' Opera del Duomo in Florence, there is an obscure but elaborate picture showing figures in a courtyard and, on the roof above, two men, of whom one carries a lamb and the other a white cat! I do not know what it is all about, but the cat is there. In the eighth-century Irish Book of Kells there are some formidable cats.

Painting, in fact, will do several things for cats. It will show us cats as they are in the everyday world. It will demonstrate the variety among cats. It will show us cats in their relations with men and with other animals. It will remind us that cats were probably often present on occasions in the human story of which the verbal accounts omit all mention of the cats. Painting restores cats to the places from which classical and biblical stories excluded them—and sometimes, in so doing, gives them great imaginative meaning.

The two great traditions which have most evidently influenced belief, legend, and story-telling in the Western world are the classical and the Biblical. As we have seen, the cat is either non-existent or unimportant in stories of Ancient Greece and Rome, and the Hebrews turned a cold shoulder on an animal that had been deified by the Egyptians; but the stories of Palestine and Greece and Rome spread in countries where the cat was domesticated, and painters in these countries soon Put The Cat In His Place—that is, right in the middle of things.

It is true that there are few cats in paintings of scenes from classical stories, and there certainly seems to be little place for them among monsters and battles or with heroes sulking in tents or pouring out the story of their woes to a Carthaginian queen. In one of the rare places in classical story where some sign of a love for domestic animals is shown, however, a painter has made the cat's claim. Much has been made of the dog, Argos, who, upon the return of his master Odysseus after twenty years of wandering to Troy and back, recognized and welcomed Odysseus, and then died. Pintoricchio, painting frescoes at the end of the fifteenth century to illustrate scenes from the *Odyssey*, painted the moment when Odysseus rejoins his wife, Penelope. Odysseus, looking remarkably young and un-jaded after his travels, strides into the room. Penelope sits at the web she has so often woven and unwoven during the years of faithful waiting. Balls of her thread lie on the floor— and with one of them a grey-and-white cat is playing. Argos had waited for Odysseus, but Pintoricchio knew that a cat, probably a line of cats, had given company and comfort to Penelope while she waited. Much of the story of women has been a story of waiting, at home, on the shore, at the pit-head; a cat has often shared such vigils. Pintoricchio has painted a truth, however unrealistic his details. The picture is now in the National Gallery in London.

In paintings of Biblical stories the cat finds his place in Italy as soon as painting moves away from the ideals of the Primitives. Some Biblical scenes cry out for the presence of cats as soon as they are translated into realistic visual terms. Paintings of the Sixth Day of Creation sometimes indicate cats among the other beasts; and, of course, cats appear when all the animals are gathered into the Ark. (There is a story that the domestic cat was created *in* the Ark, by the lion, in order to keep down the rats and mice, but painters know no such apocryphal tale.) Perhaps the most understanding painting of the animals gathering to go into Noah's Ark is one from the studio of Bassano, in Venice. There are (of course) two cats in the picture, both Tabby, with white fronts. They are taking no notice of the (very odd) elephant and giraffe in the background. One sits towards the right of the picture, quietly taking everything in; the other, in the centre foreground, is sitting under a cow— the source of milk. One feels that Noah must have found a cat's aptitude for quietly intelligent adjustment to conditions a great comfort while he was trying to deal with lemmings and peacocks.

No other story of the Old Testament produced interesting painted cats, but the stories of the New Testament, and the legends to which they gave rise, have been painted with cats in most remarkable places. Perhaps the oddest I have found is an altarpiece in the church of San Domenico in Perugia, in which the Virgin Mary, kneeling beside her well-stocked desk, is addressed by the Angel of the Annunciation—and, within a few feet of the Angel, a skinny grey cat is arching its back and erecting its fur against a little yapping dog. It is quite impossible here to assign any symbolical meaning to either cat or dog; Angel and Mary are meeting in reverential courtesy, cat and dog are scrapping, and there is no sign that either animal is friend or enemy of Angel or Virgin.

Behind the cat and dog, however, is an open doorway leading to what may well be the domestic offices of the house (there are no signs of domestic activity near Mary); and the cat's appearance in Biblical pictures is often a reminder of the everyday domestic activities that must have accompanied the more important or dramatic activities that are recounted in the stories. Thus, there is (also in Perugia) a painting by Giannicola di Paolo of Herod's banquet. The terrible story of Salome demanding the head of John the Baptist as a reward for her dancing calls up no 'normal' thoughts in most of us, particularly after some treatments of the story by *fin-de-siècle* artists. Yet the feast must have begun as an 'ordinary' feast; only the vengeful ferocity of Herodias turned it into something else. In the picture a cat and a dog stand in front of Herod's table, the dog meditating attack, the cat watching the dog with restrained but alert caution. For them, this is "one of those feasts" where they hope for scraps, and they are waiting and watching with customary jealousy, unaware that one of the chargers carries a unique load. It is fair to say that at least one of the human attendants appears quite as unconcerned as the animals.

Scenes of feasting, even of ordinary meals, are, obviously, scenes where we may expect to find cats, and we do. Indeed, among the Italian schools of painters these are the only scenes in which the cat is presented. The treatment, however, varies very much indeed, from presenting the cat as a piece of common verisimilitude to using it as a sign of a profound imaginative understanding. In a painting of the *Feast in the House of Simon the Pharisee*, by Bernardo Strozzi, nearly every detail is directed towards everyday convincingness; at the left of the picture there is a serving-table, and on this table a cat, who has evidently jumped up to find what he can, is simultaneously striking down at a dog leaping up from the floor and being driven off by servants: a cat's life! In a great *Feast in the House of Levi* by Veronese a happier cat is lurking and playing under the edge of the tablecloth, watched by a dog. This cat seems sure of his position, and he is evidently engaged in that teasing of a slower-witted creature which the sharp cat sometimes delights in. These cats are clearly not intended to add any moral or allegorical point to the painted story. They appear because the painters regarded cats as convincing commonplace accompaniments of feasting.

Cats appearing in paintings of the Last Supper, however, have sometimes been regarded as being in a different category. Sometimes, I believe, they are, but not in the meaning that has been assigned to their appearance. In a small room of the Convento di San Marco in Florence (Savonarola's monastery) there is a painting by Ghirlandaio of the Last Supper in which Jesus and the faithful disciples mostly face the onlooker, but Judas sits with his back almost completely turned to the viewer. On the floor behind Judas a cat is sitting. It has been suggested that this cat represents the devil, waiting for Judas's rapidly-approaching soul. There appears to be no evidence to support this interpretation; and it is very interesting that a more famous *Last Supper* by the same painter, in the church of Ognissanti, also in Florence, is quite extraordinarily similar to the San Marco painting in organization; even some of the differing details differ only in being transposed (though some details, such as the attitude of St John, are really different). The only difference in *content* between the two paintings is that there is a cat in San Marco, none in Ognissanti. It is very difficult to believe that Ghirlandaio would present cat-as-devil in one version of the picture, and simply not bother about it in the other. Cat simply as cat, however, might easily appear in one and not in the other. There might even be local and personal reasons for such a difference.

Cats in paintings of the Last Supper do, however, appear to be of great importance in the work of one great painter, and their importance seems to increase as the painter's life goes on. On the whole, the liveliest cats among Italian painters occur with the Venetians. (It is an oddly interesting historical point that most Venetian-painted cats are grey-tabby-with-white; this is not a particularly common colouring among cats all over the world, but it is, to this day, very common in Venice.) One of the very greatest of the Venetian painters, Tintoretto, painted the Last Supper more frequently than any other subject. Most of these paintings are still in Venice, though one or two have travelled elsewhere, for example to Vienna. In all but about two of Tintoretto's many treatments of the subject, a cat appears; and the cat becomes more, not less, important, as the painter's experience of life and of painting increases. In the first treatment (so far as we know), a painting in the church of Santa Marcuola, a dark cat sits very still in the right foreground of a formal painting of formally posed disciples. In the last treatment, the great *Last Supper* in the church of San Giorgio Maggiore, a highly naturalistic (and beautifully observed) cat is right in the middle of the foreground. He is, so far as I am aware, the first ginger cat to appear in painting!

Between the first and the last there are many treatments, and it is impossible not to feel that to Tintoretto the cat had importance, since it appeared almost invariably in presentations of the subject to which the painter constantly returned with passionate seriousness. As the paintings follow each other the cat is more and more developed, in naturalistic detail of fur, structure, and attitude. Moreover, it is not always the same cat; changes in colouring show that Tintoretto was using different living models, not simply remembering a lay figure of a common-denominator cat. There can be no possible doubt of Tintoretto's interest. The question is, whether this undoubted interest in the cat has any particular meaning in his treatment of a subject he evidently found absorbing.

I think there was such a meaning, and I think we can find a hint of the meaning by comparing a great Tintoretto painting which makes no use of a cat with one of the *cenacolos*, or *Last Suppers*, in which the cat is very beautifully used. One of the most stupendous paintings in the Scuola di San Rocco is Tintoretto's *Crucifixion*. The parts of the picture other than the central group of Christ's cross and his mourners all emphasize the lack of concentration on that group. The workmen are so busy with their job, the riders so concerned with their errands of business or pleasure, that it is quite clear that none outside the central group is presented as having any awareness of the exceptional. Tintoretto develops this separation in other paintings, and often uses a cat to make his point. Above all, he seems to use the cat to emphasize the innocence of some of the life that ignores those events which later tradition assumes must have seemed central to all but the wicked.

This becomes clear if we look at the *Last Supper* now in the sacristy of San Stefano in Venice. Here, the table of the supper is set upon a dais, diagonally placed. On the steps of the dais, between Jesus and a bearded disciple who is probably St Peter, are a small boy and a grey Tabby cat. Jesus is looking towards the disciple, but aware of boy and cat; the disciple is looking mainly towards boy and cat. The small boy and the cat are playing together, gently, pleasurably, innocently, all unaware that a meeting of great significance is taking place round the table. The significance of the supper is heightened by the unawareness of boy and cat, but only because they appear so innocent; an evidently sinful ignoring of the main action would have a limiting effect on the scene, reducing it to a mere superficial

53

opposition of actions. The special quality of meaning is brought out by the fact that it can escape the attention of the innocently natural.

This seems to be the use that Tintoretto makes of the cat in all his major treatments of this subject. For him, the meaning is so strange, so literally marvellous (as well as greatly good) that he has to show that the purely natural cannot comprehend it. In most of the paintings he accepts the hint of the "upper room" that the Last Supper was intimate, private, so that he cannot bring in many extra people to make his point. Usually, he lets a cat serve his purpose. Here is a creature highly organized, highly intelligent, beautiful, not to be accused of sin; and the creature sits, or plays, or seeks for food, innocent and uncomprehending, about the disciples' feet. Common life goes on; do not blame it when it does not understand. With Tintoretto the cat may mean the world and the flesh, but not the devil. Where he uses human beings as well as a cat for this purpose in painting this subject he sometimes uses them also for other purposes, in particular to call up memories of other parts of the story. The boy in the picture described reminds one of presentations of the boy Jesus, up to the time of the questioning in the Temple. In his final great *Last Supper*, in San Giorgio Maggiore, there are numbers of servants in attendance, most of them busily engaged in serving out food. Behind the table, however, stands one woman servant, illumined by the rays of a hanging lamp that also reveal hovering angels. In attitude and general appearance she is singularly like many paintings of the Madonna; she cannot but remind the beholder of the Madonna's part in the rest of the story, though the Madonna had no part in this scene. But here again it is the cat in the centre foreground that points the relation of the scene to the earth, loved if not "too much loved". From his first cat, Tintoretto's paintings of cats had become ever more detailed, more lovingly and carefully observed, more affectionately treated, as well as more centrally placed. This last cat is a muscular ginger tom, who seems to have lost most of his tail. He stands on his hind-legs beside the container from which a woman is lifting out shell-fish on to plates. One paw over the edge of the basket, one bony elbow characteristically angled, he is fully intent on what may come out of the basket. He is fully natural, fully innocent, and totally unaware of the light that shines on his fur from the hanging lamp. This is a portrait of a real cat, not a sketch of an imagined cat—yet his contribution to the imaginative effect of the picture is inestimable.

No other painter of comparable rank has made comparable use of the cat. Tintoretto's example, however, seems to have had occasional unexpected effects. Several anonymous *cenacolos* from his time onwards include evidently non-diabolical cats. One expects all kinds of animals from Veronese, but it is interesting to find Veronese's brother including a cat in a painting which moves from the Washing of the Disciples' Feet to the Last Supper. (Tintoretto had put a cat beside the fire when the disciples' feet were being washed.) Even the august and aristocratically-tempered Titian included a cat under the corner of the tablecloth at, of all scenes, the supper at Emmaus, where the central figure has passed beyond earthly life; and one wonders whether he had not been influenced by his younger contemporary. Cats at Biblical suppers certainly became common, not only in Veronese, but we are somewhat surprised at meeting one in Titian.

Outside Italy we occasionally find a cat very much at home with the Holy Family.

A painting by Charles le Brun (now in the Louvre in Paris), the *Slumber of the Infant Jesus*, shows a Tabby-and-white cat tucked comfortably under the heating-stove; perhaps its purring had had the lullaby effect on the baby that Kipling described when the First Woman's baby was lulled to sleep by the Cat. A *Holy Family* by Rembrandt, where the Family is highlighted in the centre of the picture, has a Tabby cat sitting quietly in the shadows of the middle distance. These cats are playing the simple and natural part in family life that they play in some paintings of domestic celebrations of religious occasions. In a *Return from the Baptism* by Louis le Nain there is a black and white cat, which also peers round a stew-pot in the same painter's *Family of Peasants*. We have already seen that Nicolas Maes shows us an old lady saying grace in the company of her cat.

In fact, the sheer homely familiarity of the cat is what sometimes brings classical or Biblical scenes alive for us in painting, and it is this that we find in paintings of domestic subjects. In Canaletto, for example, we rarely find the cat, because his wide-stretching Venetian scenes rarely look closely at dwelling-places; but there is a cat in a painting by him of the portico of a house.

It is amusing to see that, in *The Flute-Player* by Watteau (now in the Uffizi), the human adults are delicately formalized, but the two children teasing a Tabby cat with a tree-branch are very realistic, and so is the cat—who is very convincingly resenting the teasing.

Not unnaturally, we often find cats painted in those moments when they can madden their house-mates, however affectionate. The creature that you keep partly to protect your food from vermin asserts a right to choose his own share of your food—and you find him in the larder, particularly when you have a store of game in it. There are innumerable paintings of cats with game, by Jan Fyt, Rubens, and numberless other Flemish and Dutch painters. A fascinating fact about such paintings is that the cat often appears in an attitude

PENELOPE'S CAT, FROM A PAINTING BY PINTORICCHIO

55

similar to that of the cat with the bird in the Pompeii mosaic. A Tortoiseshell cat in a Jan Fyt, for example, is crouched ready to jump down into exactly the Pompeii cat's position. Piles of fish also attract cats into paintable moments—often when the cat is startled by discovery, like the kitten in Chardin's *La Raie*. In many still-lifes, in fact, an intensely alive cat points up the meaning of the French term, *nature morte*, for such pictures; the cat's nature is so far from dead!

This aspect of cat nature was bound to appeal to painters, for the cat ready to spring (or even merely longing to spring) on bird or fish shows its muscles and nerves in high tension, and to paint this tension through the fur coat is a challenge to the painter. In Hogarth's famous painting, *The Graham Children* (1742, now in the Tate Gallery, London), the cat with its paws on the chair-back, gazing at the caged bird with a longing that seems to burn through the eyes, is the most muscularly alive creature in the painting. It was when it was crouching ready to spring that a cat seemed most to interest Hogarth; in *The Staymaker* the cat under the chair is in a flattened, crouching position. The imaginative painter, free from irrelevant moral judgments, paints these moments in the joy of his response to whatever is part of created nature. The painter of *Le Bénédicité*, Nicolas Maes, also painted a picture (now in the National Gallery in London) in which a maid sleeps beside her mistress—and a cat steals food close beside the sleeping maid's head.

Yet there are, oddly enough, moments when a cat seems, quite unintentionally, to point to some of the areas where human beings have found, or invented, their morality. The small black cat at the feet of the courtesan in Manet's *Olympe*, once observed among the shadows, has a curious effect upon the observer. Slightly surprised in appearance, the little cat wears its own natural fur. The otherwise-naked tart wears a necklace, a bracelet, and slippers. The cat indicates what it does not need Freud to tell us: that it is not only an individual face with an unclothed body that turns this nude into naked. Cranach had played this trick with an unclothed *Venus* years earlier, but he had not used a cat to emphasize the significance of hat and necklace on an unclothed body.

The joyful response to what exists, because it exists, is perhaps the deepest impulse behind desires to show an earth either unfallen or perfected. Literary Earthly Paradises seem to forget the cat, perhaps because words are too slow to catch with any sense of simultaneity all that one would wish to find in such a paradise; but the happy beasts in the happy glade in Jan Brueghel's *Earthly Paradise* in the Louvre include a grey cat with a striped tail.

Perhaps the feeling that happy life *without* the cat is unthinkable not only makes the cat a loved 'pet' when he is no longer needed to protect grain, but also impels painters to recognize him as a loved creature as well as a mighty hunter. Gwen John painted a black cat, very quiet, held by a young woman in her lap; and Robert Colquhoun painted in 1945 a leaping cat ready to play with the ball a woman holds for him.

Few European painters of animals have been famed especially for their cats. Cuyp's cows (so devastatingly used by Dickens in relation to a political dinner-party) and Stubbs's horses loom too large in their pictures for cats to make much appearance. A cat in their hands is as ill-prepared-for as a tiny kitten of mine which was once approached by a country vet with the stethoscope he used for horses.

29   BLUE-POINTED & SEAL-POINTED COLOURPOINT (HIMALAYAN)

30   BLUE-POINTED COLOURPOINT (HIMALAYAN)

31   BLUE-POINTED COLOURPOINT (HIMALAYAN)

32 TORTOISESHELL-POINTED COLOURPOINT (HIMALAYAN)

33 SEAL-POINTED COLOURPOINT (HIMALAYAN)

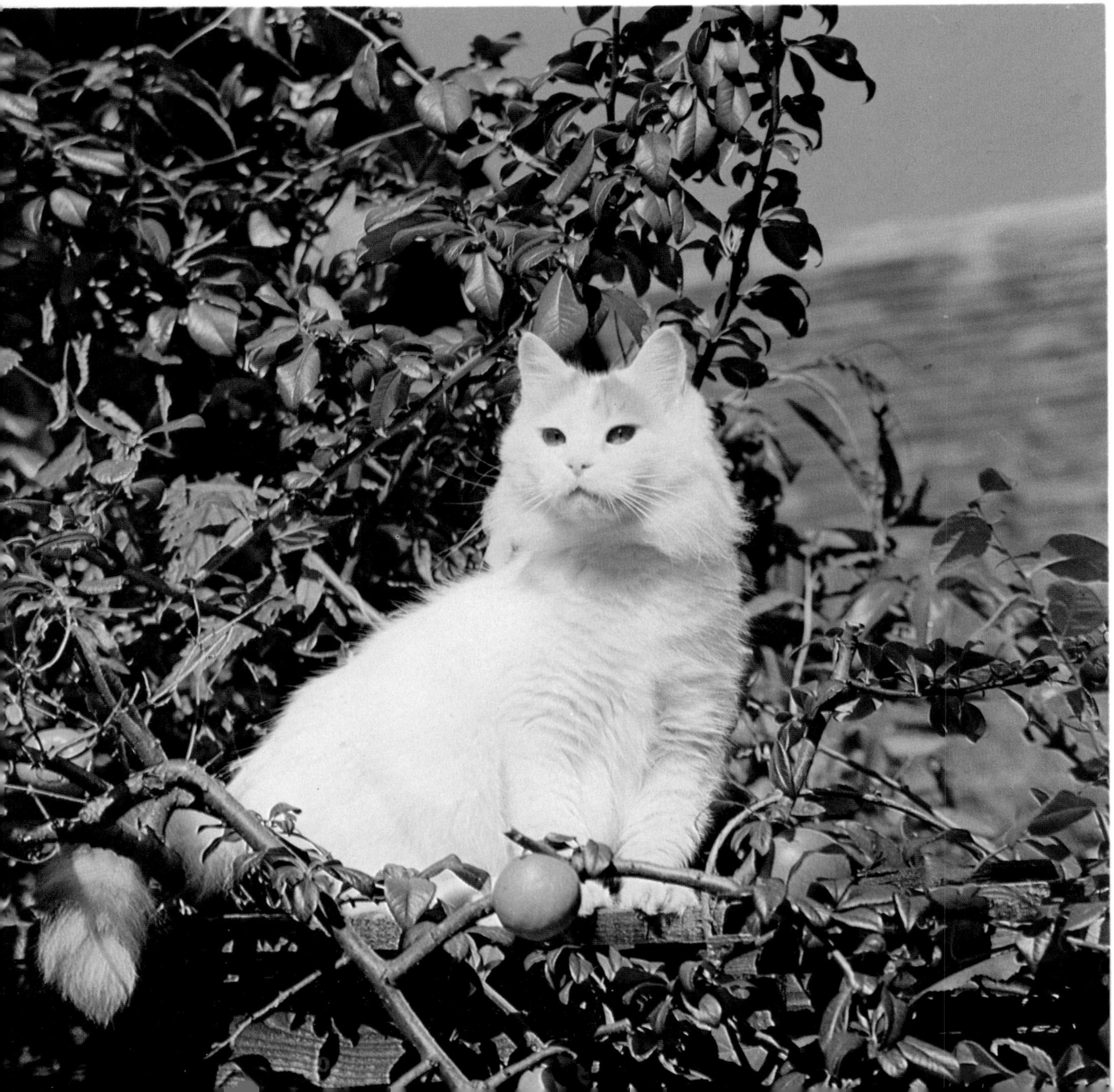

35   SHADED CAMEO

37–38   SEAL-POINTED BIRMAN

One English artist, however, was famed almost entirely for his cats. Poor Louis Wain's cats usually appeared comic, and they were taken lightly, as he intended, though very long and careful observation preceded the pictures. How long and careful, and how deep, we may now see; for the paintings of his last years of mental breakdown are still full of cats. Some of these last pictures seem, like some of Van Gogh's last landscapes, to hold the subject at a point of intensification threatening imminent disintegration. Were his cats a horror or a hope in his malady?

It is a pleasure to turn to decisive evidence (though it can hardly now be needed!) that in many a painter's studio a cat was as harmless and necessary as it was in ordinary homes. From the Netherlands of the seventeenth century and from France of the nineteenth century we have paintings of a painter at work in his studio which show a cat—as so often, right in the middle of the foreground! David Ryckaert's patchy ginger-and-tabby-and-white cat is curled up fast asleep immediately behind the painter's stool. Courbet's White Longhair is full of play—and ready to pounce on the model's draperies. What these two paintings show must have been a fact in dozens of studios.

Among the thousands of cat paintings and models in the world we have had room to look at only a few, chosen either because they are exceptionally interesting or beautiful in themselves, or because they seem to indicate strong tendencies in the plastic and visual representations of cats.

The cat does not often occur in music, and when we think we have found him, we may come to realize that we have recognized him by the guidance of words, rather than by that of music itself. *Five Eyes*, by Armstrong Gibbs, is probably the best-known song connected with cats. The setting beautifully captures the general mood of the poem; but when we analyse our response we find that our conviction that cats are involved is produced as much by the words of de la Mare's poem as by the music. The same is true of settings of Tennyson's *When cats run home*, and other poems referring to cats.

Yet we may expect cats in music. Of all the domestic animals, cats have the most varied and expressive 'music' of their own. They sing their love, their hate, their grief. This vocal activity of cats is well recognized, and non-musicians have recorded their awareness of it. There are paintings and engravings (even one attributed to El Greco) of cat orchestras and cat choirs. There are rather distressing hints of groups of cats taken round, generations ago, and sometimes, by some means, 'made' to emit sounds composing 'music'. There are even, tucked away in back rooms and junk shops, models or (worse) stuffed figures in kitten orchestras. Yet, when we come to real music, we find little feline expression. The name of *The Cats' Fugue* given to one of Domenico Scarlatti's keyboard numbers seems to have been a late christening, and there is no proof of the story that some of the melodic movement was suggested by the order in which a cat placed her paws on the keys. Composers who used bird notes (like those of quail and cuckoo in the "Pastoral" Symphony of Beethoven) or the calls of other animals (like the ass's bray in Mendelssohn's *Midsummer Night's Dream* music) have not attempted to use cat music. Perhaps it is because cats are not readily mocked that Saint-Saens did not include them in his *Carnival of the Animals*; he found it easier to laugh in music at Persons with Long Ears and Pianists.

Cats are represented in Italian madrigals of the sixteenth century, but these are rarely heard. A nineteenth-century presentation of cats in music remains one of the best. Rossini's *Duet for Two Cats* was one of the many compositions he intended for skilled amateurs in his day; it is now attempted only by professionals. It is entrancingly funny—and also simply entrancing. Rossini makes the two voices sing intervals common in cat music, he makes them "caterwaul", and he also makes them intertwine in relationships grateful to the human ear. The gaiety and grace of the duet are not unworthy of the animals represented.

Perhaps the favourite musical picture of cats, however, is to be found in Act 3 of Tchaikovsky's *Sleeping Beauty*. The dance here represents Puss in Boots's courtship of the White Cat, and Tchaikovsky delightfully scores the music with shrill "miaowings". He charmingly suggests feline coquetry encouraging the willing male until, becoming too amorous, Puss is sent scurrying away with a spiteful scratch for his pains.

The only full-scale musical work based on cats is Ravel's *l'Enfant et les Sortilèges*, a ballet-opera based on a tale by Colette. It has evoked great ingenuity in costume-designers, but one does not quite forget that its inspiration was literary.

Cats are so good at singing and dancing in their own terms, their own modes, that it is only natural that singing-and-dancing representations of them in human terms and modes should be rare. Cats do not model or draw or paint, and human artists can do much for them here. Cats do sing and dance, and there is little that human artists can add to their performance.

THE CAT IN LITERATURE

There are no literary presentations of cats as old as some of the plastic and visual treatments, but they certainly appear in literature long before our era, and in recent centuries their appearances in letters have become so frequent that it is no more possible to refer to them all than it was to list all the cat's embodiments in sculpture or painting. We can only glance here and there at cats in poetry and prose, the choice governed by accident, whim, taste—and space. Some writers who have described or referred to cats with delicacy and understanding must be left out, because we have already drawn on their works in tracing the history and the lore of the cat. We have seen, for example, how writers as far apart as Chaucer, Shakespeare, and the Brontës have used attitudes to cats almost as touchstones of character in the people they presented. We have seen how folktales became 'literature' in the hands of Perrault. We have seen cats creeping shyly or frisking merrily into the literature of nearly every century for two thousand years and more. Now we must turn to other writers, and somehow make our choice among their feline opera. Apart from chance and whim, what grounds for choice have we? First, we should perhaps limit ourselves to those works, or parts of works, where the cat is at least a principal, if not the only, object of the writer's interest; we cannot chase cats throughout all glancing references, or record them where they are merely part of the setting of a scene. Second, we should include only those writings which clearly make some deliberate attempt at literary effectiveness, omitting all merely factual statements. This does not mean that we must ignore all works by naturalists, or material in letters not written for publication. Wherever the writer has clearly sought to infuse sensuous or emotional life into his catty writing, we may regard that writing as 'literary'. We are then left with hundreds of works, good, bad, and indifferent, from which to choose. We had better choose either those which are supremely good in themselves, or those which illustrate some important or curious historical or personal attitude to cats. Many satisfy both requirements. It will be well to limit the numbers of works, so that they may, as far as possible, speak for themselves. We cannot make a sculptured cat materialize itself out of the page for the reader's delight, but we can let some literary cats appear in their original dress of words.

Among the earliest European poems about a cat is an eighth-century Irish poem, which has been translated more than once. The version given here is by Helen Waddell.

I and Pangur Bán my cat,
'Tis a like task we are at:
Hunting mice is his delight,
Hunting words I sit all night.

'Gainst the wall he sets his eye,
Full and fierce and sharp and sly;
'Gainst the wall of knowledge I
All my little wisdom try.

'Tis a merry thing to see
At our tasks how glad are we,
When at home we sit and find
Entertainment to our mind.

So in peace our task we ply,
Pangur Bán, my cat and I;
In our arts we find our bliss,
I have mine and he has his.

Quite apart from the skilled balance in phrasing, the content of this poem is attractive in its recognition of the combined independence and companionship, sympathy and self-respect, of cat and man. Accepting the simple fact that hunting mice is natural for a cat, the poet cannot help believing that labour may be seasoned by the craftsman's delight as much for the cat as for the man. Not only the kill, but the skill of the hunt, matters to these fellow-craftsmen.

An independence enforced by harder conditions was recorded in an Arabic poem of the same century. The poet, Abu Shamaqmaq, wrote:

When my house was bare of skins and pots of meal,
    after it had been inhabited, not empty, full of folk and richly prosperous,
I see the mice avoid my house, retiring to the governor's palace.
The flies have called for a move, whether their wings are clipped or whole.
The cat stayed a year in the house and did not see a mouse
    shaking its head at hunger, at a life full of pain and spite
When I saw the pained downcast head, the heat in the belly, I said,
'Patience; you are the best cat my eyes ever saw in a ward.'
He said, 'I have no patience. How can I stay in a desert like the belly of a she ass?'
I said, 'Go in peace to a hotel where travellers are many and much trade,
Even if the spider spins in my wine jar, in the jug, and the pot.'

The cat here seems to have felt that faithfulness is all very well, but there should be reason in all things! The man can hardly deny it. An Arabic poet of the following century mourned, half in earnest, half in joke, the loss of a cat that fell to her death while trying to catch pigeons. In the mock-morality of his last lines, Ibn Alalaf Alnaharwany seems oddly to foreshadow Gray's Ode of nearly a thousand years later:

Why, why was pigeons' flesh so nice,
That thoughtless cats should love it thus?
Hadst thou but lived on rats and mice,
Thou hadst been living still, poor Puss.

Curst be the taste, how'er refined,
That prompts us for such joys to wish,
And curst the dainty where we find
Destruction lurking in the dish.

Most medieval writers, apart from Chaucer, refer to the cat in proverb and moral, or in domestic advice (as for anchoresses). Towards the end of the period, Skelton's *Philip Sparrow* expresses enmity towards a cat, but it is a formal enmity, almost imposed by the nature of the poem. The young girl, Jane Scrope, is mourning for the death of her pet sparrow, and inevitably

Vengeance I ask and cry
By way of exclamation
On all the whole nation
Of cats wild and tame.

The family cat was obviously not turned out on such a plea. Even when Henryson, in his version of the fable of "The Town Mouse and the Country Mouse", described the panic that overcame the two mice when their revels were interrupted by the cat, he did not blame the cat for his nature; he still called him Gib Hunter, "our jolly cat".

In the sixteenth century there is an amusing reversal of the cat and mouse fears. George Turberville was not the passive kind of lover who wants to be a glove upon his mistress's hand. He would serve her where most she felt the need of service and, if he could be changed from a man, he would not be any creature but a cat.

I would be present, aye,
    And at my Ladie's call,
To gard her from the fearfull Mouse,
    In Parlour and in Hall;
        .   .   .   .   .   .

The Mouse should stand in Feare,
    So should the squeaking Rat;
All this would I do if I were
    Converted to a Cat.

At about the same time in France, when Ronsard (evidently an aileurophobe) was confessing his horror of cats, another member of the Pléiade, Joachim du Bellay, wrote an epitaph on a departed cat, less well-known than his epitaph on a dog, but quite as full of observation and feeling. There is delicate feeling as well as humour in this poem, but it is particularly interesting for one reason. In almost enumerating the 'points' of the cat (rather as Shakespeare enumerated the 'points' of a horse in *Venus and Adonis*), du Bellay reveals a sensitive awareness of the cat's physicality, of the nature of fur, paws, nose, and the rest. Now, this is rare in French poetry before the nineteenth century. Many animals appear in French literature, from the tales of Renart onwards, but their furriness or featheredness, their four-footedness, their sheer physical animal nature, is rarely of any

60

importance. The writers do not, apparently, take delight in the very difference of other animals from man, their different shape and texture and movement. Even Montaigne, musing, sympathetically and imaginatively, on his cat's mentality and temperament, does not invite us to feel her fur. Instead, the French writers emphasize (as is proper in fables), those parts of animal behaviour from which morals may be drawn for human use. They keep their eyes mercilessly on the moral, social, or political object. The elegance, gaiety, and sophistication of La Fontaine's fables are in no part derived from a sense of physical immediacy in the shape, skin, or movement of the animals who appear in them. His version of "The Town Mouse and the Country Mouse" is more elegant than Henryson's, but he does not give us the sense of the extreme smallness of a country mouse on a journey, or of the scrabbling scutter of panic, that we find in Henryson. When he tells one of the old cat stories his sense of the point of the story remains supreme; he is never deflected from his purpose by irrelevant response to fur or paw. Political and social points are kept as clear as in the fourteenth-century references to the impossibility of belling the cat.

It may be that some of the nursery rhymes in which cats appear originally had political meanings, but this is always difficult to judge, because of the difficulty of dating the rhymes. Most of them existed in oral tradition before they were written down, and we can never be sure of the length of their oral existence. There have been many attempts (none very satisfying) to explain the cat and the fiddle in the "Hey, diddle, diddle" rhyme. The cats in nursery rhymes, in fact, were often probably there simply because they were a familiar part of kitchen and nursery life; and the rhymes about them were readily used for nursery moralizing.

> Ding, dong, bell,
> Pussy's in the well.
> Who put her in?
> Little Tommy Thin.
> Who pulled her out?
> Little Tommy Stout.
> What a naughty boy was that,
> To try to drown poor pussy cat,
> Who never did any harm,
> And killed the mice in his father's barn.

This is only one of many variants known today, and some form of the rhyme seems to have been known at least as early as the sixteenth century. The moral lesson, however, almost certainly belongs to later generations, influenced perhaps by the rhymes deliberately composed for teaching purposes by such writers as the Misses Taylor.

> I love little Pussy,
> Her coat is so warm,
> And if I don't hurt her
> She'll do me no harm.

Rhymes of the full oral tradition can never be safely dated; few were written out before the eighteenth century, but many evidently existed long before that. Cats often appear in them, usually as objects of affection or, at least, familiarity; but the gentle attitude may have developed only in the later versions.

Reasons for increased gentleness are not far to seek, and one of them is certainly the growth of delight in observation of the animal world, of understanding developing out of sharpened seeing. As the sixteenth century moved into the seventeenth, Edward Topsell, in his *Historie of Four-footed Beastes*, described the cat like this:

> Cats are of divers colours; but for the most part gryseld like to congealed yse, which commeth from the condition of her meate; her heed is like unto the head of a Lyon, except in her sharpe eares: her flesh is soft and smooth: her eies glister above measure especially when a man commeth to see a cat on the sudden, and in the night they can hardly be endured for their flaming aspect.
>
> It is a neat and cleanely creature, oftentimes licking hir own body to keepe it smoothe and faire, having naturally a flexible backe for this purpose, and washing hir face with hir fore feet, but some observe that if she put hir feete beyond the crowne of her head, that it is a presage of raine, and if the backe of a cat be thinne, the beast is of no courage or value.
>
> It is needelesse to spend any time about her loving nature to man, how she flattereth by rubbing her skinne against ones Legges, how she whurleth with her voyce, having as many tunes as turnes, for she hath one voyce to beg and to complain, another to testifie her delight and pleasure, another among hir own kind by flattring, by hissing, by purring, by spitting, insomuch as some have thought that they have a peculiar intelligible language among themselves.
>
> Therefore, how she beggeth, playeth, leapeth, looketh, catcheth, tosseth with her foote, riseth up to strings held over her head, sometime creeping, sometime lying on the back, playing with one foote, sometime on the bely, snatching, now with mouth, and anon with foote, apprehending greedily any thing save the hand of a man, with divers such gestical actions, it is needelesse to stand upon: insomuch as Coelius was wont to say that being free from his Studies and more urgent waighty affaires, he was not ashamed to play and sport himselfe with a Cat.

Here, there is evidently far more than a purpose of communicating bare fact. The facts about a cat's fur, colour, shape, movement, and language have given Topsell such pleasure that he must try to communicate that pleasure to his readers, make them see and touch and hear the creature. For about three generations after this in England no other writer recorded cat facts so lovingly as he had done, but many must have shared his experience, and when we reach the eighteenth century we find cats in literature sharing the benefits of one of the great glories of that century—its rapidly-growing humanitarian treatment of animals. Even Pope, declaring that the proper study of mankind is man, seems to have found birds and fish more beautiful and endearing than most men. From now on, cat literature pours out of the pens and the presses. Much of it—moral tales, verse fables, poems wavering uncertainly between comedy, pathos, and bare truth—is, to say the best, mediocre. The importance of such work lies in its volume, which shows that Johnson was, in his love for cats as in many fields, simply *primus inter pares*, a greater cat-lover because he was a greater man than most. The best pieces of cat literature in the period are, in fact, the best-known;

but it is worth looking at them again both because of their intrinsic value and because they are good representatives of their kinds in the period.

Perhaps the clearest evidence of the widespread joy in cats is given in personal letters. Cowper practised the art of letter-writing for the pleasure of his friends, and he wrote this to Lady Hesketh:

I have a kitten, my dearest Cousin, the drollest of all creatures that ever wore a cat's skin. Her gambols are not to be described, and would be incredible, if they could. In point of size she is likely to be a kitten always, being extremely small of her age, but time I suppose, that spoils every thing, will make her also a cat. You will see her I hope before that melancholy period shall arrive, for no wisdom that she may gain by experience and reflection hereafter, will compensate the loss of her present hilarity. She is dressed in a tortoise-shell suit, and I know that you will delight in her.

The one word "hilarity" is enough to suggest the description he refused to give. Another experience with cats he turned into a poem, *The Colubriad*, but I think it retains more freshness in the description he wrote in a letter to Newton:

Passing from the greenhouse to the barn, I saw three kittens (for we have so many in our retinue) looking with fixed attention at something, which lay on the threshold of a door, coiled up. I took but little notice of them at first; but a loud hiss engaged me to attend more closely, when behold—a viper! the largest I remember to have seen, rearing itself, darting its forked tongue, and ejaculating the afore-mentioned hiss at the nose of a kitten almost in contact with his lips. I ran into the hall for a hoe with a long handle, with which I intended to assail him, and returning in a few seconds missed him: he was gone, and I feared had escaped me. Still however the kitten sat watching immoveably upon the same spot. I concluded, therefore, that, sliding between the door and the threshold, he had found his way out of the garden into the yard. I went round immediately, and there found him in close conversation with the old cat, whose curiosity being excited by so novel an appearance, inclined her to pat his head repeatedly with her fore foot; with her claws however sheathed, and not in anger; but in the way of philosophical inquiry and examination.

This is free from the *longueurs* which slacken some of his poems about animals, such as *The Retired Cat* (about a cat that got shut up in a drawer).

Not all those who have recognized, in Gray's *Ode on the Death of a Favourite Cat drowned in a Tub of Goldfishes*, the absurdity of its mock-heroic, and the *sotto voce* humour of the reference to the cat's proverbial nine lives, have observed also the accuracy of some of the natural detail: the "conscious tail" is a master-stroke in cat delineation.

'Twas on a lofty vase's side,
Where China's gayest art had dyed
  The azure flowers that blow:
Demurest of the tabby kind,
The pensive Selima reclined,
  Gazed on the lake below.

Her conscious tail her joy declared:
The fair round face, the snowy beard,
  The velvet of her paws,
Her coat, that with the tortoise vies,
Her ears of jet, and emerald eyes,
  She saw: and purred applause.

Still had she gazed, but 'midst the tide
Two angel forms were seen to glide,
   The Genii of the stream:
Their scaly armour's Tyrian hue
Though richest purple to the view
   Betrayed a golden gleam.

The hapless Nymph with wonder saw:
A whisker first and then a claw,
   With many an ardent wish,
She stretched in vain to reach the prize.
What female heart can gold despise?
   What Cat's averse to fish?

Presumptuous Maid! with looks intent
Again she stretched, again she bent,
   Nor knew the gulf between.
(Malignant Fate sat by and smiled)
The slippery verge her feet beguiled,
   She tumbled headlong in.

Eight times emerging from the flood
She mewed to ev'ry wat'ry god
   Some speedy aid to send.
No Dolphin came, no Nereid stirred:
Nor cruel Tom nor Susan heard—
   A fav'rite has no friend!

· · · · · · ·

The high-water-mark of eighteenth-century cat poetry is Christopher Smart's astonishing presentation of "my Cat Jeoffrey", from *Rejoice in the Lamb: A song from Bedlam*.

For I will consider my Cat Jeoffrey.
For he is the servant of the Living God, duly and daily serving him.
For at the first glance of the glory of God in the East he worships in his way.
For this is done by wreathing his body seven times round with elegant quickness.
For then he leaps up to catch the musk, wch is the blessing of God upon his prayer.

· · · · · · ·

For having consider'd God and himself he will consider his neighbour.
For if he meets another cat he will kiss her in kindness.
For when he takes his prey he plays with it to give it [a] chance.
For one mouse in seven escapes by his dallying.
For when his day's work is done his business more properly begins.
For he keeps the Lord's watch in the night against the adversary.
For he counteracts the powers of darkness by his electrical skin and glaring eyes.
For he counteracts the Devil, who is death, by brisking about the life.
For in his morning orisons he loves the sun and the sun loves him.
For he is of the tribe of Tiger.
For the Cherub Cat is a term of the Angel Tiger.
For he has the subtlety and hissing of a serpent, which in goodness he suppresses.
For he will not do destruction, if he is well-fed, neither will he spit without provocation.
For he purrs in thankfulness, when God tells him he's a good Cat.
For he is an instrument for the children to learn benevolence upon.
For every house is incompleat without him & a blessing is lacking in the spirit.

· · · · · · ·

For by stroaking of him I have found out electricity.
For I perceived God's light about him both wax and fire.
For the electrical fire is the spiritual substance, which God sends from heaven to sustain
   the bodies both of man and beast.
For God has blessed him in the variety of his movements.
For, tho he cannot fly, he is an excellent clamberer.
For his motions upon the face of the earth are more than any other quadrupede.
For he can tread to all the measures upon the musick.
For he can swim for life.
For he can creep.

64

40–41   BLACK SHORTHAIR

42   BLUE-EYED WHITE SHORTHAIR

43   ORANGE-EYED WHITE SHORTHAIR

44   BLUE-CREAM SHORTHAIR

Wild and whirling words, no doubt—after all, *Rejoice in the Lamb* was "A Song from Bedlam"—but in his inspired madness Smart has caught the power and gentleness and mystery and familiarity and glory and grace and meekness of the cat all at once. Indeed, he must convince us that "every house is incompleat without him & a blessing is lacking in the spirit". Abandoning chronology for the moment, we may give as a kind of post-script to Smart a twentieth-century poem.

Peterkin the Cat
Exultate Deo: Make a cheerful noise unto the God of Jacob

David, son of Jesse, when he twangled on his harp,
  And blessed the Lord of Hosts with all his voice—
David wasn't in it with Peterkin, my cat,
  When he calls upon his soul to rejoice!

When the rain is in the street, and the rain is in your heart,
  And there shines no light on all your sodden ways—
"This *is* a nice fire," says Peterkin, the cat!
  "Praise," says Peterkin, "Prr-rr-rraise!"

When man has got no need of you, and God is very far;
  When there lies before you length of heavy days—
"That *was* a good dinner," says Peterkin the cat!
  "Praise," says Peterkin, "Prr-rr-raise!"

"Oh, wise little beastie, spread lissome on the mat,
Can you learn me the comfort of your ways?"
  "That's more like a Christian," says Peterkin, the cat:
"The Lord likes cheerful noises," says Peterkin, the cat—
  "So Prrraise! Prr-rraise! Prrr-rr-raise!"

. . . . . .

This is a much more completely 'domestic' creature than Smart's, and Cicely Hamilton would not lay claim to Smart's inspiration, but she and Peterkin are in a straight line of descent from Smart and Jeoffry.

The great Romantics did not turn their backs on all the pleasures enjoyed by the Augustans. The "hilarity" of Cowper's kitten reappears in "a kitten's busy joy" in Wordsworth:

The Kitten and the Falling Leaves

. . . . . .
See the kitten on the wall,
Sporting with the leaves that fall,

. . . . . .
What intenseness of desire
In her upward eye of fire!
With a tiger-leap half way
Now she meets the coming prey,
Lets it go as fast, and then
Has it in her power again:
Now she works with three or four

Like an Indian conjuror;
Quick as he in feats of art,
Far beyond in joy of heart.
Were her antics played in the eye
Of a thousand standers-by,
Clapping hands with shout and stare,
What would little tabby care
For the plaudits of the crowd?
Over happy to be proud,
Over wealthy in the treasure
Of her own exceeding pleasure!

When we have read this, we are not surprised that there is room even in the austerity of *The Prelude* for a glimpse of a kitten.

Keats's wonderful capacity for outgoing sympathy was well-exercised by a veteran tom:

Sonnet: To a Cat

Cat! who has pass'd thy grand climacteric,
    How many mice and rats hast in thy days
    Destroy'd?—How many tit bits stolen? Gaze
With those bright languid segments green, and prick
Those velvet ears—but pr'ythee do not stick
    Thy latent talons in me—and upraise
    Thy gentle mew—and tell me all thy frays
Of fish and mice, and rats and tender chick.
Nay, look not down, nor lick thy dainty wrists—
    For all the wheezy asthma,—and for all
Thy tail's tip is nick'd off—and though the fists
    Of many a maid have given thee many a maul,
Still is that fur as soft as when the lists
    In youth thou enter'dst on glass bottled wall.

It was in the nineteenth century that cats walked into French literature and took possession of distinguished writers. Gautier not only wrote about his own cats in *La Nature chez Elle et la Ménagerie Intime*, but also described Baudelaire's love and understanding of cats. Baudelaire wrote several poems to and about cats, and his gift for making his language more malleable and no less accurate than it had been before was what was needed to naturalize cats in French poetry. Anatole France gave Sylvestre Bonnard a cat, Pierre Loti embodied real cats in *Vies des deux Chattes* and created imaginary cats in fiction; many French writers knew and loved cats even when they did not write about them. The line comes to a peak in the twentieth century with Colette, in whose stories cats are impulses to emotion and motives to action.

One nineteenth-century French author who wrote about cats without much affection excelled on occasion in a kind of story which developed rapidly through the nineteenth into the twentieth century. Maupassant wrote one or two famous examples of the un-canny, the macabre, short story, and it was inevitable that the cat should find its way into this *genre*. Poe's *The Black Cat* is well-known, but it cannot, for mysterious suggestion, come near *Ancient Sorceries*, by Algernon Blackwood. In this remarkable story a traveller, alighting on impulse from a train at a little old French town, is warned by a fellow-traveller, "Prenez garde, à cause du sommeil et des chats!" From there, he walks into an experience, of half-life by day and intense life by night, in a world of barely-concealed old practices of witchcraft, that a reader can never afterwards quite forget. This world is touched upon again in *The Cyprian Cat* by Dorothy Sayers, though she, as we shall see, had also a quite different experience of cats.

On this subject English and French literature seem often to come closer together than they usually do, so it is not surprising that some remarkable feats of translation have been achieved where cats are concerned. Even Beatrix Potter, with her Tom Kitten, has 'gone' beautifully into French, and the nineteenth-century Edward Lear has been magically moved over into twentieth-century French. Lear drew his own cat Foss many times, and cats occur frequently in his tales and verses. The most famous, however, is certainly the Pussy Cat who loved and was loved by the Owl; and Lear's English seems to be equally loved and loving in Francis Steegmuller's French:

The Owl and the Pussy-cat

I

The Owl and the Pussy-cat went to sea
  In a beautiful pea-green boat,
They took some honey, and plenty of money,
  Wrapped up in a five-pound note.
The Owl looked up to the stars above,
  And sang to a small guitar,
'O lovely Pussy! O Pussy, my love,
  What a beautiful Pussy you are,
      You are,
      You are!
  What a beautiful Pussy you are!'

Le Hibou et la Poussiquette

I

Hibou et Minou allèrent à la mer
  Dans une barque peinte en jaune-canari;
Ils prirent du miel roux et beaucoup de sous
  Enroulés dans une lettre de crédit.
Le hibou contemplait les astres du ciel,
  Et chantait, en grattant sa guitare,
'O Minou chérie, O Minou ma belle,
  O Poussiquette, comme tu es rare,
      Es rare,
      Es rare!
  O Poussiquette, comme tu es rare!'

II

Pussy said to the Owl, 'You elegant fowl!
  How charmingly sweet you sing!
O let us be married! too long we have tarried:
  But what shall we do for a ring?'
They sailed away, for a year and a day,
  To the land where the Bong-tree grows
And there in a wood a Piggy-wig stood
  With a ring at the end of his nose,
      His nose,
      His nose,
  With a ring at the end of his nose.

II

Au chanteur dit la chatte, 'Noble sieur à deux pattes,
  Votre voix est d'une telle élégance!
Voulez-vous, cher Hibou, devenir mon époux?
  Mais que faire pour trouver une alliance?
Ils voguèrent, fous d'amour, une année et un jour;
  Puis, au pays où le bong fleurit beau,
Un cochon de lait surgit d'une forêt,
  Une bague accrochée au museau,
    Museau,
    Museau,
  Une bague accrochée au museau.

III

'Dear Pig, are you willing to sell for one shilling
  Your ring?' Said the Piggy, 'I will.'
So they took it away, and were married next day
  By the Turkey who lives on the hill.
They dined on mince, and slices of quince,
  Which they ate with a runcible spoon;
And hand in hand, on the edge of the sand,
  They danced by the light of the moon,
    The moon,
    The moon,
  They danced by the light of the moon.

III

'Cochon, veux-tu bien nous vendre pour un rien
  Ta bague?' Le cochon consentit.
Donc ils prirent le machin, et le lendemain matin
  Le dindon sur le mont les unit.
Ils firent un repas de maigre et de gras,
  Se servant d'une cuillère peu commune;
Et là sur la plage, le nouveau ménage
  Dansa au clair de la lune,
    La lune,
    La lune,
  Dansa au clair de la lune.

By now, nearly all literatures have produced cat stories, and many of them are as "easy, vulgar, and therefore disgusting" as nightdress-case cats and pincushion kittens. Many, for obvious reasons, dwell, with varying degrees of sensitiveness, on the sufferings of cats. Many celebrate the cat's astounding powers of endurance. Some are good, and a few examples of understanding float serenely down the torrent of commonplace stuff. Masefield, for example, in *The Midnight Folk*, recognizes that all cats are individuals and, while Nibbins is always good and friendly to the hero, Greymalkin and Blackmalkin do wrong and have to mend their ways. Ruth Pitter in several poems thinks herself into cat situations, and finds ways of spelling cat language.

The Matron Cat's Song

So once again the trouble's o'er
   And here I sit and sing;
Forgetful of my paramour
   And the pickle I was in;
Lord, lord, it is a trying time
   We bear when we're expecting,
When folk reproach us for the crime
   And frown with glance correcting.

So purra wurra, purra wurra, pronkum
                           pronkum :
   Purra wurra pronkum, pronkum purr.

How much I feared my kits would be
   Slain in the hour of birth!
And so I sought a sanctuary
   Which causes me some mirth:
The surly cook, who hates all cats,
   Hath here a little closet,
And here we nest among her hats—
   Lord save me when she knows it!

Hey purra wurra, etc.

     ·   ·   ·   ·   ·   ·

Those eyes which now are sealéd fast
   Nine days against the light
Shall ere few months are overpast
   Like stars illume the night;
Those voices that with feeble squall
   Demand my whole attention,
Shall earn with rousing caterwaul
   Dishonourable mention.

Then purra wurra, etc.

But then, alas, I shall not care
   How flighty they may be,
For ere they're grown I'll have to bear
   Another four, or three;
And after all, they are the best
   While the whole crew reposes
With fast-shut eyes, weak limbs at rest,
   And little wrinkled noses.

So purra wurra, purra wurra, pronkum
                           pronkum :
   Purra wurra pronkum, pronkum ryestraw :
Pronkum ryestraw, pronkum ryestraw,
   Pur-ra—wur-ra—pronkum
Pronk . . . Foof.

                (She sleeps)

Dorothy Sayers wrote a poem that must come home to the business and bosoms of all who have had to do with cats at any time of difficulty. *War Cat* is about a cat blackmailing its owner into efforts to replace rejected food:

Only stop crying
and staring in that unbearable manner—
as soon as I have put on my hat
we will try to do something about it.
My hat is on,
I have put on my shoes,
I have taken my shopping basket—
What are you doing on the table?

The chicken-bowl is licked clean;
there is nothing left in it at all.
Cat,
hell-cat, Hitler-cat, human,
all-too-human cat,
cat corrupt, infected,
instinct with original sin,
cat of a fallen and perverse creation,
hypocrite with the innocent and limpid
                      eyes—
is nothing desirable
till somebody else desires it?

Is anything and everything attractive
so long as it is got by stealing?
Furtive and squalid cat,
green glance, squinted over a cringing
                                    shoulder,
streaking hurriedly out of the back door
in expectation of judgment,
your manners and morals are perfectly
                        abhorrent to me
you dirty little thief and liar.

Nevertheless,
although you have made a fool of me,
yes, bearing in mind your pretty
                        wheedling ways
(not to mention the four mice and the
                        immature stoat),
and having put on my hat to go to the
                        butcher's,
I may as well go.

A little Danish poem by Piet Hein briefly epitomizes a most important truth about cats.

"Roadside Conversation"

Lille kat,
Lille kat,
Lille kat på vejen!
Hvis er du?
Hvis er du?
—Jeg er sgu min egen.

Little cat
Little cat,
Little cat in the road!
Whose cat are you?
Whose cat are you?
—Damn it, I'm my own cat.

It is amusing to contrast with this the lines written by Pope for the collar of a dog given to the Prince of Wales:

I am His Highness' dog at Kew;
Pray tell me, sir, whose dog are you?

Like Piet Hein, T. S. Eliot recognized a cat's right to its self-ness, and whatever the comicalities and ingenuities of *Old Possum's Book of Practical Cats*, the Gumbie Cats, the Rum Tum Tuggers, the Jellicles, though recognizable types, all have room for the individuals among them, Macavity, Bustopher Jones, and the rest.

Many contemporary writers of fiction seem to dislike their fellow-men. This may be one of the reasons why human beings in science fiction are often anaemic and unindividualized. Where men are colourless, it might seem hopeless to search for fully living animals. Yet, even here, in some of the frightening imagined worlds of the future, we find cats restoring life, intelligence, and individuality to the bleak spaces. In a short story by Cordwainer Smith, *The Game of Rat and Dragon*, teams of man-and-cat have to protect the great space-routes from attacks of great horror and danger from deep space. Only a cat has reactions quick enough to perceive the approaching danger in time, and the partner man acts at once on the telepathically received reactions of the cat. After one dangerous encounter, a man recovers consciousness in hospital, caring for nothing but to know that his cat partner is safe. The nurse is disappointed and angry. "You and your damn cats!"

He cut off the sight of her mind and, as he buried his face in the pillow, he caught an image of the Lady May.
"She *is* a cat," he thought. "That's all she is—a *cat*!"

70

But that was not how his mind saw her—quick beyond all dreams of speed, sharp, clever, unbelievably graceful, beautiful, wordless and undemanding.

Where would he ever find a woman who could compare with her?

There may not be much purely human hope in this story, but in *Catseye*, a novel by André Norton, a man from Earth who is a mere casual labourer on another planet finds himself, while working in a pet-shop, in telepathic communication with five animals imported from Earth to be expensive pets for luxurious idlers in Korwar. The animals are a kinkajou, two foxes, and two cats—all quick, all intelligent. Together, the man and the animals live through an exciting adventure story, facing dangers from a most evil enemy. Though all the animals are quick, the two cats are quickest and most intelligent of all, and it is they who help most in judging where dangers lie, and compel themselves to face what they most dread. The unspoken communication between the man and the animals grows deeper and fuller and warmer, and love and respect grow with it. At last, when evil and danger have been partly overcome, partly evaded, the man and the animals are allowed to live free in the wild spaces, of forest and hill and plain, of Korwar. The Head Ranger of the spaces has recognized that something wonderful is growing in the understanding between the man and his animals, particularly his cats, and he sees in that the best hope for his universe. Troy and Simba and Sahiba may find the way to a shared life that is both natural and peaceful.

We tried to see cats as they emerged out of the dark backward and abysm of time. This glimpse into an imagined future sees them still as brave, beautiful, clever, independent, but loving to a man's heart's content.

VIGNETTE BY THOMAS BEWICK, 1797

71

THE VARIETIES

THE LONG-HAIRED CATS

There are very many theories as to the origin of cats with long, flowing coats, but very few facts. According to Helen Winslow in her *Concerning Cats*, all the long-haired cats originated "from the Indian Bengalese, Thibetan, and other wild cats of Asia and Russia". The source of her information is unknown to the author. There are a number of small wild cats in these areas, but nothing really like the domestic cats with the long, silky fur.

The *manul* or Pallas's cat was once regarded as a possible ancestor, but there are fundamental differences which are now considered to make this unlikely. The *manul* weighs about seven pounds, being silver-grey in colour, with striped markings, and a short, thick, ringed tail. The ears are low on the broad head, and the side whiskers are most peculiar. The coat is thick, but certainly not long.

For many years it was presumed by several zoologists that the European wild cat was responsible. Inter-breeding is known to take place, but again there are certain differences, so this theory too has been discarded. The fur of the European wild cat is beautifully marked, very thick, but far from long and silky, and the tail is club-like.

It is an established fact that the Longhairs have been known in Turkey and Persia for over three hundred years. It is considered that the long fur probably started as a mutation in the first place, and, because of the attractive appearance, the cats were thought more of than those with short coats and were therefore cherished.

It is said that the Crusaders returning from the Holy Wars brought back with them, among their treasures, these very rare cats. It is a nice thought, but there is no definite evidence to substantiate this. They did appear in Italy at the time of the Renaissance, when much was made of "things of beauty". Travellers from the Far East certainly brought them to Europe, and at one time they were known in England as "French" cats, as it was said they came from France.

The first in Britain were the Angoras, so called because they came from Angora, the former European name for what is now the capital of Turkey. Later came the Persians from Persia (now Iran). The type of these two breeds differed greatly, although both had long fur. The Angoras had narrower heads, taller ears, and were more slenderly built, while the cats from Persia had broad, round heads, smaller ears, and shorter bodies. The fur texture also differed, that of the Angoras being soft, fine, and silky, while the Persians were more woolly. The Points of Excellence given in Harrison Weir's *Our Cats* referred to the differences in the two breeds, and also mentioned the Russian Longhair, which apparently had an even more woolly coat, and a shorter tail.

With certain exceptions all the Longhairs should have broad, round heads, with good

45–46   BRITISH BLUE

47 CREAM SHORTHAIR

48 BRITISH BLUE

49–50   BROWN TABBY SHORTHAIR

51   SILVER TABBY AMERICAN SHORTHAIR

52 SILVER TABBY SHORTHAIR

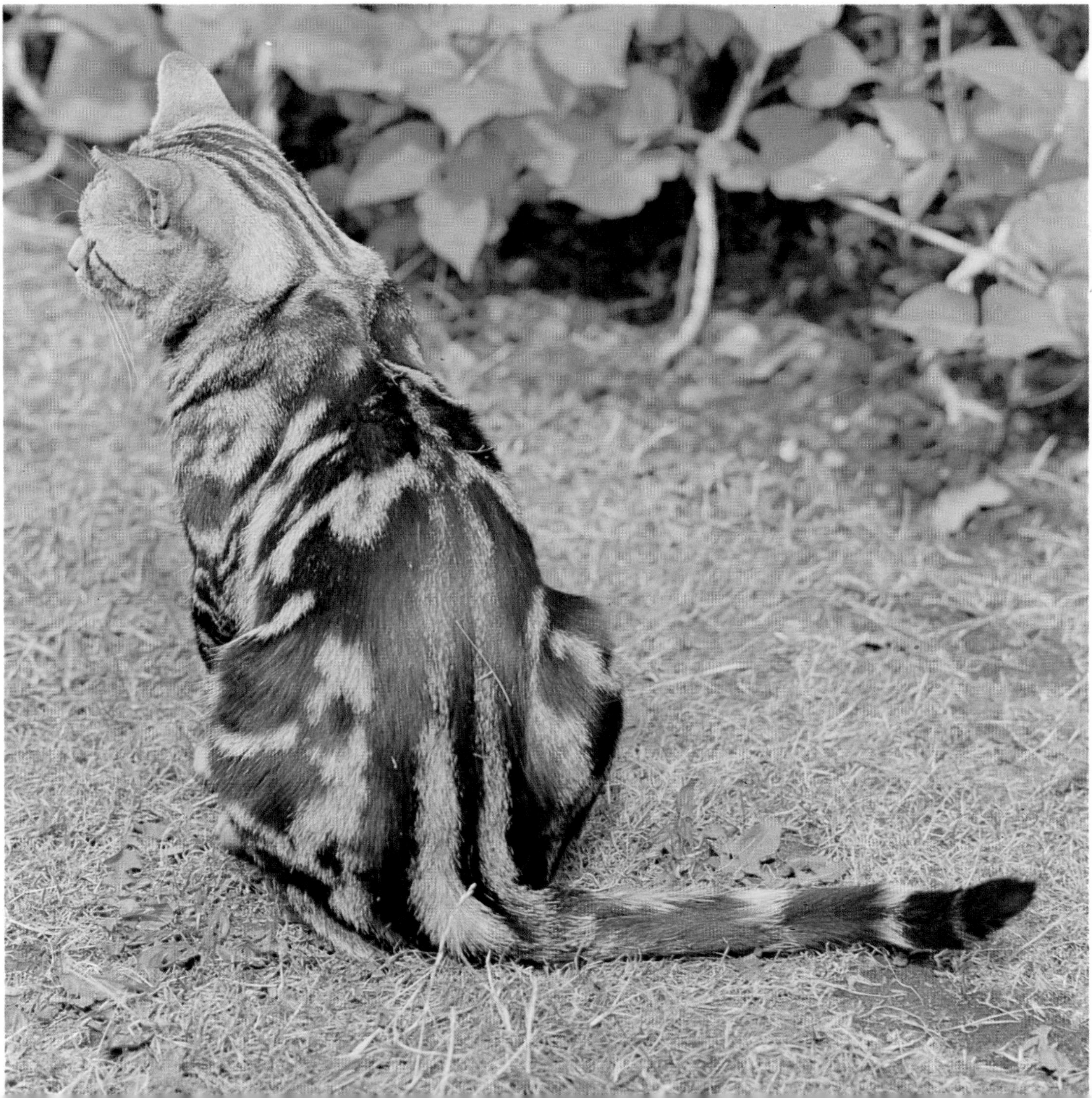

53–54   RED TABBY SHORTHAIR

55   TORTOISESHELL AND WHITE SHORTHAIR

56   TORTOISESHELL SHORTHAIR

57–58   MANX

width between the ears, short noses, full, well-developed cheeks, small, tufted ears, and large round eyes. The body should be cobby and low on short, sturdy legs. The tail should be short and full, kinks not being permitted. Through judicious breeding and using certain strains, some varieties are bred closer to the required standards than others. Often too, in experimental breeding, it can be many years before the desired type is obtained.

There are still Longhairs in Turkey, but they are not so easy to find these days. There are two known breeds, but unfortunately no records have been kept, so they have no pedigrees there.

The following information has been kindly given by Dr M. Sandikçioğlu, of the Veterinary Faculty of Ankara University.

In some foreign literature all long-haired cats are named as "Angoras", but the Ankara cat is a breed with special characteristics of its own. It may be difficult to find full-blooded (pure-bred) Ankara cats, but it is still possible. It is very easy to see many similar cats in Ankara and in the Ankara region. The characteristics and habits of the Ankara cat are:

Colour: Usually white, but can be smoke and black too.

Hair: Long, bright, soft, shiny like silk, longer on the neck and part way down the shoulders than on any other part of the body.

Head: Large, round, and massive. Nose pink-coloured, broad and short.

Ears: Medium size. Well tufted.

As a breed characteristic, pure-bred Ankara cats are always deaf.

Eyes: Large and full, placed well apart, bright, and different in colour. One is blue and one is yellow. The Black and Smoke do not have different colour eyes; their eyes are usually yellow, and they are not deaf. Congenital deafness has been recognized for many years in blue-eyed white cats.

Body: Short and very cobby. Well-furnished short tail.

Limbs: Strong and short, massive. Pads are pink.

Ankara cats are really beautiful, and very proud-looking. They are very clever cats.

It is interesting to note that an attempt is being made in the United States to reintroduce the Angoras, and a definite breeding programme has begun in an endeavour to popularize once more the original long-haired cats.

The other variety in Turkey comes from the Van area. A pair of these were brought over to England some years ago, and have been bred from so successfully that they have now received recognition, and been given a breed number (see Turkish Cats, page 88).

Gordon Stables, in his *Domestic Cats*, refers to the Longhairs as the Asiatic cats, saying that "they are of extremely affectionate and loving dispositions, and so fond of other animals, such as dogs, pet rabbits, guinea pigs, etc. They are so beautiful and so cleanly, and if kept in a clean room, take such care of their pelage, that I only wonder there are not more of them bred than there are." This was written in 1876, and in a few short years the position had changed drastically, with many people deploring the fact that the original British cats were having to take a back seat to the rapidly increasing numbers of the foreign Longhairs. Gordon Stables called the Shorthairs the European or Western cats, and said "the cats with long fur were the Asiatic or Eastern cats, also known as the Persian or Angoras, according to the difference in the texture of the coat".

When the two varieties were mated together by the early fanciers it was found that the Persian characteristics were dominant, so gradually all the Longhairs were classified as "Persian". In fact, Frances Simpson in *The Book of the Cat*, published in 1903, says that "in response to many inquiries from animal fanciers, I have never been able to obtain any definite information as to the difference between a Persian and an Angora cat", and she went on that it was her intention to confine her division of cats to long-haired or Persian cats, and short-haired or English or foreign cats.

Eventually all Angora and Persian cats were referred to as Longhairs, but today it is still possible to find cats with differing coat textures, one being soft and silky, and the other fine and more inclined to stand away from the body. Ironically enough, cats with Angora type are now usually referred to by judges in their reports as having poor type.

The first standards gave the self-colour varieties as White, Black, Blue, Grey, and Red, with the Tabbies being Brown, Blue-Silver, Light Grey, and White. Gradually, however, new colours were added as more knowledge on genetics was discovered. The type too was improved through selective breeding, until today many of the Longhairs are very close to the required standard, or perfection.

BLACK LONGHAIR

Considering the number of pet black cats there are around, and the many people who believe they bring good fortune, it is surprising to find that the pedigree varieties, both long- and short-haired, are comparatively rare.

According to Harrison Weir, the first Black Longhairs in Britain were one of the original Angora varieties, and there were also those with the Persian type, but both were difficult to obtain and most sought after. He said that the best one he ever saw belonged to Mr E. Lloyd: "It was called 'Mimie' and was a very fine specimen, usually carrying off the first prize where-ever shown." It wore a handsome collar, on which was inscribed its name and victories. The proud owner said that it had bought the collar out of its winnings, and also paid for its own food, and that it was "his friend and not his dependant".

Frances Simpson said too that "the Persian of very great value is all black, with a very fluffy frill, and orange eyes". She said also that she had read of one black queen that came straight from the land of cats and the palace of the Shah itself. Apparently it was "moderate in size, slightly built, with an expression so foreign that it amounted to weirdness; this cat could with a dash of imagination have been worked up into the incarnation of a spirit, a soothsayer, the veiled beauty of a harem, a witch, snake charmer, what you choose; but always remain something far apart from prosaic England, something tinged with romance and the picturesqueness of the mystical East. This black cat was undoubtedly a typical Persian."

Despite all this, there were very few entered at the early shows, and during the past century there has been little increase in numbers, although some of the Blacks exhibited have been magnificent cats.

One of the earliest Blacks was "Satan", owned by the Hon. Mrs McLaren Morrison in the 1890s. He was a winner every time he was exhibited. Mrs A. M. Benest's Champion "Dirty Dick" was another famous winner, and sire of a number of well-known early cats. In America Mrs Clinton Locke of Chicago imported many Longhairs, including a pair of beautiful Blacks called "Black" and "St Tudno". "King Max", belonging to Mrs E. R. Taylor, took innumerable prizes at the Boston Shows in 1897, 1898, and 1899, and was valued at one thousand dollars. Blacks from Britain are still exported all over the world, and the prefixes "Deebank", "Bourneside", "Chadhurst", and "Petravian" appear in the pedigrees of many winning overseas Blacks. In the United States there are really superb specimens, with the Grand Champion, "Vel-vene Voo-Doo of Silva-Wyte", now unfortunately dead, being so outstanding that his name invariably crops up whenever Blacks are mentioned. They are far more popular in the United States than anywhere else.

The kittens when young may have greyish-brown fur, and the dense, shining black coat may not be seen in its true beauty until it is an adult. Indeed, sometimes they are registered as Smokes.

74

It is said the rustiest-looking kitten often turns out to be a Champion.

The best Blacks have been produced from Blues in the past, with resultant improvement in type. They may be used in breeding Whites, strange as it may seem, and are also useful as studs for the Tortoiseshells, Tortoiseshell and Whites, and Bi-colours.

The type is as for all Longhairs, with the big, round eyes being a deep orange or copper, forming a beautiful contrast with the jet-black coat. A green rim is considered a fault. A black coat is difficult to keep in perfect show condition, as it takes on a rusty hue very quickly.

WHITE LONGHAIR— BLUE-EYED, ORANGE-EYED, and ODD-EYED

The last few years have seen a tremendous increase in the popularity of the White Longhairs in nearly all countries interested in pedigree cats. It is probably because they are so appealing, and to anyone who is undecided as to which colour he prefers, a small, pure-white, fluffy kitten with tiny tail held upright proves irresistible.

They are probably the oldest known variety of cat with long fur as, according to Turkish experts, the first Angora (Ankara) cats were always white, usually with blue eyes and frequently deaf. The Whites which came from Persia apparently had amber eyes, and did not suffer from deafness. Whites first arrived in England from France, so were frequently called French cats, and were said to be very valuable, particularly if not deaf.

Not all Blue-eyed Whites are deaf. Many are born with a few black hairs in the coat, often on the head, and, although a fault, it is welcomed by breeders, as it is usually found that such kittens have good hearing. It is very rare for those with orange eyes to be deaf. Odd-eyed Whites occasionally suffer from complete deafness or may be deaf in one ear only, but often have good hearing.

At the beginning of the century the majority exhibited had blue eyes, few with amber or orange eyes being bred. The blue-eyed cats usual-ly had typical Angora type, the noses being too long and the ears too tall, and even if there was only one White with orange eyes in the class, because it had Persian type, it invariably won. Because of this, and in an effort to breed Blue-eyed Whites with no deafness, cross-breeding was tried. Unfortunately, although the type was improved, the eye colour was lost. In a few short years practically all the Whites had orange eyes and were given a separate breed number in 1938. In Britain this is still the case, but in the United States and Canada, mainly through odd-eyed breeding, there are outstanding specimens with deep-blue eyes.

It is not essential to mate White to White to have a White litter, for when mated to Blacks, Blues, or Creams there may be both coloured and White kittens born. They are useful as studs for Tortoiseshells and Whites, and also for Bi-colours. Cross-breeding has produced Orange-eyed Whites with enormous round eyes and excellent type, but in Britain it is still difficult to produce an outstanding Blue-eyed White. This situation may change in the near future, as the Governing Council of the Cat Fancy have now decided to grant the odd-eyed variety a breed number, instead of classifying them as "Any Other Variety", which will help the breeders to produce full pedigree stock.

As all kittens are born with blue eyes, it may be difficult to tell until they are eight or nine weeks old, or even older, to which variety they belong.

One of the earliest Whites in Britain said to have "taken the cat world by storm" because of his marvellous size and fantastic coat was "Masher". He had wonderful blue eyes. Mrs Clinton Locke imported his grandson "Lord Gwynne" from England to the United States. He had outstanding eye colour too and was a constant winner.

Helen Winslow, in her *Concerning Cats*, published in 1900, tells of a White Persian called "Tommy". He had been imported from Persia to the United States in 1889. "He was captured in a wild state," she says. The poor thing was kept in a cage for a year, because he could not be tamed. Eventually he accepted domesticity, was valued at five hundred dollars, and won several prizes. Another White, "Grover B. the Mascotte", from Philadelphia, won a twenty-five-dollar gold medal in 1895 for being the heaviest white cat. He weighed over twenty pounds and his value was given at one thousand dollars. He had come from Malta, and always wore a one-hundred-dollar gold collar.

In England Mrs P. Cattermole's "Lotus" cats have produced many prize-winning kittens, both blue- and orange-eyed. These have been exported all over the world.

There are now several very good Orange-eyed Whites appearing at the shows. Mrs J. Hogan's Champion "Snowhite Herald", a male, many times "Best in Show", has been described as "near perfection", while Miss E. Sellars's Champion "Coylum Marcus" won the British Ambassador Award of the White Persian Society (U.S.A.). He is valued at £1000, and attends shows with his own security officer. Mrs E. Durbin's "Nineveh" Whites, bred in Britain, have been exported all over the world. In Canada Mr E. Johnston's Grand Champion "Halton Ridge Moontreasure" is an outstanding Copper-eyed White female, while Grand Champion "Simbelair's Aristocrat of Castilla", bred by Mrs L. Weston, is a most wonderful Odd-eyed White and winner of a number of trophies. In the United States Mrs M. Lohne, president of the White Persian Society, has the Grand Champion "Silva-Wyte-Alladdin of Sanida", but there are so many good ones that it is impossible to mention them all.

The kittens when first born have a pinky look, which soon goes as the fur grows. The type should be as for all Longhairs, the head being round and broad with plenty of space between the small, well-covered ears. The nose should be short and the cheeks full. All varieties should have long, flowing, pure-white coats, with full frills. The fur should be soft and silky, not woolly in texture. The blue-eyed cats should have eye colouring of a really deep blue, but so often they are too pale, while the orange-eyed, referred to as copper-eyed, should also have deep-coloured, never amber, eyes. The odd-eyed should have one blue and one orange or copper, both deep-coloured.

The Black and White Club in England looks after the interests of all the Whites, and as a specialist club proposes judges for these varieties.

BLUE LONGHAIR

These are still referred to in most countries, including Britain, as Blue Persians, after the supposed country of origin, but this is not strictly correct, as the Blues we have today bear little similarity to the first arrivals from Persia. Selective breeding and discarding during the past eighty years have produced outstanding specimens, very close to what is considered ideal for this variety. Many have gorgeous type, long, flowing, even-blue coats, and enormous ruffs around the heads.

Harrison Weir considered that all blue-coated cats were merely lighter-coloured forms of the black cats, and that the first Blues were the result of mating Blacks with Whites.

At the first shows they appeared in the "Any Other Colour" classes, and indeed that is exactly what they were. A motley crew indeed, as some had tabby markings, and others white patches, while the colour varied from a pale grey to almost black, and the eyes were green. Frances Simpson exhibited the first true Blues at the Crystal Palace in the 1880s. Her kittens were said to have been the purest blue that had ever been seen. Unfortunately, she gave no details as to how they were bred. More good-coloured Blues appeared, and in 1889 a class for "Blue self-coloured without White" was introduced. So popular was this classification that a year later it was divided into male and female, with Miss F. Simpson's male "Beauty Boy" being the first male winner, and Mrs H. Thompson's "Winks" the first female. "Beauty Boy" proved to be a very good stud, as did Mr A. Clarke's "Turco", Miss Bray's "Glaucus", and Mrs W. Singleton's "Moko", while Mrs W. Hawkins's "Wooloo-mooloo" became the most famous stud cat of his time.

It is from these cats that the Blue Persian fancy throughout the world is descended. As the coat colour improved, breeders also endeavoured to produce Blues with big, round, deep-orange-coloured eyes, instead of wholly green or green-rimmed, a very bad fault. As now, they were the most popular Longhairs, and by 1899, at a cat show in Westminster, there were forty-eight females and forty-two males.

1901 saw the foundation of the Blue Persian Cat Society by Miss F. Simpson which still flourishes today and holds a well-attended specialist show annually, with the best of the variety from all over Britain being entered. British-bred Blues are eagerly sought after by overseas buyers for quite large sums.

Between the Wars many good champions appeared at the shows, one being the well-known "Mischief of Bredon", whose name may still be found in many of the pedigrees today. Miss E. Langston's "Dion of Allington" and Lady Eardley Wilmot's "Gentleman of Henley" will also be remembered by many of the older fanciers.

The Second World War put an end to cat shows in Britain for some years, and few kittens were bred. Immediately after the cessation, as if by magic, Blues rapidly emerged into the limelight once again, with such well-known breeders as Mrs M. Brunton, of "Dunesk" fame, and Mrs J. Thompson, with the "Pensford" affix, producing outstanding kittens. "Foxburrow Frivolous", bred by Mr P. Soderberg and owned by Mrs Thompson, is now probably the most famous sire of all time. His name can be found in the pedigrees of many winning Blues, Creams, and Blue-Creams throughout the world. Mrs L. McVady's "Gaydene" cats are also excellent examples of this variety, and Mrs E. Burrows's "Orion of Pensford", bred by Mrs J. Thompson, has been practically unbeaten on the show bench, and many times "Best in Show".

A good Blue has all the characteristics required in the Longhair standard. These are good, broad head with width between the small, tufted ears, well-developed cheeks, short nose, and large, round eyes, deep orange or copper in colour. The body should be cobby and low on the legs, with a short and full tail, never tapering. Kinks are not permitted, and are considered as faults. Other faults are white hairs in the fur, tabby markings, or shadings. The Blue is one of the typiest of our cats, but in the United States the noses may be even snubbier. This is frowned on in Britain, as it has been found that such cats frequently have 'weepy' eyes, which is also considered a fault. They are renowned for their great wealth of coat, and although any shade of blue is permitted, as long as it is even right down to the roots, the paler shades seem to be more popular.

Not all Blues are perfect—in fact, some seem to revert to the Angora type, having ears that are too upright and noses that are too long, and these would never do well at shows.

Those with excellent type and coat length have been used over the years to improve other varieties, and have been mated to Blacks, Whites, Creams, and Blue-Creams (see Creams and Blue-Creams). They were also used by the late Mr B. Stirling-Webb in the production of his first "Briarry" Colourpoints.

CREAM AND BLUE-CREAM LONGHAIR

Because of their close breeding connection, it is convenient to write of these two varieties under the same heading.

Cream Longhair

The first Creams appeared by accident, and were regarded as 'sports' and apparently little valued. They were referred to as "Fawns", and usually sold as pets or, according to Frances Simpson, were sent to America, where apparently they were more appreciated than they were in England.

A Persian bred by Mrs Kinchant, "Cupid Bassanio", born in 1890, was the first recorded Cream in Britain. Another early Cream was "Ripon", once owned by Lady Marcus Beresford and then sold to Miss Cockburn Rickinson. Lady Marcus Beresford's name crops up continually in connection with many varieties in the days of the early Longhairs, but as at one time she owned one hundred and fifty cats it is not surprising that she had a number of prize-winners and champions among them.

The first Creams shown had many markings and shadings in the coat, and were certainly not pure Devonshire-cream colouring, as many are today. The type was poor, and fanciers tried many cross-breedings in an effort to improve this, with the result that, knowing little of genetics, and using Reds, the majority born were males, and the variety practically died out. Even-

77

tually it was discovered that Blue and Cream matings produced the best kittens. From this cross-breeding Blue-Creams were also produced, but it was not apparently realized for some years that this all-female variety could be used to produce spectacular Blues and Creams, with excellent type. The Blue-Creams were not recognized in Britain until 1930.

In the United States the Creams made rapid progress, with Mrs Clinton Locke breeding many fine specimens, with very good type and colour for those days. One in particular, "Jessica", was a beautiful kitten.

By the early 1930s a number of British fanciers had worked hard to produce a Cream with pure colouring and no reddish tinge, and cats bearing the cattery names of "Hanley", "Culloden", "O' the Combe", and "Bredon" were constantly winning at the shows. Perhaps one of the best known was the late Captain W. H. Powell's Champion "Biscuit of Hanley", a magnificent male renowned for his type and colour, with a pure, pale, soft, full coat. His sire was Champion "Mischief of Bredon", one of the outstanding Blue studs of his day. Captain Powell also owned another lovely Cream, Champion "Shot of Hanley", and it is from these two famous cats that many of the Creams today can trace their ancestry. The Second World War brought breeding practically to a standstill, though kittens from this strain were kept and treasured, and were bred from shortly after the War ceased.

One of the most notable exhibits at the first shows after the War was Champion " Widdington Warden", bred by the late Mrs M. Sheppard, a lovely pale, unmarked Cream. He laid the foundation for the famous Widdington Creams, now bred by Miss E. Sheppard. This lovely shade of cream is still maintained, and may be seen in Champion "Widdington Orion", one of the present-day studs who traces his ancestry to Champion "Biscuit of Hanley", through Champion "Wonderland Honeybunch", bred by Mrs O. Ruffell.

The Pensford cattery owned by Mrs J. Thompson, and famous throughout the world, has made a valued contribution to the breeding of Creams and Blue-Creams, through her famous Blue stud, Champion "Foxburrow Fri-

volous", siring such well-known Creams, all champions, as "Oscar", "Sherry", and "Paul of Pensford".

Modern prize-winning Creams include Champion "Dalan Sabin", bred by Mrs B. Barron, Champion "Startops Sans Souci", bred by Mrs D. King, and the "Wildfell" outstanding Creams bred by Mrs B. Wright.

The characteristics are as for the other Longhairs, with strong physique, a long, dense, silky coat of pale to medium cream, but pure and sound right through to the roots. The large, round eyes should be a deep-copper colour.

Creams may be used in breeding a number of varieties, as follows:
  Cream male mated to a Blue female:
    Blue-Cream females.
    Blue males.
  Cream female mated to a Blue male:
    Cream males.
    Blue-Cream females.
  Cream male mated to a Blue-Cream female:
    Cream males and females.
    Blue males.
    Blue-Cream females.
Two Creams may also be mated together. They may also be mated to Tortoiseshells, Tortoiseshell and Whites, Blacks, Whites, and Bicolours.

Blue-Cream Longhair
The Blue-Creams are sex-linked, being invariably female. Due to the cross-breeding, the type is usually outstanding. In Britain it was at first a patched cat, as it still is in North America. At first, it was called "Blue and Cream Mixed". In the United Kingdom it should have the two colours well intermingled, giving a shot-silk effect, with neither colour predominating. To see a good Blue-Cream at the height of her perfection is a sheer delight, but it is still very difficult to get away from patching, blue usually predominating, particularly on the head and legs. A cat with heavy patches looks like a Blue Tortoiseshell. A blaze on the face is permitted, but solid paws are frowned upon, as is a reddish tinge in the coat. The eyes may be deep copper or orange.

There have been several good pastel-coloured queens shown in Britain recently, including

Champion "Barwell Athene", bred by Mrs D. Fawell, Mrs J. Thompson's Champion "Opal of Pensford", and Mrs L. McVady's Champion "Dalan Amanda".

SMOKE LONGHAIR

When well presented this is one of the handsomest of cats, for, as the standard says, "it is a cat of contrasts", with a white undercoat, deeply tipped with black. From a distance it may be mistaken for a Black, and it is not until the animal walks that glimpses of the white may be seen.

In a good specimen, the broad, round head has a full, silver ruff forming an excellent contrast to the dense, black mask of the face, with the small ears delicately tufted with silver, and big, round, deep-orange or copper-coloured eyes.

It is also possible to have a Blue Smoke, with blue replacing the black. It is a very pretty variety, but there is not so much contrast as in that of the Black.

The type is usually very good, but it is not an easy thing to breed a specimen with a perfect coat and all the points required. Smoke may be bred to Smoke but, unless care is taken in choosing the right male, the kittens may fail in type. A Black may be used most successfully, and some fanciers have tried matings with Silver Tabbies, but this has often resulted in the introduction of tabby markings, particularly on the head. Such markings may be exceedingly difficult to breed out.

The kittens are black when born, and it may be three weeks before there is any sign of white in the fur. Even then it is exceedingly difficult to pick out a future champion in a litter for at least six months, especially if from a Smoke and Black mating. Many excellent examples have been exhibited, though unfortunately neutered and useless for breeding, having been sold as young kittens showing little promise of the beauty to come.

The first Smokes were bred by chance, and originated from matings between three self-colours, Black, White, and Blue. Silver Tabbies, Shaded Silvers, and Chinchillas all played their

part in producing the early Smokes. They were first exhibited in the "Any Other Colour" classes, but numbers increased and by 1893 there was a Smoke class. The fashion in England was for very dark cats, but the United States preferred the paler coats, and several cats which failed to win prizes crossed the Atlantic to gain the titles of Champions. "Watership Caesar" was English-bred, and after being imported by Mrs M. Thurston was "Best in Show" at one of the American shows.

Breeders found it exceedingly difficult to breed Smokes, although a number of crosses were tried, and the entries in this class at the shows became less and less.

There was one outstanding example, still spoken of with admiration by some of the older fanciers, Champion "Backwell Jogram", belonging to Mrs H. James. From his photographs, he had excellent type and wonderful contrasting colouring.

Recent years have seen a great revival of interest in this variety and, starting with the "Kala" strain bred by Miss D. Collins, a number have appeared at the shows well able to compete favourably with any other Longhairs. Prize-winning strains are those bearing the prefixes of "Bircotte", "Canella", and "Almondhill", among others.

TABBY LONGHAIRS

Gordon Stables, in *The Domestic Cat* (1876), speaks of the Tabbies as "the real old English cats—the playmates of our infant days and sharers of our oatmeal porridge". He was probably thinking of the cats with short fur, but, even so, those with long coats have always been liked as house pets, often being neutered. They have wonderful personalities, are very decorative, and have a reputation for being good ratters. The majority of the pets are probably the result of mis-mating or mixed-matings, and very few have markings conforming to the required standard. This is the same as for the Shorthairs: briefly, butterfly wings on the shoulders, two necklaces on the chest, ringed tail and legs, with the flanks and saddle having deep bands of contrasting colour. The face should have delicate markings on the cheeks, spectacles around the eyes, and a letter "M" on the forehead. In the short-coated varieties this pattern, or the failure to have such markings, may be seen clearly enough, but in the long fur they may be difficult to discern, particularly if the coat has been brushed up. The markings on the back are often too solid.

The origin of the long-haired Tabby is obscure. Harrison Weir said that they were not true Angoras, and gave details of one from Russia. Apparently, they were mostly dark-brown Tabbies, with dark markings, but not very clear and distinct. The characteristics he mentions are interesting in that the body is described as larger than that of the Angora and Persian, with shorter legs, the tail being short, thick, and woolly, and the eyes large, and of bright-orange colour. In fact, if used in matings with the Angoras and the Persians, the result would be the typical Longhair of today. The writer has tried to obtain information on the variety from Russia, but no records appear to have been kept there.

It was also said that these cats did not care for warmth and did not mind cold weather. This is very true of many long-haired cats; the writer's never sit by a fire and adore snow. Of course, short-haired Tabbies mated to self-coloured long-haired cats can, by selective breeding, be used to improve the markings, and this is what probably happened in the early days of the fancy.

Britain recognizes the Brown, Red, and Silver, while North America and other countries have Blue, Cream, and Cameo Tabbies as well.

BROWN TABBY LONGHAIR

At the early cat shows the classes for this variety were well filled, with many splendid animals being exhibited.

Among early winners were Miss F. Simpson's "Persimmon", sire of many prize-winning kittens, and Miss Southam's "Birkdale Ruffie". This cat won the special prize given by King Edward VII, when Prince of Wales, for the best rough-coated cat in the show. This was a framed autographed portrait of the Prince. "Birkdale Ruffie" sired a son, "Master Ruffie", said by the judges to be perfect in every point.

North America too showed a great liking for the Brown Tabbies, and many were imported from Britain. One, "King Humbert", arrived there in 1885, and was said to be so outstanding that his owner, Mr E. Barker, refused an offer for him from a millionaire of one thousand dollars. "Arlington Hercules", a prize-winner at the Westminster Show in 1902, also did well when exhibited in the United States by Miss L. Johnstone, the secretary of the Beresford Club.

In spite of all this early popularity, the numbers of Brown Tabbies have gradually decreased over the years. It may be due to some extent to the practice of mating Brown to Brown, which produced kittens with poor type, or mating to Black causing too solid markings.

The kittens when young are dark in colour, with the pattern appearing as the fur grows. The long, flowing coat should be a rich, tawny sable and the markings dense black, the short, full tail being regularly ringed. The type is as for other Longhairs, with the large, round eyes of a hazel or copper colour. Faults are a white chin, a white tip to the tail, and brindling.

The late Miss J. Fisher of "Hadley" fame exhibited a number of prize-winning Browns between the Wars whose names still appear on pedigrees today, while Mrs J. Paddon's "Trelysstans" are still doing well today, as are the "Jungle" cats belonging to the Lamberts.

This variety's interests are looked after in England by the Red, Cream, Tortie, Blue-Cream and Brown Tabby Society.

RED TABBY AND RED SELF LONGHAIR

Red Tabby Longhair
Red Tabbies were shown in the same classes at the early cat shows as Browns, but they were often poorly marked, or had white hairs. A specialist club was founded in England in 1900, The Orange, Cream, Fawn, and Tortoiseshell Society, its aims being to improve the type of cat bred, and to encourage the breeding of such coloured cats. These Orange cats were the forerunners of the Reds, the majority being self-coloured rather than tabby, but as the classification at the shows was for "marked or unmarked

59   SPOTTED

60   CHARTREUX

61   SPOTTED

62   CHARTREUX

63   BI-COLOURED SHORTHAIR

64   CHINCHILLA AMERICAN SHORTHAIR

cats" it did not really matter. The fashion, however, appeared to favour the unmarked cats. These would have been known as Red Selfs now, and were few and far between. The type was frequently poor, and nearly all had white chins and white tips to the tail. They often appeared in litters from Tortoiseshells, but not being pure bred were usually males.

By the 1920s, through various cross-matings, including using Blacks, the colour had deepened, the type had improved, and marked cats were preferred. It was probably a case of "Hobson's choice", as it was found impossible to breed the Reds without some tabby markings. Mrs F. Fosbery bred several "Eastbury" champions, and Mrs E. Neate's studs included the Champion "Red Leader", while Champion "Swinton Dinna Forget", owned by the Hon. Mrs Clive Behrens, appeared on nearly all the Red pedigrees, and was responsible for the great improvement in the colour. The numbers at the shows increased, helped by the kittens bearing the "Hendon" prefix of Mrs G. and Miss L. Campbell-Fraser. There are several breeders today, with Mrs N. Rosell's cats bearing the "Bruton" prefix invariably appearing among the winners.

Nowadays the type is very good, and many have excellent tabby markings. These may be seen clearly when the kittens are first born, disappear as the fur grows, and reappear as the adult stage is reached.

Characteristics and pattern of markings are as for the Brown Tabby, with the long, silky coat being a deep, rich red, the deep-red, mahogany-coloured markings to be clearly defined. Faults are pale chins, white tips to tails, and the tummy fur being paler than the rest of the coat. The eyes should be a deep, rich, red colour.

They are popular in North America, with the standard being close to that of the British. There is also a variety in the United States referred to as "Peke-faced". These are both tabby and self Reds, with ultra-type, the head resembling that of the Pekinese dog. In the 1910 catalogue of the National Cat Club Show Miss F. Simpson exhibited "Little Pix" in the Any Variety class, giving the breed as "Pekingese" (imported).

Red Self Longhair
Although the Orange, the forerunner of these cats, was often without markings, it appeared to be impossible to improve the colour without the use of Red Tabbies. This, unfortunately, also meant introducing tabby markings, and the variety practically died out.

Very few are entered at the shows today, and these invariably have markings on the head and shadow rings on the tail. The colour of the one or two exhibited is invariably outstanding, as is the coat texture and type. It has been suggested that a cross with a 'hot' Cream is good, but while this may help to lose the markings it may result in paler coats. If it is found possible eventually to produce Red Selfs to order, it would be most useful for breeding Tortoiseshells and Tortoiseshell and Whites. When the breeding is pure Red, the kittens may be male and female, and not, as is commonly supposed, all males.

The standard requires that the long, silky coat should be a deep, rich red, with the type as for other Longhairs, and the large, round eyes a deep-copper colour.

SILVER TABBY LONGHAIR

This is a variety which has not achieved the success it should have done, as a good specimen is most striking with ground colour of pure, pale silver and the contrasting dense-black pattern of the markings. At a National Cat Club Show sixty years ago, there were nearly thirty in the Silver Tabby class, whereas today ten would be a large number. It must be remembered that in those days standards were not so high, and many entered in the class then would now be referred to as "Any other Variety". In fact, at a 1902 cat show a judge wrote that the class was well filled, but that many of the entries should have been marked "wrong class".

It became less popular with the arrival of the Chinchilla, which it is said it helped to produce, and often the markings were so diffused that the cats were more Shaded Silver than Tabby. The type too was poor, the noses being long, and the ears too tall, and it proved difficult to find suitable studs to use to improve these faults. Blacks were tried, but often the markings were too solid, and the pattern in no way filled the requirements set out in the standard.

A noted winner in the 1920s was Miss Anderson Leake's "My Lady Dainty of Dingley". Apparently she had excellent markings, and beautiful hazel eyes. Champion "Devon Pixey" was exported to the United States to become a Grand Champion there. He was bred by Miss E. Clarke, and excelled in eye colour and type. Mrs M. Greenwood has bred a number of modern champions of this variety bearing the "Wilmar" prefix.

The kittens are born dark, and it is not until the fur has grown that the pale-silver ground colouring is seen, but by the age of six months it should be possible to pick out a future champion.

The type should be as for other Longhairs, with the body cobby on short thick legs. The long, dense coat should have a ground colour of pure, pale silver, with decided jet-black markings, with any brown tinge being a drawback. The full frill should form a frame around the face. The pattern of markings should be as for the Brown and Red Tabbies. The eyes may be green or hazel, but some fanciers still prefer yellow or orange, although these colours would now be faulted.

BLUE TABBY LONGHAIR

Blue Tabbies were exhibited at the early shows at the Crystal Palace. These cats had ground fur of bright blue, and jet-black markings, and were entered in the "Any Other Colour" class. For some reason or another they gradually died out, and none have appeared at the shows for years.

In North America and several other countries there is a recognized variety of Blue Tabbies with long fur, but the colouring in no way resembles that of the early English cats. The characteristics should be as for all the Longhairs. The ground colouring should be a pale-bluish ivory, with distinct, contrasting markings of a very deep blue. The pattern of markings is as given for the other Tabbies. The nose leather should be the colour of old-rose and the eyes a brilliant copper. Although very striking in appearance they are comparatively few in number, possibly because it is difficult to produce such a cat with the correct pattern of markings.

CREAM TABBY LONGHAIR

Cream Tabbies are also recognized in North America. The ground colouring should be pale cream with contrasting markings of buff or cream, and eyes a brilliant copper.

CHINCHILLA

Frances Simpson, in *The Book of the Cat*, written in 1903, starts her chapter on this variety with the words, "Perhaps no breed or variety of cat has been so much thought about, talked about and fought about in the Fancy as the silver or chinchilla Persian." This was certainly true, as there were arguments about the name, the classes, and the colouring required. It was a variety that arose by chance. Mrs C. Vallence bought a kitten, smoke in colour, which was the result of a Blue Persian mismating. "Chinnie", or "Mother of Chinchillas", as she was afterwards referred to, was eventually mated to a Silver Tabby. Incidentally, the fact that she was called "Chinnie" proves that the name "Chinchilla" had been thought of even before the breed was officially named.

In 1885 "Chinnie" was mated to "Fluffy 1", a very pure Silver, and a female from this litter, "Beauty", eventually produced "Silver Lambkin", the first Chinchilla stud. He lived to a great age, and it is to him that the variety owes its great success and popularity throughout the world today. He was said to be fantastically beautiful, massive in size, with cascades of silvery-white fur. He may be seen stuffed at the Natural History Museum at South Kensington, London. Anyone who goes to see him expecting to find an example of these ethereal beauties we have nowadays must be warned, however, that either time has dealt very harshly with him, or reports of his famed beauty were much exaggerated.

One of his sons, Champion "Lord Southampton", was sold to Lady Decies for £60; according to one writer of the time "this was the largest sum that had ever been given in England for a cat of any variety". Another famous son was "Waterships Caesar", winner of the "Best in Show" gold medal at the Boston, U.S.A., Show in 1902. Two clubs were formed in Britain to promote the breeding of the Silvers, one being the Silver Society, eventually called the Silver and Smoke Persian Cat Society, and the other the Chinchilla Club. These two clubs amalgamated, and still flourish as the Chinchilla, Silver Tabby, and Smoke Cat Society.

Prior to 1894 the only class for Silvers was "Silver Tabbies, including Blue Tabbies, with or without White", but after this date, to satisfy the fanciers' demand, there were special classes for Chinchillas. The Silver Society said that they "should be as pale and unmarked silver as it is possible to breed them . . . the dark tippings to be slight and faint".

Chinchilla kittens when first born frequently have dark coats, shadow tabby markings, and ringed tails. This was not realized at first and breeders sold these 'ugly ducklings' very cheaply, and then were most distressed to find that they often turned out to be "Best in Show" specimens.

Although the standard called for light-coloured coats many dark cats kept appearing and were entered in the shows. Their breeders objected when their entries never won prizes, so a further class was put on for the Shaded Silvers; instead of silver tippings, the dark edges were permitted to run a considerable way into the fur. The faces and legs, too, often had tabby markings, so the lovers of the lighter Chinchillas often referred to the new variety as "Spoilt Tabby", much to the annoyance of their breeders. There were also classes for long-haired Silver Tabbies, and frequently their markings were very indistinct. To add to the confusion, breeders themselves were not sure which variety they had, and entered the cats in whichever class appealed to them the most. At some shows officials went round before the judging started in an attempt to sort them out. When a cat at one show won the special prizes for both the Chinchillas and the Shaded Silvers it was decided to drop the latter classes. After this the breeders concentrated on producing Chinchillas with really pale coats, or Silver Tabbies with a definite pattern of markings.

Miss E. Langston, whose prefix "Allington" appears on most Chinchilla pedigrees throughout the world, has been breeding for nearly forty years, and has done so much to bring this variety to such a high standard that a Chinchilla has been "Best in Show" on many occasions. Champion "Langhorne Winsome", bred by Mrs Aubrey and owned by Miss A. Steer, was an outstanding specimen that achieved fame in 1950 by winning a "Best in Show" title at the age of twelve and a half. The late Mrs H. McLeod's "Thame" Chinchillas too have been exported to the United States and many other countries. To come to the more modern-day breeders, Mrs M. Turney's "Bonavia" cats are considered to be among the most glamorous ever seen, and both these and Mrs E. Polden's "Poldenhills" lovely specimens have been seen by millions in the Press and on television.

For many years the Chinchillas lacked stamina and were too fine-boned, and to overcome this Mrs M. Turney imported several from the United States carrying the "Kutekit" and "Silver Mesa" prefixes. This had the desired effect, and many outstanding kittens resulted, often being exported back to America. Now there are a number of fanciers producing really excellent stock, very close to standard, and bearing prefixes such as "Sonata", "Ivelholme", "Fishermore", "Hartlands", and "Jemari", among others.

The type should be as for the other Longhairs, with the large, expressive eyes emerald or blue-green in colour, rimmed with black or dark brown, with the tip of the nose brick red.

The full, flowing coat should be a pure white, delicately ticked with silver, giving a sparkling appearance. Too heavy tickings are considered as faults, as are yellow or brown tinges in the fur, and bars or patches.

In Britain, as a result of cross-breeding Chinchillas with Blues, there are Blue Chinchillas, blue replacing the white coat. The type is usually outstanding, because of the breeding, but mating an emerald-eyed cat to one with orange eyes means loss of eye-colour. The cats do not breed true, not being pure-bred as yet, so they are exhibited in the "Any Other Colour" classes, and cannot compete for championships.

SHADED SILVER LONGHAIR

There is no standard for these in Britain now, although many appeared at the shows in the late 1890s. As mentioned in the section on Chinchillas, their classes were dropped in 1902 due to the difficulty in differentiating between the Silver Tabbies, the Chinchillas, and this variety. The Silver Tabbies should have long, silver hair with a pattern of dense-black markings, with the Chinchillas having pure-white fur, lightly ticked with black, while the Shaded Silvers have no markings but heavy tickings giving a shaded effect. The ticking should give the appearance of a mantle shading down from the sides, face, and tail, with the legs the same tone, the overall effect being much darker than a Chinchilla. The eyes may be green or blue-green, delicately outlined with black. Faults are any tabby markings, brown or yellow tinges in the coat, and yellow eyes.

They are still very popular in the United States, where they do very well at the shows. There are a number of Grand Champions, with excellent type, broad heads, small ears, and gorgeous large, round, green eyes. In fact, they represent excellent examples of all that is required in the long-haired cats.

TORTOISESHELL LONGHAIR

Although the Tortoiseshell is a very old variety it has very little known history, and experts agree that the breed probably occurred, and still does, by accident, being the result of chance matings.

A good specimen is one of the most colourful of cats, with a patched coat of red, cream, and black. The patches should be bright in colour, but frequently there is too much black, giving a sombre effect. Each patch should be entirely separate, with no brindling or any white hairs.

This is another all-female variety, males being few and far between, and then usually proving to be sterile; if they do sire, their offspring are generally found to have tabby markings, and are not true Tortoiseshells. Many tales are told of enormous sums being offered for males, but there is probably very little truth in them, as unless he was able to sire a male would have very little value.

A Tortoiseshell female will certainly produce a variety of kittens, and one mated to a Black had in one litter a Black, a Red, a Cream, a Tortoiseshell, and a Blue-Cream kitten. A self-coloured male bred from a Tortoiseshell would be very good to use as a stud as, mated to a cat like his mother, there would be a fair chance of some Tortoiseshell kittens resulting. A breeder would be ill advised to use a Red Tabby, as this could result in tabby markings appearing, which may be exceedingly difficult to breed out.

In the early days of the cat fancy there were many fanciers interested in producing this variety, but few managed to do so. However, there were one or two splendid cats seen at the shows. Miss K. Sangster's Champion "Royal Yum Yum" was bred from a Black and a Tortoiseshell, and another one that did very well, winning many prizes, was "Snapdragon", afterwards exported to the United States. Later Captain G. St Barbe's Champion "Anne Goodcat" became well known between the Wars. Because of the difficulty in breeding, the classes at the shows have never increased very much in size. Miss N. Woodifield's cats bearing the "Pathfinders" prefix usually do well, as do those bred by Miss M. Rodda with the "Chadhurst" prefix.

The type should be as for the other Longhairs, and is frequently very good, because of the cross-breeding with outstanding self-coloured males. The coloured patches should be brilliant, and a cream or red blaze from the forehead to the nose, although not mentioned in the standard, is favoured, and certainly adds character to the face. The legs should be patched as well as the body, and even the ears should be broken. Solid legs are a fault, as is brindling or white hairs in the patches, and there should be no tabby markings. The eye colour may be deep orange or copper. The kittens are very dark when first born, and it may be a month or two before it is realized that the coats really are patched. They have a reputation for being highly intelligent, and because of their scarcity the demand exceeds the supply.

TORTOISESHELL AND WHITE (CALICO) LONGHAIR

Although this is one of the very old varieties, and also one of the most striking with its gaily coloured coat of red, cream, and black patches interspersed with white, it has no known origin and comparatively little definite history in the cat fancy. It is a female-only variety, any males born invariably being sterile. Although from time to time males had apparently sired it is impossible to find out if this was true, and also if the male really was a Tortie and White, with no tabby markings.

Tortie and Whites were, and still are, found frequently on farms, where a number of cats intermate and produce kittens of all colours. They are said to have been the earliest cats known in New England, having been taken there from England by the first settlers. They have always been much liked in Japan, and it is believed by many a seafaring man that to have one on board ship will bring good luck and calm seas. Because of the patched coat they were once known as the Chintz cat in Britain, and are still referred to as Calico in North America.

Although a pedigree variety, and produced from cross-breeding, it has never been possible to breed them to order, as many a would-be breeder has discovered. Even from matings with a self-coloured male it is very rare to find a kitten like the mother in the litter.

To Miss N. Woodifield in England this was a challenge, and she was determined to find out if it was possible, by long-term planned breeding, to work to a pattern of matings and in the end be almost sure that Tortie and Whites would appear. It has taken her over ten years to follow such a plan, but it has been most successful, and she has now bred many champions.

She discovered that mating good-coloured queens to top-line, solid-coloured Persian males lessened the chances of a Tortie and White turning up, and has proved that a male correctly bred will reproduce Tortie and Whites with a queen carrying no Tortie and White in her pedigree. Because of this she decided that most breeders were working on the wrong lines, and that it was more important to concentrate on the male side and produce studs that were capable of siring Tortie and White kittens. Her pedigrees now have six generations behind them.

The head should be broad and round, with full cheeks, short, broad nose, and small, well-placed ears, and the large, round eyes may be orange or copper. The body should be cobby on short, well-boned legs, and the short tail should be very full. The long, flowing coat should be of black, red, and cream, broken into patches, with white. The markings should be well balanced, but it is exceedingly difficult to find a cat perfectly patched. The head, ears, legs, and tail should also carry the colours. Faults are an excess of white, tabby markings, bars and rings, and white hairs in the patches. A white blaze on the head is allowed, although not mentioned in the standard.

Until Miss Woodifield's "Pathfinders" cats appeared on the scene, Tortoiseshell and White Longhairs had been few in number at the shows. At the Westminster Show in 1903 there was only one entry, "Mary 2", owned by Miss Yeoman, but her photograph shows some tabby markings. Lady Marcus Beresford imported one, though it is not known from where, named "Cora". This cat is said to have had perfect type, and beautiful colourings, but died at an early age from dropsy. At the National Show in 1910 three were entered, one belonging to Mrs Slingsby, a well-known fancier at that time, and her Champion "Rosette of Thorpe" won a number of prizes. Between the Wars Mrs G. Yeates, wife of the chairman of the Governing Council of the Cat Fancy of those days, exhibited her Champion "The Mock Turtle". From a Tortie and White, "Josie", Mrs D. Axon bred a number of litters, usually containing a kitten like the mother. When mated to a Blue male this cat had, among others, a beautiful, brightly-coloured kitten, afterwards to become Champion "Noxina", which was for many years a great attraction at the shows. Mrs J. Newton bred many outstanding "Carne" kittens, while Mrs P. Chapman had considerable success with her "Bridgeway" prefix. There are now more exhibited than there have ever been since this variety was first recognized, and the "Pathfinders" and other British-bred Tortie and Whites are now being exported to many other countries.

While endeavouring to breed the Tortie and Whites, Miss Woodifield noted that kittens with coats of blue, cream, and white also appeared. They are the dilute of the Tortie and Whites, and the same principles apply concerning breeding, except that to keep the colours pale it would be possible to use champion Blue and Cream males as studs, thereby producing really outstanding type and pale coats.

BI-COLOURED LONGHAIR AND SHORTHAIR

Within the last year or two these have been officially recognized in Britain, but cats with two-coloured coats are among the oldest English cats known. Black and whites known as Magpies, with markings as for the present-day standards, were entered at early cat shows. There were also others with differently marked two-coloured coats. These were the Black and Whites, as distinct from the Magpies, having white chests and noses, and four white feet. Other colours included the White and Black, and the Red and White. They were produced by cross-breeding, and were looked on by many simply as pets, and were exhibited under "Any other Colour".

The official British standard first set proved to be too exacting as regards the markings, and has now been amended as follows:

Any solid colour and white; the patches of colour to be clear and evenly distributed. Not more than two-thirds of the cat's coat to be coloured, and not more than one-half to be white. Face to be patched with colour (white blaze desirable in the Shorthair). The eyes may be deep orange or copper in colour for the Longhairs, with the additional colour of yellow for the Shorthairs.

The pattern of markings is the same whether for long- or short-haired cats. A fault is intermingling of the two colours. Before amendment, the pattern of markings was required to follow that of a Dutch-marked rabbit. This proved impossible to reproduce, with the consequence that challenge certificates were withheld by the judges,

and at the moment of writing there are only two Longhair champions—"Pathfinders Goldstrike" and "Pathfinders Pacemaker"—and one Shorthair—"Primlington"—though with the change in the standard there will probably be several more in the near future.

Miss N. Woodifield of the "Pathfinders" prefix has bred many long-haired and short-haired Bi-colours, and has been responsible for the re-establishment of this variety. She found that they appeared constantly in litters when she was endeavouring to breed Tortoiseshell and Whites. Frequently the sires are self-coloured champions, so the type and coats are usually good.

The long-haired variety should be typical in type, with broad head, full ruff, cobby body, and short, full tail. The coat should be long, flowing, and silky, with the two colours being entirely distinct from one another.

The Bi-coloured cats with short fur should have British type, short, close coats, and the same pattern of markings.

COLOURPOINT (HIMALAYAN)

As far back as 1922, in Sweden, the possibility of producing long-haired cats with the Siamese coat pattern was thought of, and a Siamese was mated with a White Persian, but nothing more seems to have been done to further the variety. Later, in the United States, Mrs V. Cobb and Dr C. Keeler experimented with cross-matings between Siamese and Persians, and eventually produced long-haired cats with the required Siamese coat pattern, but lacking type. The Second World War put an end for the time being to any further efforts to improve this.

In 1947, in England, a cat with long fur, with the required colourings but no known pedigree, was brought to the late Mr B. Stirling-Webb to be mated to one of his studs. He was surprised to see that she had Persian type and, being interested in genetics, he decided to see whether he could breed a similar, but better, cat with full pedigree. Although it is possible to breed a long-haired Siamese in only two generations, the difficulty is to produce a specimen with a broad, round head, rather than the wedge-shaped head of the Siamese, and with big, round eyes, instead of almond-shaped eyes, but preserving the bright-blue colour. He kept closely to a set pattern of breeding and eventually, with the help of the best Black and Blue Longhairs available, he achieved his ambition, with the new variety being granted recognition in Britain in 1955.

Meanwhile, in the United States, not realizing that an experiment on similar lines was proceeding elsewhere, Mrs M. Goforth had also seen a similar cat, and she too began planned breeding on similar lines. This was very successful, and in 1957 these cats were recognized, being called Himalayan, as the coat pattern resembled that of the Himalayan rabbits. Fundamentally, there is little difference between the British and American varieties.

In both countries the variety proved very popular, and a number of fanciers took them up with enthusiasm. In a very short time Mr Stirling-Webb's "Briarry" Colourpoints became world famous, and have been exported all over the world, including the United States. Another breeder in England, Miss D. Collins of the "Kala" prefix, developed an entirely different strain, which proved to be most useful.

Mrs S. Harding of "Mingchiu" fame worked closely with Mr Stirling-Webb until his death, when she took over the best of his stock, and by selective breeding continued to improve the variety. Both Seal and Blue Colourpoints were produced from the first experimental breedings, and then, by further selection, Chocolates and Lilacs were bred, and now Red and Tortoiseshell Colourpoints are appearing.

The kittens are cream in colour when born, with the point colouring appearing as the fur grows. This colouring continues to darken until the full adult stage is reached, and forms a splendid contrast with the long, cream coat. The head should be broad and round, with a short nose and well-developed cheeks, the ears being small and tufted. The big, round eyes should be a clear, bright, decided blue, as deep as possible. Pale eyes are a fault which keeps appearing at the moment, but efforts are being made by several fanciers, using selected strains only, to improve the colour. Any similarity in type to the Siamese is considered most undesirable and incorrect.

The points colouring should be seal, blue, chocolate, lilac, red, or tortoiseshell with the appropriate body colour—i.e., cream, glacial white, ivory, magnolia, off-white, or cream respectively. The tails should be short and full, the same colour as the points, and kinks are considered defects.

In the United States, the Himalayan colours are as given for the Colourpoints in Britain, with the addition of the Flamepoint, having delicate orange, flame-coloured points.

Both countries have specialist Colourpoint clubs, with the British club catering for Rex-coated and "Any Other Variety" cats as well.

BIRMAN
(SACRED CAT OF BURMA)

There is occasionally some confusion between the Birmans and the Burmese, but the latter is a short-haired variety, and when the two are seen together there are no points of similarity, even in the colouring.

The Sacred Cats of Burma were first seen in France in 1925, and is a definite French variety, most if not all Birmans coming from French stock.

Although like the Colourpoint (Himalayan) the coat pattern of the Birman resembles that of the Siamese, here the similarity ends, as the Colourpoint should have typical long-haired type and the Birman more like that of the original Angoras. However, there is one great difference, which is very striking. The four paws should be pure white, producing a glove-like effect. The white on the back paws should extend up the back of the legs, finishing in a definite point. Apart from this, the colouring and points are as for the Siamese, although the body fur may have a golden-beige tinge. The shape should be long and low on sturdy legs, while the head should be wide, but strongly built, with full cheeks. The eyes should be almost round, a bright China blue in colour.

The original variety was Seal-point, but Blue-points are now appearing in Britain, and in the United States Chocolate and Lilac are also

87

recognized. The points colours are as for the Siamese.

In Britain Mrs E. Fisher and Mrs M. Richards were responsible for the first importations from France. These were a male, "Nouky de Mon Rève", bred by Madame S. Poirier, and a female, "Orlamone de Khlaramour". Other importations followed, and now there are several champions bearing the "Paranjoti" prefix, and many prize-winning "Praha" and "Mie-Hua" kittens, some of which have been sent to the United States.

TURKISH

History has it that the first cats with long coats came from Turkey. These were the Angoras or Ankara cats, self-coloured, mostly white, and having an inclination to deafness, but in the Van district, also in Turkey, there were other long-haired cats.

These cats had the same type—i.e., short, wedge-shaped heads with large, well-feathered ears, and long noses. The bodies were long, but they were distinctive in having auburn markings on the faces and ears, and auburn-ringed tails. Apart from the markings the white coats were long, soft, and silky. Instead of eyes of blue, or one blue eye and one yellow, the cats from the Van district had eyes of light amber, with pink-skinned rims.

Miss L. Lushington and Miss S. Halliday saw several of these cats when touring Turkey, and were intrigued by their unusual markings, and also by their fondness for swimming in the shallow streams. With great difficulty they managed to find an unrelated male and female, and eventually brought them to England.

This pair produced a litter exactly like themselves. Others were imported, and it was found that they bred true, and also that they all had normal hearing. They were registered by Miss Lushington under the prefix "Van".

Unfortunately, no records had ever been kept in Turkey, so there could be no pedigrees provided for the first arrivals, and it has taken many years to get the necessary proven four generations of pure breeding. This has now been done, and the Governing Council of the Cat Fancy has recognized them, granting them a breed number, and they have their own classes and championship status. They are cats of great charm, and are of particular interest, having the original Angora type.

Possibly because of their country of origin they have very full, long coats in the winter, but lose most of it in the summer. Some have small auburn patches on the back, but these should not be considered a bad fault in an otherwise good specimen.

MAINE COON

As far as is known, because no records have been kept, the Coon cats of Maine originated through the cross-breeding of cats arriving at that port from ships from all over the world, and definitely were not, as one theory propounded, the result of a racoon mating with a cat, which is an impossibility. Miss I. Mellen, in *A Practical Cat Book* (1939), says they were originally White Angoras brought from Turkey. Mrs E. Pierce, owner of a number of Maine cats between 1860 and 1900, writing in Frances Simpson's *Book of the Cat*, refers to having owned a Blue-eyed White herself, but also said that the Maine coast was rich in specimens of the long-haired Brown Tabby. According to her there were so many different cats there because kittens were often taken on board ship to amuse the children during the long voyages often remaining when the ships departed again. Cross-breeding and interbreeding and the fairly severe winters eventually produced a race of strong, massive animals with thick coats of all colours and markings.

Exhibitions of the Coon cats were held long before the first official cat show in Madison Square Gardens in 1895, with one of the cats, "Richelieu", belonging to Mr Robinson, winning at many shows in Boston, New York, Philadelphia, and Bangor (Maine) in the early 1880s. At these exhibitions there were sometimes as many as one hundred entries, and, as it was long before pedigrees were thought of, it is presumed that the Best Cat was chosen entirely on condition and looks.

No-one really appreciated the beauty of the

65 ABYSSINIAN

66–67   ABYSSINIAN

68   ABYSSINIAN

69   RED ABYSSINIAN

local cats until the shows started, and it was realized that many of the cats being imported, often at a very high price, had their counterparts in Maine, and so the summer visitors to New England were soon buying kittens and taking them to all parts of the United States. The majority of these kittens were pets, and were neutered, and did little to spread the variety across the country.

In 1953 the Central Maine Cat Club was organized, holding a show each year in Maine to choose the State Champion Cat, and there are now other societies also specifically for breeders of the Coon cats.

Mrs Robert Whittemore has been breeding these cats for many years in Maine, and has now succeeded in obtaining recognition for them. They are unknown in England.

In appearance the coat is not as long as the Longhair (Persian), but is thick and fairly coarse. The type is very much as for the Angoras, the head being long and pointed rather than round. The ears are more upright, and the nose a little longer. It is a massive cat on high legs, with a fairly long body and long, bushy tail. The colour may be self, or patterned, often with tabby markings. The variety is noted for its high intelligence and cleverness.

THE CAMEOS

These have been developed in North America by selective breeding during the last ten years or more, and there are now a number of possible variations. Basically, they have ticked or shaded coats, as in the Chinchillas, Shaded Silvers, and Smokes. The type and other characteristics should be as for all Longhairs.

Shell Cameo or Red Chinchilla

This was the first one produced, and a good example is a strikingly beautiful cat, with a white undercoat and delicate red tickings, giving a sparkling effect. The eyes should be a brilliant copper in colour, rimmed with rose. Tabby markings and too heavy tickings are faults.

Working on the same lines as the Americans, British and European breeders have been endeavouring to produce this much admired variety, and one or two have been appearing at the shows, particularly in Holland.

Shaded Cameo or Red Shaded

This is as for the Shaded Silver with red replacing the black shadings, giving a general red appearance. The shadings must be definite, so that there is no confusion with the Shell Cameo. The eyes should be a brilliant copper colour, with rose-tinted rims.

Smoke Cameo or Red Smoke

Like the Black and Blue Smokes, this cat should have a contrasting coat: the undercoat should be white, deeply ticked with red, with the white not being seen until the cat moves. The mask of the face and the points should be red. The full ruff and the ear tufts should be white, and the eyes a deep copper.

Cameo Tabby

The pattern of markings should be as for the other Tabbies, with ground colour or off-white, and the markings a distinctive red. The eye colour should be as for the other Cameos.

CHOCOLATE SELF AND LILAC SELF LONGHAIR

From time to time, possibly because of a mismating in the first place, a cat appears in the "Any Other Colour" class with a coat colour not seen before and, because it is so attractive, breeders toy with the idea of producing a new variety with similar colouring. This is not as easy as it may seem. There are many things to be taken into consideration, such as finding the right males to use, setting the eye colour, and the type. This may take years, with constant disappointments, and sometimes it proves impossible to get the necessary generations—i.e., parents, grandparents, and great-grandparents—of pure breeding behind a cat before consideration can even be given to a recognized standard.

However, dedicated fanciers often do succeed, through careful and patient selective breeding, and so a new variety is born. In Britain there are now two new self-coloured cats with long coats appearing. One is the Chocolate Self, which the late Mr B. Stirling-Webb was working on at the time of his death, and which has now been bred by Mrs S. Harding, continuing along the same lines. The coat should be the colour of milk chocolate, uniform all over, and the eyes deep orange or copper in colour, with the general characteristics as for the other Longhairs. The type has not yet reached the high standard required, but doubtless this is only a matter of time.

There is also another 'man-made' breed being exhibited with long, lilac-coloured coats. The characteristics should be the same as for the other long-coated cats. Mrs S. Harding is working hard to produce these with good type.

BALINESE

Produced in the United States and Canada by selective breeding by dedicated breeders over a number of years, but not yet known in Britain, the Balinese has now been granted full championship status by the Cat Fanciers' Association, Inc., and other associations.

The standard given for this dainty cat with the "grace and ethereal beauty of a Balinese dancer" is for a cat with Siamese type and coat pattern but with a longer, silkier coat of two inches or more in length.

Apart from the coat pattern there is little similarity between the Colourpoints (Himalyans) and the Balinese, the former being long-haired cats with Persian type, whereas the latter is definitely Siamese in type.

The head is wedge-shaped rather than round, almost triangular in shape, with a long, straight nose, and large, pointed ears. A striking feature is the deep, vivid-blue eyes, almond in shape. The body colouring may be slightly darker than that of the Siamese, but the points should be just as clearly defined. Four colours are recognized.

Quiet, affectionate cats, their increasing popularity may be judged by the numbers now appearing at the shows in North America.

KHMER

These may be seen in Europe, but are not recognized in other continents. Long-haired cats with a Siamese coat pattern, they closely resemble the Birmans, but do not have the gloved paws. The ground coats are golden cream, the points—*i.e.*, mask, ears, legs, and tail—being dark brown.

ANY OTHER COLOUR (LONGHAIR) AND ANY OTHER VARIETY (SHORTHAIR)

As there were very few colour classes at the early cat shows, many exhibits were entered as "Any Other Colour or Variety". Most varieties, before gaining recognition, appeared under this heading, even Blue Persians.

As the shows grew larger, and more varieties were bred, better classification was given, with the entries in the "A.O.C." classes becoming less and less. It was, however, decided to keep the classification at the shows, as it is still useful for showing cats not answering any specific standard; it also provides a 'show-case' for any new variety, 'man-made' or otherwise, that may appear.

No challenge certificates are given, as there is no set standard, so there are no champions under these classifications.

THE SHORT-HAIRED CATS

At cat shows up to 1895 in Britain the short-haired cats were considered to be more important than the Longhairs, and appeared in far greater numbers, but the swing began in 1896, with the National Cat Club at the Crystal Palace Show putting the Longhairs first. By the early 1900s the Longhairs were in the majority, with just a few Shorthairs being exhibited. It must be remembered that this was in the days before the Siamese achieved their world-wide popularity.

The Short-Haired Society was founded in 1901 in an endeavour to increase the interest in all Shorthairs, and to encourage the breeding of a pedigreed British cat which would conform to the standard laid down by that Society and was accepted by the Governing Council of the Cat Fancy. The same year saw the beginning of the British Cat Club, founded by Sir Claud and Lady Alexander, the well-known Sussex breeders and exhibitors of Shorthairs for many years. This is not now in existence.

Prior to the first cat shows and before breeding to order was even considered possible, the majority of cats in the British Isles were short-coated, descendants of those brought to these shores by the Romans, and, taking the domestic pets into consideration as well, this is probably still so today.

These cats had intermated freely over the centuries and, as quarantine was unthought of, others were constantly arriving, brought here by sailors and travellers. The results were cats of varied colours, many with tabby markings. The Short-Haired Society chose colours from the wide variety offered, and each breed was given a number and a Standard of Points. The set standard is in reality a description of the ideal cat for which to aim in breeding, and helps eliminate faults, such as white patches in Blacks, large ears, long bodies, and narrow heads.

It is interesting to note that although there were a great many mixtures of colours from which to choose, the self-coloured—i.e., the same colour all over—and the tabby-marked cats were considered to be the most desirable for the purpose of establishing the British cat as a pedigreed animal. The exceptions were the Tortoiseshell and the Tortoiseshell and White. Bi-coloured cats had appeared at early shows and were judged according to Mr Harrison Weir's Points of Excellence, but these were not recognized by the society. A different standard was also put forward for a Magpie cat. This was most exacting, but was not accepted until as recently as 1966, when it was renamed Bi-colour, with the markings required to be the same as that of a Dutch rabbit. In 1955 the Blue-Cream Shorthair was introduced, and in 1966 a very old variety, the Spotted, again received recognition.

A cat may be registered as pedigreed if three generations of his ancestors are registered British Shorthairs, even if of varying colours. For instance, a British Black male and a British Tortoiseshell female could produce a champion Red Tabby male. The same rule applies to crosses between Black, British Blue, Blue-Cream, Cream, and in fact all the British Shorthairs, but it would be wise to study the genetic principles governing dominant and recessive colours and coat patterns before experimenting.

By careful selection over the years fanciers have produced strong, sturdy animals, with broad chests, and having medium-length bodies on legs of good substance, in proportion to the body, on neat, well-rounded feet. The broad, round heads have well-developed cheeks, short noses, and small, slightly rounded ears. The tails are thick at the base, well set, with the length in proportion to the body.

The American Shorthairs are similar to the British Shorthairs, with some differences in standard, while the Exotic Shorthairs have more long-haired type.

It is possible that they are descended from the same cats, as the first domesticated ones in America were thought to have been taken there by the Pilgrim Fathers. All were house pets to begin with, but, as in Britain, standards were set and recognition granted.

At first in the United States, all the Shorthairs were known as Domestic, but gradually two types emerged, the original having heads that were full cheeked, a little oblong in length, medium to large bodies on medium, heavily-muscled legs, and the other type having round and massive heads, short noses, and cobby bodies on low legs. As the latter frequently had some long-haired breeding in the pedigrees, it was decided that there should be two recognized varieties, the first being known as the American Shorthair and the second as the Exotic Shorthair.

The American Shorthair colours are the same as given for the British, with the addition of Red Self, Chinchilla, Shaded Silver, Black Smoke, and Blue Smoke. As well as the Silver, Brown, and Red Tabbies recognized in Britain, there are the more unusual Blue and Cream Tabbies.

Although the noses are slightly more snub, in appearance and coat the Exotic Shorthairs are very like the British cats. They are recognized in the same colours as the American Shorthairs, but with the following possible colour variations: Shell Cameo, Shaded Cameo, Cameo Smoke, and Cameo Tabby.

The Shorthairs are renowned for their calmness and readiness to adapt themselves to any situation. They are very intelligent and readily respond to affection. The coat is important, and must never be fluffy. It should be firm to the touch, short, fine and close, not woolly.

Mating British to British very often tends to cause a loss of type, with a certain snippyness creeping in. Some breeders advocate an occasional out-cross with a Longhair of similar colour; although there is then the danger of introducing a certain fluffiness into the coat, it should ensure good, round heads, with big, round eyes.

The recognized colours in Britain are as follows:

White with blue eyes	Tortoiseshell
White with orange eyes	Tortoiseshell and White (Calico)
White with odd eyes	Spotted
Black	Bi-coloured
British Blue	Manx (This is usually included in the British group, although there are slight differences in the standard, apart from the taillessness which is unique.)
Cream	
Blue-Cream	
The Tabbies: Silver	
Red	
Brown	

BLACK SHORTHAIR

The short-haired cat with a dense-black coat is one of the oldest varieties known, and is often seen in the home as a pet. It is difficult to appreciate that there is a Black pedigreed cat, unless one can compare a champion with a mongrel. Most pets will be found to have a white locket under the chin, and fail on type and eye colour. It is possible to get a very good black coat from a Siamese mismating, but the type will invariably be Foreign, and the eyes green.

Characteristics are as for all the British cats, but the adult coat should be a shining jet black right to the roots, and the eye colour deep copper or orange. Kittens are sometimes placed at a disadvantage at shows, as the coats may be rusty or greyish in colour when young.

A Black is very useful for breeding the newly-recognized black and white Bi-colours, Tortoiseshells, and Tortoiseshell and Whites.

There has been no great increase in numbers exhibited over the years, possibly due to the fact that there are so many pets of similar colour. In the 1910 National Cat Club Show at the Crystal Palace there were three males and five females. Dr Prior showed two, "The Verger", a male, and "Nocturna", a female; the price in the catalogue was given at £100 each, which was fantastic for those days. At the National Cat Club Show at Olympia in 1967 there were two adults only, and three kittens. The female Champion "Teign Tammy", to mention just one, owned by Mrs L. Silcock, has been producing some excellent kittens.

WHITE SHORTHAIR— BLUE-EYED and ORANGE-EYED

One of the most striking of the British Shorthairs is the White, particularly if having eyes of deep, sapphire blue and a short, fine, close coat of dazzling white. There is also an orange-eyed variety, when the eyes must be a real golden orange or copper in colour. Frequently a cross-mating will produce a cat with odd eyes—that is, one blue eye and one orange eye. Recognized in Britain, they do not yet have championship status as they do in the U.S.A. and Canada. It is very difficult to breed an outstanding specimen with deep-blue eyes. Two Blue-eyed Whites mated together may produce poor type and pale eyes; in an endeavour to improve this, breeders sometimes use other self-coloured cats, but while this may improve the type, it may mean introducing the wrong eye colour.

Early books on cats often refer to the Whites as being slow and moody, but it was not always realized that there is an element of deafness in this variety, particularly the blue-eyed variety, and it was often because the cat did not hear the owner calling that it failed to respond. Breeders nowadays endeavour to avoid using strains that are known to suffer from deafness. Even a deaf cat will respond to signals and vibrations so, apart from the danger of not hearing traffic if it strays on the road, it is not the severe handicap one might suppose.

Gordon Stables, in his *Domestic Cats*, says that a Black is often afflicted with kleptomania, while a properly educated White is "as honest as the day". Referring to the colour, he says, "White as driven snow, if intended for a show cat, if not a very little black wonderfully improves the constitution." It is a fact today that kittens born with some black hairs, particularly on the head, rarely suffer from deafness.

The newly-born kittens have a pink appearance, which soon goes as the fur grows in length. As all kittens have blue eyes when young it is difficult to show definitely for the first few months what the eye colour will ultimately be, so it is unwise to register too soon. By three months, if the eyes are still a bright blue, they should remain so.

Although much in demand the numbers are still comparatively small, and White studs are few. White males when mated to Tortoiseshells may produce Tortoiseshell and Whites, and are also useful for cross-mating for breeding the Bi-coloured Shorthairs.

The Whites have a reputation for gentleness, and are very affectionate, highly inquisitive, and usually keep themselves immaculate, although some breeders do bath their exhibits prior to the shows. Naturally, the coat is all important; it should be a pure white, untinged with yellow or any other marks or staining.

Early breeders of this variety included Sir Claud and Lady Alexander with "Ballochmyle Billie Blue Eyes", and "Ballochmyle Snow King." Only blue-eyed cats were recognized in the shows of those days, and often the eyes were a "wishy-washy" blue and the coats too open. Later Miss T. Cochrane's Champion "Chelsea White Ensign" and Champion "Chelsea Fairy Flan", and Champion "Blythswood Douglas" owned by Mrs C. McCowatt, did much to improve the variety. Miss A. Codrington has had some very good "Watermill Whites", and Mrs C. Betts of the "Dellswood" prefix has exhibited some pretty kittens recently.

BRITISH BLUE

The first short-haired blue cats were thought to have come from Russia (see Russian Blue), but right from the days of the early cat shows it was realized that there were two distinct types, so there must have been resident blue cats. Mr E. E. Jung, an early authority on Shorthairs, wrote in *The Book of the Cat* (1903). "There seems to be a great difference of opinion as to the shape and make of head of these cats. Some judges look for a round, full head of the English-bred cat; others, the long head of the Eastern variety." He believed it depended on the country from which they originated, and said that the specimens from Malta had the round heads and more of the British-bred type than those from Archangel. Of course, blue cats have frequently appeared on farms in litters from Tortoiseshells and Tortoiseshell and Whites, so that is probably where they came from.

An early winner in 1911 was "Blue Peter", owned by Miss Cochrane, who also had Champion "Chelsea Thistledown", "Speedwell", and "Grey Dawn". Champion "Ballochmyle Blue King", owned by Lady Rachel Alexander, and "Blue Boy", belonging to Mr S. Woodiwiss, also did well at the shows, and appear way back on many of the pedigrees, as did Champion "Chelsea Twilight", belonging to the late Miss H. Hill Shaw.

Many breeders of the Russian Blues in the 1930s became interested in the British Blues, and names began to appear which are still remembered today. Mrs Abell bred "Twink of Blagdon", which was a constant winner, as was "Micky of Odersfelt", belonging to Mrs Dimberline, while Mrs Amor Crouch had Champion "Capermudge", an outstanding Blue, responsible for siring many good specimens, and whose name is still appearing on pedigrees. The Rev. B. Rees, a noted Shorthair breeder, bred Champion "Sylvan Joey" in 1943, said to be the most perfect example of a British Blue ever shown. Unfortunately, he failed to sire, but his litter brother, "Sylvan Timmy", was responsible for founding many of the good strains seen today.

The British Blue is the most popular variety of the Shorthairs, and often comes very close to the required standard, with good, round head on a sturdy body. The colour may be a light to medium blue, but must be level in colour throughout, with no white hairs or tabby markings. The big, round eyes may be copper, orange, or yellow. The variety is now renowned for its sturdiness and imperturbability, although an early writer declared that they had "delicate constitutions".

There are many breeders today, with the classes at the shows being well supported. Mrs J. Richards "Pensylva", Mrs K. Savage's "Bonaventura", Mrs I. Johnson's "Jezreel", and Mrs S. Beever's "Fendale", to mention just a few, are all prefixes featuring constantly among the winners.

The male British Blue makes a useful mate for the all-female Blue-Cream. Such a mating may produce Blue-Cream females, Blue females, Cream males, and Blue males. A British Blue female mated to a Cream may have Blue-Cream females and Blue males, but a male British Blue mated to a Cream female could have Blue-Cream females and Cream males.

CREAM SHORTHAIR

This is a comparatively rare variety and, some fanciers think, fairly new, but Lady Rachel Alexander bred them many years ago, and in the 1930s her "Ballochmyle Cream Cracker", Miss Bowley's "Galbre", and Mrs Harpur's "Cream Courtier of Plaicey" were always among the winners. Mrs J. Cattermole of the "Mingswyck" prefix was responsible for a revival of interest in the breed. By mating a long-haired Cream female to a British Blue, the Rev. B. Rees's "Sylvan Timmy", a litter of three Cream males and two Blue-Cream females resulted. They were all short-haired, but unfortunately only the two Blue-Creams lived. One of these was mated to another British Blue, "Sylvan Quickee". Among the kittens she had was a Cream male, which was called "Mingswyck Apollo", and also a Blue male, "Mingswyck Blue Prince"; the last-named ultimately became a champion and his name appears in a number of pedigrees.

About this time, the late Mr G. Allt found that his long-haired Cream, Champion "Danehurst Princess", had mismated with a stray ginger tom. Among this litter was a short-haired

Cream female, "Mingswyck Marylyn". The two mated together and eventually produced a litter of all short-haired Creams.

Unfortunately, many of the early Creams had bars, markings, and ringed tails, and the challenge certificates were usually withheld. By careful selection these have been eliminated to a great extent, although sometimes the tails have shadow rings. Mrs J. Richards has produced some outstanding specimens bearing the "Pensylva" prefix, with the desired deep, rich, cream colour.

Having British Blue in the pedigree, many Creams excel in type, having good, broad heads, with well-developed cheeks, small ears, and big, round copper or orange eyes.

If Cream male is mated to British Blue female, Blue males and Blue-Cream females may result, but a Cream female mated to a Blue male may have Cream males and Blue-Cream females; a Cream male mated to a Blue-Cream female may have Blue males, Blue-Cream females, and both male and female Creams. Or again, if a Cream male is mated to a Tortoiseshell or a Tortoiseshell and White many varieties are possible, as some may resemble the mother, and the kittens may even include Blue-Creams.

The kittens are charming, lively, alert, and usually a delightful colour when young, but even if unmarked it is possible for bars and rings to appear as the fur grows, and also for a reddish tinge to develop, which is a bad fault.

BLUE-CREAM SHORTHAIR

Often excelling in type, this female-only variety —as any males born would probably be sterile— may be produced from cross-breeding Blues and Creams, and Creams and Tortoiseshells (see British Blues and Creams for possible kitten colours).

In Britain the coat should be of the pastel shades of blue and cream softly intermingled, without patching, although a cream blaze on the forehead is permitted. This effect is difficult to produce to order, and often results in cats with cream patches on the body, and solid paws.

In Canada and the United States Blue-Creams should have cream patches, and the short, thick coat should be a distinct blue, never intermingled. In fact, what is a bad fault in one country can be considered correct in others. In Britain the large, round eyes may be copper, orange, or yellow, never green, while in the United States they should be a brilliant gold.

They make excellent mothers and, depending on the stud used, have the most fascinating colour variations in their kittens.

TABBY SHORTHAIRS

It has been said a number of times that if all the cats in the world were allowed to mate together the result would be Tabbies of many colours. From experience it is known that a Tabby can appear most unexpectedly; the writer once had a short-haired silver mackerel Tabby with black markings, produced as the result of a Chinchilla mismating with a Black Shorthair, which, when mated to a Blue, had an outstanding Brown Tabby kitten with all the correct markings. On the other hand, when endeavouring to breed pedigree stock it is sometimes extremely difficult to get the exact pattern of markings required, and only by careful selective breeding is it achieved.

The pattern set by the Governing Council of the Cat Fancy states that there should be delicate pencilling markings on the face, with lines forming spectacles around the eyes, the cheeks being crossed with two or three distinct swirls, and a mark like an "M" on the forehead. The chest should have necklaces of two unbroken narrow lines, usually referred to as "Lord Mayor's chains". Looking down on the back of the cat, it should be possible to see distinct markings forming a pair of butterfly wings. The flanks and saddle should have deep bands of contrasting colour, and the legs and tail should be ringed. A distinct vertical line should run down the spine with a minor parallel stripe on each side. Markings should also be clearly seen on the stomach.

The markings should stand out distinctly from the ground colouring.

Many kittens of self-coloured varieties, both long-haired and short-haired, have shadow tabby markings when first born, but these fade with growth.

Silver, Red, and Brown Tabbies are the only colours recognized in Britain at the moment, although Yellow and Blue were exhibited at the early shows, and Blue and Cream Tabbies are still included in the American Shorthair standards.

There is also a pattern of markings referred to as "Mackerel-striped". Here the markings should be as dense as possible, and completely distinct from the ground colour. The rings should be as narrow and numerous as possible, and run vertically from the spine towards the ground.

BROWN TABBY

A famous champion, "Xenophon", was exhibited at the beginning of the century. Said to represent the "ideal" with a rich, sable-brown, ground-coat colour, he won more money and special awards than any other Shorthair exhibited up to that time. He seemed to have belonged to several owners, finally being bought by Lady Decies.

Although there are very many pet Brown Tabbies, a good pedigree specimen is comparatively rare. A few have been exhibited at recent shows, bred by Mrs B. and Miss E. Lambert of the "Jungle" prefix and Mrs P. Absalom with "Brynbuboo". The pets very rarely have the correct ground colouring, being more greyish-brown than the rich sable required in the standard. The markings should be dense black, and there should be no white. A white chin often does appear, and is considered a fault.

RED TABBY

Red Tabbies should be a definite red, both in the background colour and the deeper red mahogany markings, never the ginger or marmalade colouring seen so often in pet cats. The pattern must show up distinctly. There should be no white in the coat, particularly at the tip of the tail.

The type is frequently very good, being typically British. The eyes may be hazel or orange. At a show in 1910 fourteen Red Tabbies were entered, far more than there would be at any show today. In the male class "Gainsborough Redjacket", belonging to Mr E.

Oliver, was priced at £100, while in the same class "Ginger Jim", belonging to Mr C. Buxton, was for sale at only £2. Unfortunately, it is unknown which, if either, was the winner.

Miss G. Hardman of the "Killinghall" prefix has bred some excellent specimens in recent years, and has more than once had a "Best in Show".

It is quite incorrect to say that all the Reds are male. In pure breeding, with Red on both sides, a litter may contain both males and females. It is when one parent is not pure bred, although the other is, that the kittens produced may be Red males and Tortoiseshell females.

SILVER TABBY

One of the most popular of the short-haired Tabbies, and now appearing at the shows in quite large numbers, the Silver Tabby is most striking in appearance, with the dense black markings contrasting well with the body colour of pure silver. There should be no brownish or yellowy tinges or brindling in the coat. The type is usually good, and typically British. The eyes may be green or hazel in colour.

When first born the tabby markings show up clearly in the kittens, but often, when a few weeks old, they appear smudged and possibly greyish, clearing again as the coats grow.

Champion "Jimmy" was well known at the early shows, as were the Silvers owned by the Hon. Mrs McLaren Morrison, and the "Sedgemeres" of Mr S. Woodiwiss. In the mid-thirties there were very few shown, but Mr Kuhnel's "Double Gift" did well, as did a well-known neuter, "Silver Penny", owned by Mrs Burl. Today we have many breeders, and mention must be made of the cats bred by Mrs M. Thake with the "Silverseal" prefix, which have helped popularize this variety, as also have the "Elvaston" cats bred by Mrs E. Grant-Allen, those bearing the "Culverden" prefix of Miss F. Robson, and the "Lowenhaus" cats of Mr R. Pearson.

All the Tabbies have a reputation for being sturdy, healthy animals, alert and lively, of happy disposition, making ideal pets. Perhaps because of their ancestry, they are very independent, yet show affection readily.

70   RUSSIAN BLUE

71–72   RUSSIAN BLUE

73   BROWN (SABLE) BURMESE

74   BLUE BURMESE

75–76   BROWN (SABLE) BURMESE

TORTOISESHELL SHORTHAIR

The ideal Tortoiseshell is a cat with a patched coat, with black and light- and dark-red patches equally balanced and entirely distinct from one another. At least, that is the requirement of the recognized standard, and it should be the aim of breeders to achieve this. Although the Tortoiseshell is one of the oldest varieties known, and often may be seen on farms, where the cats mate together indiscriminately, it is exceedingly difficult to produce one to order.

The farm cat is rarely up to pedigree standard, as there should be no brindling in the coat or any intermingling of the colours, nor should there be any white hairs. The legs, feet, and ears too should be patched, as well as the body and head. A red blaze on the head is favoured. The eyes may be orange, copper, or hazel.

Because the variety is almost invariably female, one reads of gigantic sums being offered for Tortoiseshell males, but there is rarely any truth in such rumours since, although they do turn up occasionally, they prove to be sterile.

A male was exhibited at the Crystal Palace by Mr Smith in 1871. He was apparently quite overcome at the interest his cat aroused, but there is no mention of it ever siring kittens. In the later shows Champion "Ballochmyle Samson", owned by Lady Rachel Alexander, won many championships and prizes, as did Champion "King Saul", belonging to Mrs Herring.

A self-coloured male is the best stud to use, as a Tabby may produce kittens with stripes, rather than patches, but even so it is impossible to predict what colours the kittens will be. Some fanciers never manage to breed them, no matter what coloured stud is used. They appear sometimes in litters from Tortoiseshell and Whites.

The kittens are very dark at birth, the bright colours appearing as the fur grows. They are alert, very forward, and highly amusing, the type usually being very good.

TORTOISESHELL AND WHITE (CALICO) SHORTHAIR

This is one of the most attractive of the Shorthairs, particularly if bred close to the required standard, with clear, distinct patches of red and black and the addition of white. The type should be as for all the British varieties and is frequently good. Like the Tortoiseshells, it is virtually an all-female variety, although an occasional male has appeared. At one of the early shows three Tortoiseshell and White males were entered; one, "Totty", belonging to Mr Hurry, was valued at £100, but no references have been found to any kittens by him.

Known as the Calico cat in the United States, they were once referred to as "Chintz and White" in England, where they were also known as Spanish cats.

Miss N. Woodifield of the "Pathfinders" prefix has succeeded in breeding them by using strains she has produced through selected matings, entailing the use of the recently recognized Bi-colours. Harrison Weir said as far back as 1889 that, "if Tortoiseshell and White are desired, then a black and white male may be selected" (used), but apparently the early breeders did very little about selective breeding, and failed to realize the importance of his statement.

Unless a strict breeding plan is adhered to it is practically impossible to breed this variety to order. If no Bi-colours are available one of the self-coloured cats is the best stud, particularly if bred from a Tortie and White. The kittens in the litters may be of various colours, and may even include a Blue-Cream. Using a White may result in an uneven balance of the colours, with white predominating.

MANX

The Manx is unique among all the domestic cats in being completely tailless, and this has been responsible for the many legends as to its origin, some even referring to the Ark.

As many breeders have discovered to their cost, it is very difficult to produce a Manx with three generations of pure breeding, as taillessness mated to taillessness may produce a lethal factor, resulting in the death of the kittens. It is for this reason that stumpy (partially tailed) or even tailed cats are used in the breeding; this means that Manx are registered in the supplementary, not the full, register of the Governing Council of the Cat Fancy.

Manx were exhibited at the first cat shows held in England, but it is obvious that they were not always true Manx, as some show reports refer to "knobs" and even stumps. In fact, Harrison Weir in his book *Our Cats*, published in 1889, says that "it differs from the ordinary domestic cat in being tail-less, or nearly so, the best breeds not having any".

Japan, Borneo, and Malaya have cats with hooked or stumpy tails, but apparently none completely tailless, with a hollow where the tail should start, as required in the Manx standard.

The Manx is usually classified with the British Shorthairs, but it differs from them in several respects, apart from the lack of tail. The round head should be slightly larger, the nose being longish, with the cheeks prominent. The ears are rather wide at the base, tapering slightly off to a point.

In appearance it is a square-looking cat, with short back and deep flank, with a round rump, and a decided hollow or dimple at the end of the back-bone, where the tail should begin. The coat is double, with soft topcoat, and thick under-coat. The eye colour may vary, being yellow or greenish, orange, or possibly blue if the fur is white. Any coat colour or pattern is permitted.

A Manx may be born in a litter from one tailless and one tailed parent, or a Manx mated to a stumpy, and some authorities state that it is possible for both parents to be tailed, providing they carry the Manx gene. Two Manx may produce tailed kittens.

They have the reputation for being highly intelligent, good hunters, and, despite the lack of tail, intrepid tree-climbers.

Many breeders in the British Isles and the United States are producing and exhibiting superb specimens, while the Isle of Man has established a cattery at Noble's Park, Douglas, which may be visited, and from which kittens may be ordered.

The Manx Cat Club was formed in 1901, and later amalgamated with the Short-Haired Society, also formed in 1901. One of the earliest champions was a tabby named "Katzenjammer", belonging to Mrs H. Brooke, while the late Sir Claud and Lady Alexander were famed for their "Ballochmyle" Manx.

In the 1920s and 1930s, the late Miss H. Hill Shaw owned several outstanding Manx, including Champion "Finchley Boy" and Champion "Katzenjammer's Ghost", the latter being considered near perfect. Miss M. Sladen of "Stonor" fame has also shown and bred many champions over the years, while there are in Britain today the "Rosental", "Brightwell", "Manxtown", and "Dreemskerry" strains, among others, appearing constantly among the winners. "Manninagh Mona", sent from the Isle of Man cattery to the United States a few years ago, became a champion in a very short time, and added considerably to the interest already shown in the breed there. The numbers of Manx are on the increase, with many being exported all over the world from the British Isles to would-be owners intrigued by these quaint, unique, and very affectionate cats.

SPOTTED

This is one of the oldest varieties known; in fact, there is a mosaic discovered in Pompeii now in Naples Museum showing an excellent example of a spotted cat with a bird. It is very like those seen at the shows today.

Harrison Weir, in *Our Cats*, published in 1889, tells of a hybrid, produced from a domestic cat and an English wild cat, taking first prize in the Spotted Tabby class at a Crystal Palace show. Once fairly common, the variety gradually died out, and for many years was scarcely seen. It did crop up once or twice by chance in pet cats, with the spotting being exceptionally good. The last few years have seen a revival of interest in the "Spotties", and recognition has been granted again, resulting in outstanding specimens being exhibited, and even winning "Best in Show" awards.

The type should be as for other British cats, with broad head, well-developed cheeks, and short nose. The body should be well-knit and powerful, and the legs of good substance. Any colour background is allowed, but the spots should be of a suitable colour, and must be distinct, standing away from the background. Bad faults are stripes and bars, but these are permissible on the face and head. The eye colour should conform with the coat colour.

Recent Spotted winners have included those bearing the "Culverden" prefix, bred by Miss F. Robson, Mr R. Pearson's "Lowenhaus", Mrs J. Richards's "Pensylva", and Mrs. J. Higgins's "Zephyr". All colours have been seen, and have included many Silvers, several Browns, and a few Reds.

CHARTREUX

Harrison Weir, writing in his book *Our Cats* in 1889, gave a whole list of names for the short-haired cats with blue fur, among them being the Chartreux. Although one or two have been imported into England, this is definitely a French variety.

They are thought to have originated in South Africa and been taken to France by the Chartreux monks, hence the name.

They are distinctive cats, very like the British Blues, but with slight differences, particularly as regards the coat colouring. This is more a bluish-grey rather than blue. Massive in size, they are well muscled with broad chests. The heads are large, but not quite so round as those of the British cats, but the jowls are more powerful. The eyes should be yellow or orange in colour.

They make wonderful pets, being gentle and intelligent, and have the reputation of being excellent rat-catchers.

AMERICAN SHORTHAIRS

In addition to those detailed below, colours are as for British Shorthairs: White, Black, Blue, and Cream; Red, Brown, and Silver Tabbies; Tortoiseshell, and Tortoiseshell and White (Calico). The body type should be as for other American Shorthairs.

Red
This is a cat with a short, thick, even coat of brilliant red, with body and head shape as for the other American Shorthairs. There should be no markings or shadings, and the eyes should be a brilliant gold.

Chinchilla
The undercoat should be pure white with black tickings, as for the long-haired variety, with eye colour of green or blue-green.

Shaded Silver
As for the Chinchilla, but the black tippings to form a mantle, as in the Longhairs, with eyes of green or blue-green.

Black and Blue Smoke
Except that the fur is short rather than long, the standard is the same as given for similar colours in the long-haired varieties. Although not a recognized variety in England, an exceptional specimen was exhibited a few years ago.

Blue Tabby
A cat with a pale, bluish-ivory ground colouring, with tabby markings of a deep blue, forming a definite contrast. The eyes should be a brilliant gold in colour.

Cream Tabby
As for other Tabbies, but the ground fur to be a very pale cream with buff or deeper cream distinctive markings. The eyes should be a brilliant gold.

EXOTIC SHORTHAIRS

These are comparable with the British Short-hairs, having similar standards, but they also have the following colour variations in addition to those mentioned in the British Shorthair section:

Chinchilla	Blue Smoke
Red Self	Red Smoke
Shaded Silver	Cameo Smoke
Shell Cameo	Cream Tabby
Shaded Cameo	Blue Tabby
Black Smoke	Cameo Tabby

All the standards are as required for the long-haired colours, the body being of definite Long-hair or Persian type, but, of course, the fur should be medium in length, while being soft in texture.

THE FOREIGN SHORTHAIRS

This group contains the Siamese, which are dealt with in a separate section, the Abyssinians, the Russian Blues, the Burmese, the Chestnut Brown Foreign, the Rex and the Korats (U.S.A.). With slight differences in type and body shape, and in comparison with the British Shorthairs and the Longhairs which require exactly opposite characteristics, the Foreign varieties have wedge-shaped heads, fairly large prick ears, almond-shaped eyes, long, graceful bodies on tall, slim legs, and long, tapering tails. They should never be massive cats.

Of all the pedigrees, they most closely resemble in outline the original domesticated cats in Egypt, but the coat colours vary considerably. Several are man-made breeds, while for the others it is claimed that they originated from the countries they are named after. In most countries, however, it is difficult to find any such cats, but it must be remembered that the type and often the colouring has been altered to a certain extent by selective breeding, and the majority do not now resemble the resident cats of their country of origin.

Perhaps because of their exotic appearances, they are sometimes thought to be delicate, but, if from good stock and correctly fed when kittens, they usually live long, healthy lives. They like warmth more than the Longhairs, but this is understandable when comparing the fur length.

They greatly dislike being on their own for long periods, and much appreciate the constant companionship of their owners. Many like travelling around in cars. If trained correctly when young they will take readily to leads.

RUSSIAN BLUE

Today the Russian Blue is definitely a Foreign Shorthair, with long, graceful body, a longish face, and narrowish skull, with short, close coat of a clear blue colour, but from 1880, when it was first seen on the show bench, there seems always to have been confusion as to the type required and much argument as to the origin.

Referring to the early writers, Charles Ross wrote in 1867, in *The Book of Cats*, that "Blueish grey is not a common colour; these species are styled Chartreuse cats and are esteemed rarities." In 1876, Gordon Stables wrote of "the Blue Cat being of delicate constitution and of a sad slate colour". He said they had the merit of being extremely gentle, and that pure blue cats were very rare and greatly prized. Harrison Weir wrote in 1889 that they were shown under a number of names "as the Archangel cat, then Russian blue, Spanish blue, Chartreuse blue, and lastly, and I know not why, American blue". In his opinion it was not a distinct breed, but merely a light-coloured form of the black cat. In the United States at that time they were known as the Dark Maltese, as there was a tradition that they came from Malta.

At the end of the last century Mrs Carew Cox, a well-known fancier of this variety, referred to short-haired Blues, with faint tabby markings, being imported from the north of Norway, and said they were known as "Canon Girdlestone's breed"; but who the Canon was appears to be unknown. She owned many Blues, including one, "Kola", from the town of Kolås. This cat was blue with white and "changed hands more than once whilst at sea, and was finally exchanged at the London docks for a leg of mutton". She imported several from Russia, with such names as "Lingpopo", "Fashoda", and "Yula", so any cats whose pedigrees can be traced way back can claim to have real Russian blood in their lineage if such names are included.

By the beginning of the century, probably because the early fanciers knew nothing of breeding techniques, and cats were mated indiscriminately with those with British type, it was difficult in most cases to distinguish between the British and Foreign varieties. Frances Simpson said that when collecting illustrations for her *Book of Cats* she was showered with photographs, but was quite unable to pick out one type from the other. Classes at the shows were for "Shorthaired Blues", with both varieties entered. The judges invariably gave the first prizes to cats with British type, much to the discontent of the owners of the Russian cats. Eventually the name "Russian" was dropped and they were called "Foreign Blue Shorthairs". It is not understood how the name change helped in any way, for a 1910 National Cat Club show catalogue still gave only the one class, with cats such as "Ivanovitch", obviously a Russian, and "Ballochyle Bumpums II", owned by Lady Rachel Alexander, who specialized in the British Blue, competing against each other, among others. The late Miss M. Rochford of the "Dunloe" prefix did much to improve the Russian cats, and many were exported all over the world, several to the United States.

In 1948, after much discussion, the Governing Council of the Cat Fancy decided that the cats could revert to the old name of "Russian". This, perhaps, would have helped the variety, but unfortunately, due to the War, suitable studs were not available, and breeders, over-anxious to improve the type, mated their cats to Siamese and other varieties. As a result, instead of improving, many faults appeared, such as Siamese type, wrong-coloured eyes, and ringed tails, and often the much admired silvery sheen on the coat completely disappeared. Championships were frequently withheld, and the Russian Cat Club, seeing little future for the variety, was dissolved. This distressed a number of well-known breeders, who banded together and drew up a revised standard, which was eventually accepted by the Governing Council. By keeping to a strict breeding programme the Russians have now recovered much of their early charm, the numbers being exhibited are gradually increasing, and an association has been formed in Britain for interested fanciers.

The British standard says that the Russian differs from the British Shorthair in being lithe, long, and snaky, and fine in bone. The primary feature, and one which distinguishes it from all other cats, blue or otherwise, is the coat, which should be short, close, and lustrous, and of a sealskin-like texture. It is also longer in the leg than the British cat.

The colour should be clear blue, with the medium shade being preferred. The adult cat should be free from tabby markings or shadings, although these may sometimes be seen in kittenhood. The coat should be double, giving a distinct silvery sheen. The short, wedge-shaped head should have a flat skull and prominent whisker pads. The large, pointed ears should be wide at the base and set vertically to the head, the skin of the ears being thin and translucent, with very little inside furnishing. The almond-shaped eyes should be a vivid green, the tail fairly long and tapering.

The Russians are always referred to as quiet cats, not over-demonstrative but very attached to their owners. Some have scarcely any voice at all, and are very shy, but they are invariably dignified.

ABYSSINIAN AND RED ABYSSINIAN

Abyssinian
The Abyssinian is a slender, essentially graceful cat, with a proud walk, and of all the pedigree cats today most closely resembles those portrayed in early murals and statuettes of the Ancient Egyptians and regarded by them as sacred.

The shape of the head and the general appearance of a good specimen is almost identical to that of several of the Egyptian bronze cat statues. We owe their veneration in Egypt, and thus their existence today as pets, if the breed is the same, to the chance that the tribe with the cat as its totem eventually triumphed over all others in the Nile Basin and founded the Egyptian civilization. The ancestors of the Abyssinian cats were mummified and given reverent burial.

The caffre cats and the smaller jungle cats are generally accepted as being the forerunners of the domestic cats, and here again there is a close resemblance in colouring and, in some cases, the distinctive ticking. The Abyssinian is often referred to as the "Bunny" cat because of the similarity in colouring to that of the British wild rabbit, but the ruddy coat of the Abyssinian is far richer in colour and the ticking more definite, although this may have been improved greatly by selective breeding over the years since the name was first given.

Apparently the first Abyssinian seen in England was "Zula", said to have been brought here by Mrs Barrett-Lennard in 1868. Some authorities doubt this, but it was the year the British forces returned from Ethiopia, so perhaps there is some truth in it.

They were first recognized in 1882, and Harrison Weir refers to them as "a variety of the tabby cat", but says "this can scarcely be called a tabby proper, as it is nearly destitute of markings, excepting sometimes on the legs and a broad black band along the back". He also says that a hybrid from an English wild cat and a domestic cat will produce a cat with similar markings. The standard today calls for the fur to be short, fine, and close, but his Points of Excellence says that there should be "Soft, rather woolly hair, yet silky, lustrous, and glossy, short, smooth, even, and dense"! In these points he also mentions the Abyssinian Silver Grey, or Chinchilla, with silver instead of brown ground colour. Over the years, kittens with these colours have appeared in one or two litters, and have occasionally been exhibited, but when judged the coat is usually referred to as "cold", not conforming with the standard. During the past year or two several have been seen at shows with silvery or blue coats.

Among the early fanciers was Mr L. Wain, the cat artist, who owned several. Frances Simpson mentions Mr S. Woodiwiss's "Sedgemere Bottle" and "Sedgemere Peaty" as being "superlative", with rich coat colouring, but says

that the majority of the early specimens had heavy stripes and were too dark in colouring. As now, the difficulty was to breed a specimen with no white, and there was trouble at an early cat show when a judge did not place an outstanding cat because it had a few white hairs, giving the first prize to a dark, almost sooty, Abyssinian. This has been known to happen at modern shows too.

The first recorded Abyssinians in the United States belonged to Miss J. Cathcart, and were exhibited in Boston in 1909, but it was not until 1934 that a pair, "Woodroffe Anthony" and "Woodroffe Ena", were sent to the United States by Major S. Woodiwiss, who was then the honorary secretary of the Abyssinian Cat Club. Other imports followed, which included an outstanding male, Champion "Ras Seyum", and soon Abyssinians were appearing at many of the American shows. The Second World War stopped importations for a while, but shortly after the cessation the late Mr W. Price imported a female from the well-known British Taishun cattery, and the flow started once more, founding many good blood lines in the United States and Canada. Today there are far more Abyssinians in North America than in Britain, although there they are increasing all the time. The standard in the United States and Canada is exceedingly high, and, to mention just one of many, those bearing the "Chota-Li" prefix have particularly good colouring. British-bred cats bearing the "Taishan", "Contented", and "Nigella" prefixes appear frequently in the list of champions in Britain and many other countries.

Abyssinian cats are of Foreign type—although the head is not as long as that of the Siamese, and the tail is broader at the base and not so whip-like. The standard says they should be of medium size, never large or coarse. The particular difference between an Abyssinian cat and other cats is that the fur is 'ticked'—that is to say, each hair has two or three bands of colour ending in a black tip.

In colour they should be a rich, ruddy brown, ticked with black, and the underparts should harmonize, preferably being orange-brown. This subtle colouring gives the cat a glowing look. It has black pads, and this colour extends up the back of the hind legs. The cat has an intelligent expression, with ears constantly on the alert and large, expressive eyes.

A good specimen should have no barring or tabby markings, and no white, except for a little round its chin which is undesirable but permissible.

Red Abyssinian
In 1963 another colour variety, the Red Abyssinian, which lacks any black pigment, was recognized by the Governing Council of the Cat Fancy and given a breed number. The type is the same as for the standard Abyssinian, the difference being in the colour. The body colour is rich, copper red, doubly or preferably trebly ticked with darker colours. Lack of distinct contrast in the ticking is a fault. The richer the body colour the better; a pale colour is a bad fault.

The belly and inside of the legs should be deep apricot, to harmonize. The tail tip is dark brown and this may extend along the tail as a line. A spine line of deeper colour is permissible. The nose leather is pink. Pads are pink, and set in brown fur which extends up the back of the legs. Eye colour is as for the standard Abyssinians.

The chief charm of the Abyssinians lies in their devotion to human beings. They have great self-confidence, perhaps inherited from the time when they were worshipped as gods by the Egyptians.

BURMESE—BROWN (OR SABLE) AND BLUE

The first recorded Burmese was a female, brown in colour, imported from India into the United States by Dr J. Thompson in 1930. It is difficult to know why the name "Burmese" was given in the first place, as apparently there are very few similar cats in Burma. For want of a male of the same colouring, she was mated to a Siamese. Eventually, through selective breeding, pure breeding became possible and the Brown Burmese was recognized in the United States in 1936 by the Cat Fanciers' Association, Inc.

The first Burmese did not appear in Britain until after the Second World War, when a pair was imported by Mrs L. France. The female was in kitten, but lost her litter during the long period of quarantine. She was re-mated and it is from her progeny that the majority of the British Burmese are descended. Several other imports followed, including Champion "Laos Cheli Wat", a female, and "Gas Gatos de Foong", a male, brought over by Mr V. Watson. The male's name still appears on many pedigrees today. The first British champion was "Chinki Yong Jetta", a granddaughter of one of the original female imports, now eighteen years old, and living happily with Mrs J. Merry, a breeder and judge of Burmese. A second male, "Casa Gatos Darkee", soon to become a champion, was imported in 1952. "Jetta", mated to him, produced two champions, "Chinki Golden Gay" and "Chinki Golden Goddess", the latter now living with Mrs H. Waldo-Lamb, a well-known breeder of Burmese. It was from "Darkee", mated to his daughter, Champion "Chinki Golden Gay", that the first Blue Burmese appeared. The first Blue stud was "Lamont Blue Burmaboy", soon to become a champion, but his son, Champion "Ballard Billin", still at stud in 1968 and owned by Mrs R. Knowles, was the first Blue champion.

Later, Champion "Darsham Khudiran" was imported, and being of an entirely new strain did much to improve the breed. The next ten years saw the Burmese, both Blue and Brown, becoming increasingly popular, with such well-known champions as "Kingsplay Fei-Fo", "Sablesilk Bimbo", "Dewpoint Nimrod", and "Copplestone Lun-Tha", among others, siring many prize-winning kittens. An outstanding Blue, Champion "Arboreal Blue Leela", bred by Mrs J. Dyte and owned by Miss M. Mack, is said to be one of the most beautiful Burmese ever seen, with several judges saying that they are unable to fault her.

In 1964, through planned breeding, it was found that it was possible to produce Cream Burmese, and during the early phases of the experiment Tortie and Blue-Cream Burmese were born in several litters. These mated back to Brown and Blue Burmese had both red and cream kittens, but it was decided to concentrate on the cream, as the more attractive colour. The Creams and Blue-Creams now have breed numbers in Britain, but do not yet have championship status.

The Blue Burmese are not recognized in the United States, but the breeders there have produced Champagne Burmese, said to be a pure-bred colour variation of the 'sable' Burmese, carrying a gene for diluting the pigmentation on the brown spectrum. British breeders are following this colour variation with interest, and several have already been imported.

Although Foreign in type, there should be no close resemblance to the Siamese shape, as the wedge-shaped head of the Burmese should be shorter, with the ears slightly smaller. The body should be medium in size, dainty and svelte, with proportionately slim legs, the hind legs being slightly higher than the front. The tail should be long and tapering to a point, with a slight kink at the extreme tip only being allowed. The almond-shaped eyes should be yellow and slant towards the nose in the true Oriental fashion. Squints are not permitted.

In the adult Brown the body should be a solid, rich, dark, seal brown, shading to slightly lighter on the chest. Kittens may show a slight contrast between the body colouring and points, but this is a fault in the fully grown cat. The kittens when born are *café au lait* in colour, with the coat darkening as the fur grows.

The same characteristics are required for the Blue, but the adult body colour should be a bluish grey, darker on the back, with a silver sheen to the coat. The eyes should be yellowish green.

Although from the same stock originally, the Burmese in the United States and Canada have slightly different type, the heads being rounder and the bodies shorter. They are usually referred to as Sable, rather than Brown as in Britain. They are exceedingly popular, almost rivalling the Siamese. Among so many outstandingly good Burmese there, it is difficult to pick out one, but Grand and International Champion "Kittrik's Guing Ho of Silkwood", a Canadian Burmese, has done particularly well, becoming a Grand Champion when only a year old.

In Britain there is one specialist Burmese Club, while North America has a number of such clubs, so the Burmese interests are well catered for.

HAVANA (CHESTNUT BROWN FOREIGN)

This is a typical example of a variety which came into being through selective breeding. Apparently brown self-coloured cats had been known in 1894. Mrs L. French had two, an imported queen with the delightful name of "Granny Grumps", and her son "Timkey Brown". These chocolate-coloured Siamese were popular on the Continent, and appeared on show benches.

The early breeders, however, understood so little of the principles of heredity governing the production of these brown cats that the breed soon died out.

Yet the method is simple. A black or blue self-coloured cat of Foreign type is mated to a Chocolate-pointed Siamese. The resulting litter will be all black. All kittens will be carrying the required chocolate factor, and when mated among each other, or to a Chocolate-pointed Siamese, they are capable of producing progeny of Black, Seal-pointed Siamese, Chocolate-pointed Siamese, and Self-coloured. The proportion of brown to other coat patterns is 3:16, so that several litters may be born before one brown cat is produced. Early breeders may have been puzzled by the fact that a Seal-pointed Siamese carrying chocolate may be used to produce Browns, but a Siamese carrying seal only will produce only Blacks or Seal-pointed Siamese.

The late Mrs I. Munroe-Smith, well known for her "Elmtower" Chestnut Browns, bred her first self-brown kitten "by accident". One of her Siamese queens chose her own mate in the shape of a Black Longhair; the results were, as was to be expected, all black kittens, but one of these mated back to her Siamese grandfather produced a self-brown kitten. This was a male, "Elmtower Bronze Idol", later to become very well known and the sire of many kittens of his own colouring. In 1953 a group of breeders, including Mrs Munroe-Smith, the late Miss E. von Ullman, and Mrs A. Hargreaves, realized that, by scientific breeding, it was possible to produce these rich chestnut-brown-coloured kittens to order. The first name given to the variety was Havana Brown, but this was changed

77–78   HAVANA

79   DEVON REX

80   CORNISH REX

81   CORNISH REX

82   KORAT

83–84   SEAL-POINT SIAMESE

to Chestnut Brown Foreign in Britain when granted recognition in 1958, to avoid any confusion with the Havana rabbits, which were being bred for their coats. The breed was once again officially known as Havana in Britain in 1971. They are still comparatively rare cats, but Mrs S. Warren of the "Senlac" prefix has produced several fine specimens, as has Mrs M. Dunnill of "Sumfun" fame, Miss P. Turner with the "Scintilla" cats, and Mrs B. Stewart who bred Champion "Sweethope Coffee Bud", to mention just a few breeders.

The Havana or Chestnut Brown is a cat with Foreign type, fine in bone, with graceful proportions. The short, glossy coat of rich chestnut brown should be even in colour throughout, and the pads of the dainty, oval-shaped feet a pinkish shade. The head should be long, well proportioned, and narrowing to a fine muzzle, with the ears being large and pricked. The body should be long, lithe, and well muscled, with a long, whip tail. Kinks are not permitted. The slanting, oriental-shaped eyes should be green. Dark points, tabby markings, and white hairs in the coat are counted as faults.

The kittens are most attractive, with soft, downy fur of rich brown, opening their eyes when only a week old. They are exceptionally lively and loving, and very forward, making most entertaining companions.

REX—CORNISH AND DEVON

One of the most fascinating of the new breeds of cats is the Rex cat, with its alert air and curly coat. These cats are almost unique in the history of the fancy, as they are the result of a mutation of nature, which has produced a difference in the structure of the hairs of the coat.

Although there had for some years been tales of curly-coated cats in the West of England, it was not until 1950 that the first curly coat was recorded. This was a kitten with a curly red and white coat that was born in a litter of ordinary farm kittens on Bodmin Moor in Cornwall. The owner, Mrs Ennismore, realized that its coat had a similarity to the coats of the Astrex rabbits

which she had bred. Her veterinary surgeon contacted the well-known geneticist, A. C. Jude, who did microscopic tests on the coat hairs of the kittens, and then declared that the kitten appeared to be a new mutant.

On Mr Jude's advice, the kitten was reared to maturity and then mated back to his dam—a normal-coated Tortoiseshell, who produced more curly-coated kittens in her next litter. Mrs Ennismore decided to call this new breed "Rex cats", because of their similarity to the Astrex rabbit, and the original mutant was named "Kallibunker"—a name now famous throughout the world.

Shortly after this the well-known experimental cat breeder, the late Mr B. Stirling-Webb, obtained a cream and white Rex male from Mrs Ennismore, and he began a planned programme of outcrossing to Burmese and British Shorthairs. Normal-coated hybrids mated to Rex resulted in plain-coated hybrids, but in the back-cross of hybrid to Rex the ratio of Rex kittens then produced was 1:1.

In 1960 another curly-coated male kitten was found by Miss Cox near a tin-mine in Buckfastleigh, Devon. As she had heard of the Rex cats she contacted Mr Stirling-Webb, who bought this new kitten, which he named "Kirlee". It was thought that "Kirlee" must be a relation to the Rex cats found in Cornwall, but when he was mated to "Kallibunker's" offspring, only normal-coated kittens resulted. After numerous test matings it was assumed that "Kirlee" was of a different genetic make-up from "Kallibunker". A similar breeding plan was therefore evolved for "Kirlee", and his off-springing Rex kittens resulting from back-crosses were again 1:1.

Under the guidance of Mr Stirling-Webb a group of breeders was formed to specialize in Rex breeding, and the two types of cat were provisionally called Gene 1 and Gene 2 Rex. When, in 1967, the Governing Council of the Cat Fancy granted recognition to Rex they became Cornish and Devon. It is particularly interesting to know that in 1948 Dr Scheur-Karpin of East Berlin found a Rex mutant, which she named "Lammchen". This cat produced numerous Rex kittens which are known as German Rex.

Then, in 1964, a Rex mutant was born in a litter of normal-coated kittens bred by Mrs Stringham of Oregon, U.S.A. This kitten, "Kinky Marcella", was the founder of the American strain of Rex.

In each country it has been proved that the Rex gene is recessive, and will always breed true when mated to its similar genotype. Though there are some variations in each type of Rex coat it seems that all Rex cats are lacking in guard hairs and the normal intermediate awn hairs—in fact, their coats closely resemble the down (or under) coat of normal cats. In spite of this, Rex cats are extremely hardy, and love to go out in all weathers. The Devon Rex occasionally produce kittens with very poor coats, but breeders of integrity have these kittens neutered so that they cannot be used for breeding.

While all Rex cats have the long lines of body and limbs that in England are called 'Foreign type', there are distinct differences between the Cornish and the Devon Rex. Whereas the Cornish has a medium-to-long head with high-set ears and a straight head, the Devon Rex has a short wedge head with a clearly defined "stop" and whisker break, full cheeks, and low-set, wide-based ears. The Cornish Rex coat is short and dense with a tendency to curl while the Devon Rex coat, though also short and dense, is wavy rather than curly.

Experimental Rex breeding has shown that any coat pattern or colour can be "rexed", although it seems that pure white Rex top the poll in popularity.

Since the Rex breed was officially recognized by the Governing Council of the Cat Family Rex classes at all the large shows have been well filled, and there are already four Cornish Rex champions. The very first Cornish Rex champion was Mrs Bygrave's "Noend Crinkle", a beautiful Blue-Cream bred by Mrs E. Aitken and sired by "Riovista Kismet", Mrs A. Ashford's Canadian Rex import.

"Amharic Kurly Katie" was the first Devon Rex champion. She is a most attractive Black Rex, owned by Mrs G. Genty, bred by Mrs M. Knight, and sired by "Ampharic Piccanninny Pixie".

There are now two clubs specializing in Rex cats—the colourpoint, Rex-coated, and A.O.V.

Club, which was Mr Stirling-Webb's original club, and the Rex Cat Club, which was formed in 1964.

Although cat-lovers are drawn first by the Rex cats' lovely coats, probably the greatest attraction lies in their personalities. Rex are great extroverts, abounding with affection and intelligence, and with an almost human sense of fun.

KORAT

According to the Korat Cat Fanciers' Association in the United States, the Korat cat is a very old breed in Thailand, regarded highly by the Thai people and considered to bring good fortune. They are not recognized in Britain—indeed, the writer does not think they have been seen here, although Mrs Richard Negus, writing in the Cat Fanciers' Association of America's Year Book, says that a blue cat from Thailand was "exhibited at a cat show in London in 1896 by a young Mr Spearman, an Englishman just home from Thailand, who defended his 'Blue Siamese' when challenged by stating that there were others in Siam from where he had brought it". She also says that there were Korat cats in America in 1934, but nothing is known about them.

The first pair of Korats for breeding were imported to the United States from Thailand in 1959 by Mrs J. Johnson, but over the years many other importations have followed, and there is now a rapidly expanding number of breeders of this variety. It has a recognized standard, granted by the Cat Fanciers' Association, Inc., which says that it is rare even in Thailand, and because of its unusually fine disposition is greatly loved by the Thai people. The cat has a self-coloured coat with a distinctive silver sheen, is medium in size, but muscular. From the front, the head is heart-shaped, and the ears large and rounded; the large, luminous eyes should be a brilliant green-gold when adult. The tail should be medium in length, rounded at the tip, with a tiny kink only permitted. The fur is short to medium, glossy, and close-lying. The colour must be a definite blue all over, but tipped with silver. The Korat Cat Fanciers' Association is being very strict about the breeding of these "bringers of good fortune" cats, and is endeavouring to ensure that the variety is kept pure bred. They are also recognized in Canada and South Africa.

The kittens are born silver-blue and keep that colour all their lives, although the actual shade may differ, according to the region from which the original importations came, some being much darker than others. They are gentle, loving cats, quiet by nature, and make excellent companions.

FOREIGN WHITE SHORTHAIR

This is an attractive, well-balanced cat of Foreign type, fine in bone and of graceful proportions. It has been produced by carefully selected matings, and has taken several years to perfect. A provisional standard has been accepted by the Governing Council of the Cat Fancy, but championship status has not yet been granted.

The coat should be pure white, with no black hairs, although occasionally kittens have a few black hairs on the head, but these usually go with the change of coat. The fur should be short, fine, glossy, and close-lying, never thick or standing away from the body. The head should be wedge-shaped, with large, pricked ears, wide at the base. The body should be medium size, and the tail long and tapering. Kinks are not permitted. The oriental-shaped eyes may be golden yellow or bright blue in colour.

Because of the interest shown in this new variety in Britain there is now a Foreign White Cat Society and a Foreign White Cat Fanciers' Association.

TONKANESE

The Tonkanese is now making its appearance in Britain and is the result of cross-mating a Siamese with a Burmese, but has no standard or championship status as yet. It is short-haired, with body of medium length. It is also being bred in the United States. This is most interesting when one remembers that the first Burmese to arrive there was mated to a Siamese in the first place.

SIAMESE CATS

There are many legends and stories about the origin of the Siamese, but few facts: they may or may not have been the Royal Cats of Siam, or the guardians of the Buddhist temples in Bangkok.

It is diverting to reflect on the stories that the first Siamese imported to England was a present to the British Consul-General from His Majesty, the King of Siam, or alternatively that it was stolen from a temple and smuggled out of the country, though not by the Consul-General, but these stories cannot be substantiated.

The Consul-General referred to was Mr O. Gould, and history has it that he brought the first pair of Siamese to England from Bangkok in 1884, the progeny being exhibited by his sister, Mrs Velvey, at the Crystal Palace Show in 1885. These were cats with the definite Siamese coat pattern, and apparently, according to many writers, were the first seen in Britain. This is rather puzzling, as Mr Harrison Weir says "on reference to the Crystal Palace catalogues from the year 1871 until 1887, I find that there were fifteen females and only four males, and some of these were not entire". If the first pair did not arrive until 1884 and were exhibited in 1885, surely Mr Harrison Weir, who was responsible for the first official show in 1871, would have known this? Why, therefore, should he go through the catalogues for all those years, instead of the last two, to find out the number of Siamese in the country? Because of this they must have been known in Britain prior to 1884; in fact, a pair were exhibited at the 1871 show. He also says that "I have always understood the Siamese were not allowed to be exported, and were only got by those so fortunate as a most extraordinary favour, as the King of Siam is most jealous of keeping the breed entirely in Siam as royal cats." This would account for the small numbers.

Apparently they had been known in Siam (now Thailand) for more than two hundred years, but authorities differ as to their origin before this. Some considered that they were semi-albinos, hence the light coats, and that they were possibly bred from the Malay jungle cat. Others prefer to give the credit to the Egyptians. The shape and outline is similar, but there is no evidence of cats with such colourings in Ancient Egypt.

Mrs Vyvyan and Miss A. Forestier Walker were among the first to own Siamese in Britain, and many of the prize-winning strains today are descended from their famous "Tiam O'Shian". Other early owners included Lady Dorothy Nevill and Sir Robert Herbert, while the Duke of Wellington was responsible for importing a number. Mrs Vyvyan is credited with bringing a whole family of Siamese to England in 1886, and she is quoted as saying that "Most of the kittens have crossed eyes and kinks in their tails. They live on fish and rice boiled together and need a great deal of care, owing to their delicacy. The kittens are difficult to rear."

The difficulty in rearing in those days was unfortunately very true. A great deal of it was probably due to the change of climate, and the kittens' complete lack of immunity to any infection that was around. Often after shows whole catteries were almost wiped out, for this was long before the days of injections and vaccines for cats. The early fanciers also tended to treat their Siamese as 'hot-house plants', and while they like warmth, and indeed need it, when very young, over-heating can be as bad, if not worse than, the cold. In time, it was a case of the survival of the fittest, and over the years they have adapted themselves most remarkably to the vagaries of our eccentric climate. Once over kittenhood they are certainly as healthy as any other cats, some living very long lives indeed.

In England in 1896, "Wankee", from Hong Kong, was the first Siamese champion. He belonged to Mrs M. Robinson and, judging from his photograph, he was a most beguiling cat, but according to the present-day standard possessed every fault possible. He had a round head, very un-oriental eyes, sturdy paws, and a rather thick tail—in fact, except for the colouring, more like the British Shorthairs of today.

The original cats were dun-coloured, with points of dark, chocolate brown, apple-shaped heads, and sturdy bodies—rather portly cats, in fact, with round eyes and thick tails. Many had squints, and kinks in the tails, which are still liked by some fanciers, but are definite faults according to today's standards. They have been more or less bred out, and generations of selective breeding have established cats with long, graceful heads, almond-shaped eyes, large ears, slim bodies with long, whip tails, and delicate legs and feet. In some cases, unfortunately, in attempting to achieve the perfect wedge-shaped heads required, weak chins resulted. Their voices, however, remain the same, and the characteristic banshee-like notes of some calling Siamese queens have to be heard to be believed.

The numbers increased very slowly at first, possibly because of the high mortality rate of the kittens. In 1907 a breeder wrote that these cats were practically unknown to the general public. *Our Cats* magazine for March 1912, which printed for that month the kittens registered with the Governing Council of the Cat Fancy, listed a whole page of Blue Longhairs, but gave only two Siamese kitten registrations.

Since those days the numbers of Siamese registered each year have rocketed beyond all belief and, whatever their origin, they are now known in practically every country in the world, having been exported from Britain in the first place.

The Siamese Cat Club was founded in 1901, and by 1902 had thirty-one members, but by 1915, probably due to the First World War, the membership had dropped to nineteen. The first standard of points was drawn up in 1902. The club today is the largest specialist cat club in Britain, possibly in the world. The president is the well-known writer, Sir Compton Mackenzie. It runs an annual show, with the cream of all the Siamese cats in the country being exhibited.

The first Siamese in America appeared there in 1895, imported from England, and were, at first, slow to gain popularity. In fact, in books written by the early fanciers, they were only given the most casual of mentions. Helen Winslow in her *Concerning Cats*, written in 1900, says "They are extremely pretty, with blue or amber coloured eyes by day, which grow brilliant at night. These cats also frequently have the kink in the tail, and sometimes a strong animal odour, although this is not disagreeable." She goes on to give details of the type, which sounds very much the same as ours today, but then says "The body is of a bright uniform colour, and the legs, feet and tail are usually black." Frances Simpson, in her *The Book of the Cat*, written about the same time, says that the "love of Siamese cats had not yet developed in America, and specimens of the breed are few and far between". Lady Marcus Beresford sent out two good cats to Mrs Clinton Locke, and several fine litters were reared.

The numbers of Siamese in Canada and the United States now are much greater than those in Britain, although they are still the most popular variety here. In Australia, Tasmania, and New Zealand too they are rapidly increasing. South Africa, with its increasing cat fancy, also favours Siamese, but in Europe, while there are many Siamese, the writer feels the Longhairs are still the first love.

The Official Standards of Points have been carefully drawn up with a view to helping uniformity in judging at shows. There are Seal-points, Blue-points, Chocolate-points, Tabby-points, Red-points, Tortoiseshell-points, and Any Other Dilutions, but the standard, type, and shape of all Siamese cats, whatever their colour varieties, are the same. They should be:

Medium in size, body long and svelte, legs proportionately slim, hind legs slightly higher than the front ones. Feet small and oval, tail long and tapering, straight or slightly kinked at the extremity. Head long and well proportioned with width between the eyes narrowing in a perfectly straight line to a fine muzzle. Ears rather large and pricked wide at base. The body, legs, feet, head, and tail all in proportion, giving the whole a well-balanced proportion. Eyes Oriental shape and slanting towards the nose.

Squints and kinks are not encouraged. A squint is officially defined as "when the eyes are so placed that they appear to look permanently at the nose", and the operative word is "permanently" because many Siamese squint occasionally for many reasons. The characteristic kink is also regretted by some, but one kink leads to another, and a tail with not one but three kinks in it is not a pretty thing, and it is therefore advisable to try to breed them out.

It is difficult to maintain the pale adult coats which are so much admired, and which were more common in the early Siamese, possibly because they were considered delicate and were coddled. There is no doubt that Siamese living in unnaturally over-heated places keep their lighter coats. In tropical countries they are pale coated but their contrasting points are poor, while in Northern countries, where it is colder and damper, they develop darkish, woolly coats, which again lose contrast with points, so it seems that, if healthy out-of-doors cats are wanted, they will tend to have darker coats. On the other hand, with the darker coats often comes the deeper blue eye colour, which is required.

Although the Siamese with their long, slender lines have a 'delicate air', they are often deceptively heavy when picked up, and are well muscled when looked at closely.

SEAL-POINT

The first Siamese were seal-pointed, with markedly pale coats and very dark points but poor type. It was in the early 1940s that the type began to improve through selective breeding. Notable cats at that time were those bearing the "Prestwick" prefix, of world-wide fame, bred by Mrs Duncan Hindley, Mrs O. Lamb's Champion "Morris Tudor", and those belonging to Mrs E. Kent, now Chairman of the Siamese Cat Club. Mrs P. Lauder also showed many prize-winning kittens.

The Seal-point is the most popular of all the colour varieties, and an outstanding specimen may come very close to the ideal standard. The points should be a clearly defined seal brown, with the body colour cream, shading gradually into pale, warm fawn on the back. The oriental-shaped eyes, slanting towards the nose, should be a clear, brilliant, deep blue.

CHOCOLATE-POINT

Chocolate-points, with points the colour of milk chocolate, had been known from the earliest days of the Siamese, but had been rejected by the fancy when two early fanciers, Miss E. Wentworth-Fitzwilliam and Mrs L. French, had championed their cause. They came back into favour when the late Mr B. Stirling-Webb exhibited some of his excellent "Briarry" Chocolates. Mrs I. Keene bred a most beautiful male, Champion "Killdown Jupiter", afterwards neutered.

In the Chocolate, the standard is the same as for Seal-point, except that the points colour should be that of milk chocolate, with the body colour ivory all over, the shading, if at all, to be the colour of the points.

BLUE-POINT

The first champion Blue-point "Sayo of Bedale", was bred by the late Mrs P. Wade, one time chairman of the Siamese Cat Club, the cat eventually being bought by Madame d'Ollone and taken to New York. The classes at the shows are always well filled, and although at one time this variety was considered to be too heavy in body and not fine enough in bone, careful breeding in recent years has produced outstanding cats. Mr J. Shewbridge's Blue-point Champion "Tamruat Sophar" was Best Siamese at a recent National Cat Club Championship Show, a great achievement when one considers there were nearly four hundred and fifty Siamese entered. The best kitten too was a wonderful Blue-point, "Bru-Bur-Baby", bred by Mr B. Burlton.

The Blue-points should have the ears, mask, legs, paws, and tail all the same colour blue; the ears should not be darker than the other points. The body should be a glacial white, shading gradually into blue on the back. The Oriental eyes should be a clear, bright, vivid blue.

Some credit must be given to the champions of over thirty years ago, for they were the ancestors of many of the winning cats today. Most pedigrees seem to go back as far as Champion "Bonzo", a winner of a number of firsts at shows many years ago. Names such as Champion "Jacques of Abingdon" and Champion "Blue Seagull" may also be found in old pedigrees, and people in those days wishing to breed Chocolates or Blues asked eagerly which cats were likely to carry the appropriate genes.

LILAC-POINT

One must not forget the Lilac-points, a variety rapidly increasing in numbers and now rivalling some of the earlier colours in popularity. These first became known in Britain through the unceasing efforts of the late Mrs K. R. Williams, of "Doneraile" fame, although they had been established in the United States for many years before this. They were not experimentally-bred, but first appeared in a litter having two Blue-point parents carrying the chocolate factor necessary to produce Lilac-points. It was found that Lilac mated to Lilac will always breed true to colour. Mr A. Colin-Campbell of the "Colgrave" prefix has bred many outstanding Lilac-point champions, and Mrs E. Fisher and Mrs E. Biggie have also helped by breeding very fine specimens in the past.

The standard is as for all Siamese, with the points of a pinkish-grey colour, and body colour of off-white (magnolia) shading to tone with the points. The eyes should be a clear, light, but vivid blue. A fault sometimes is a tail showing a chocolate colour rather than lilac.

RED-POINT

The end of the Second World War saw the start of experimental breeding. The late Mr B. Stirling-Webb bought "Georgie", the fluffy-coated Siamese queen from whose progeny he eventually established the lovely Colourpoints. Dr N. Archer undertook the work of breeding Red-points, not an easy task, and one that must have taken a long time, as it was not until 1952 at the Southern Counties Cat Club's Championship Show that she exhibited the first Red-pointed Siamese and his Tortie-pointed sister. The late Miss A. Ray also bred and showed a number of Red-points at the National Cat Club shows. In the U.S.A., Mrs Rolling and Mrs A. de Felippo, working on similar lines, achieved the same charming results. These are now recognized, with the type as for all Siamese; the points should be a bright, reddish gold, with the body colour white, shading, if any, to apricot on the back. The eyes should be a bright, vivid blue.

TABBY-POINT

Although it is a well-known fact that mismating by a Siamese usually results in black kittens it has also been proved possible for the kittens to be born bearing "the dominant colouring of a non-pedigree parent distributed in the typical Siamese coat pattern". This happened in 1965, when a Siamese was mated by a roving Tabby cat, and a most attractive kitten with striped points resulted. Several breeders became interested in the possibility of breeding such a variety. Siamese with tabby markings had been known in the United States and also in Europe for many years, and undoubtedly had appeared in Britain before this, but had received little or no attention.

Experimental breeding was carried out for a number of years, but because of the difficulty of producing four generations of pure breeding, by mating like to like, recognition was slow in being granted. Eventually the various Siamese cat clubs in Britain co-operated and agreed on a standard which was acceptable to the Governing Council of the Cat Fancy. There had been disagreement as to the name, one club calling the cats "Lynx-points", and another "Shadow-points", but recognition was given to the name "Tabby-point".

The Tabby-point is typically Siamese in every way, with the same long, lithe lines, differing only in that the points are definitely Silver Tabby—that is, silver with black stripes. The body colour should be pale and free from markings, with the mask showing clearly defined stripes, especially around the eyes and nose, and distinct markings on the cheeks. The legs should have broken stripes of varied size, with solid markings on the back, while the tail should be definitely ringed, ending in a solid tip. The eyes should be a brilliant, clear blue, and the ears black with a thumb mark.

Mrs Duncan Hindley, writing in her book *Siamese Cats Past and Present*, says, "The new breed of Tabby-point Siamese excels in eye colour which is rather exceptional, as at one time it was said that a pale-coated cat generally had paler eyes too. Here again it is selection in breeding."

TORTOISESHELL-POINT

By cross-matings it has proved possible to produce Siamese with variations in the points colouring. All are typically Siamese in looks and character. An example of this is the recently recognized Tortie-point, with well-broken tortoiseshell markings on the mask, ears, feet, and legs. The body colouring should be pale and the eyes a vivid blue. This is an all-female variety.

ALBINO

It has been found possible in the United States to breed an all-white Siamese, with typical Siamese characteristics and coat. It is not pink-eyed. Such a variety is not recognized in Britain, but is akin to the Foreign White Shorthair.

ANY OTHER DILUTIONS

Carrying the breeding experiments a stage further other point colourings have been produced, and while not yet eligible for challenge certificates may be registered in Britain as Breed 32c.

Cream-points. The points should be between the colour of rich Devon cream and pale sand.

Chocolate-Cream Points. The chocolate-cream points should be quite distinct from the pale body colouring.

Blue-Cream Points. Cream and blue blending to produce a misty effect in the points. This is a female only variety.

Lilac-Cream Points. Lilac replacing the blue, making the points very pale.

All these varieties have typical Siamese characteristics.

85   BLUE-POINT SIAMESE

86   CHOCOLATE-POINT SIAMESE

87–88   BLUE-POINT SIAMESE

THE CAT FANCY

THE AUSTRALIAN AND NEW ZEALAND
CAT FANCY

Australia

There have been pedigree cats in Australia for more than seventy years, the earliest being chiefly Longhairs of British origin. A few Seal-points were imported, but it was not until the Second World War that pedigree-cat breeding really started, and Australian blood lines were developed. Today, the Siamese head the popularity list, but all varieties are known, and any new breed soon makes its appearance. There is still a steady importation of British stock.

Every state of Australia has at least one governing body to which all breed and specialist clubs are affiliated. New South Wales has a council governed by the Royal Agricultural Society, which stages a show in April of every year including a large cat section.

This show is the highlight of the year and cat owners from all states exhibit there. An interesting rule laid down by this society is that a delegate shall be detailed to attend the shows organized by various affiliated clubs as the RAS representative, who will then report to the council on the conduct of the show in general.

The New South Wales RAS also registers cats and kittens from other states, thus keeping a valuable record of the overall fancy. This is not the practice of the other states, though many breeders take advantage of this service and thus a fairly complete register for the whole of Australia is maintained. Many shows are held annually in various places such as Parramatta, Bondi, Austen, Gordon, Newcastle, and so on.

New South Wales was the first state to start a cat fancy, seventy years or more ago. Judges appointed by the RAS are free to judge at inter-state shows, New Zealand shows, and so on, should they so wish.

Victoria has more than one governing body, the oldest being the Governing Council of the Cat Fancy of Australia, formed in 1928, which has affiliated clubs in Queensland, Tasmania, and Western Australia. There is also the Feline Control Council, formed in 1962 and governed by the RAS of Victoria, which stages a week-long show in Melbourne every September, and a two-day cat show held in the Mitchell grandstand, the RAS judges having a reciprocal arrangement to judge in other states and New Zealand. Although judges from both councils are free to judge inter-state they are debarred from officiating at shows organized by the opposition council in the State of Victoria. They may judge only at the shows organized by the clubs affiliated to the respective councils, and this procedure also applies in other states having more than one council.

Queensland has more than one governing body, the largest being the Council of the Federated Cat Club, established in 1959, to which the Siamese and Shorthair Society is affiliated. The principal show is held in Brisbane City Hall.

Perth, Western Australia, has a governing body now affiliated to the Royal Agricultural Society of Western Australia, with several clubs running shows in various places.

Tasmania's governing body is also affiliated to the Royal Agricultural Society of that state and runs annual shows in Hobart and Launceston.

Adelaide, South Australia, has, so far, one governing body only; it is a fairly young fancy but growing very rapidly.

There are pedigree cats in the Northern Territory, where an official cat fancy has been set up, and in all probability shows will soon be held under its auspices.

Many shows are guaranteed by various organizations; entry fees are small, and no money prizes are given as a general rule, other prizes given by the patron and members being presented at the end of the day. Show procedure follows the continental pattern as to method and judging.

Practical and oral classes are arranged to train judges and stewards, and those that pass consider themselves fortunate. A judge is issued with a licence which is reviewed annually and can be revoked if thought necessary.

Australian judges use the English standard of points for some breeds, but they tend to differ in their interpretation from state to state, especially with the newer breeds. An attempt is being made to adopt a general standard for all states, however. This is very necessary because of exhibitors showing in the various states and being confused by different interpretations of the standard for the same cats, some of the shows being affiliated to one council, some to another.

New Zealand

The Governing Council of the Cat Fancy of New Zealand stages a large show in Auckland, and the Pedigree Persian Cat Fanciers of N.Z. Inc. holds an all-Longhair show in Wellington annually or bi-annually. Various cat clubs are affiliated to the council. In both Australia and New Zealand most varieties are well represented, being descended from English stock reinforced from time to time by further imports. These countries have beautiful cats and a flourishing fancy.

THE CAT FANCY IN CANADA

In keeping with every other aspect of life in Canada, the cat fancy has progressed by leaps and bounds.

The picture today has changed immensely since 1906, when the Royal Canadian Cat Club first sponsored a show. Of the 192 entries, the majority were "handsome cats without known pedigree", the only pure-bred cats in the show being Persians. The Siamese did not make an appearance in Canadian shows for several more years. Gradually other pure breeds were introduced into the country, many of which were English imports. Today, after many years of careful, selective breeding, Canadian-bred cats are taking top honours in all breeds and taking "Best in Show" awards across Canada and the United States.

In 1961 the Canadian Cat Association was formed and started registering pure-bred cats—the first such registry in Canada. Until then breeders had registered their cats with one of the American associations. The CCA has grown steadily and has member clubs in many parts of Canada. However, there are many clubs that are still affiliated with one of the larger international organizations with headquarters in the United States (*e.g.*, the Cat Fanciers' Association, the American Cat Fanciers' Association, the American Cat Association). As the interest in pure-bred cats increases from year to year, new clubs are formed, and new breeders are producing fine kittens from the large selection of excellent show specimens now available in Canada. At present there are thirty-five active clubs, planning shows and helping new cat owners to understand the importance of good feeding, careful breeding, regular grooming, and ideal conditions.

Apparently, Siamese cats are the most popular breed in Canada at the present time, with the

Persians running a close second. The Himalayans (Colourpoints) are ever increasing in popularity, as are Abyssinians and Burmese. However, all the recognized breeds are seen at Canadian shows including Havana Browns (Chestnut Brown Foreign Shorthairs), Rex, Russian Blues, Manx, Red Colourpoint Shorthairs, American Shorthairs, and even the new hairless mutation known in North America as the Sphinx.

Among the well-known names of today which have done so much to elevate the pure-bred cats to their present enviable position are, in the west, Mr and Mrs A. Davison's "Chatsiam" Siamese, Mr and Mrs B. Borrett's "Chestermere" Himalayans, Mr and Mrs A. Maling's "May-Ling" Abyssinians, and Miss J. Jeffries' "Rio Vista" Burmese; in the east, three catteries have excelled with their Siamese—Mrs M. Buckner's "Queens Canada", Mrs M. Elliott's "Shan Ling", and Mrs M. Steward's "Sunshine". The east also claims such famous Shorthair catteries as Mrs S. Bray's "Silk-wood" Burmese, Mrs E. Field's "Chota-Li" Abyssinians and Russian Blues, and Mr and Mrs J. Graham's "Suen" Russian Blues. In Persians, Mr E. Johnston's "Halton Ridge", Mrs E. Warwick's "Rondolay", and Mr and Mrs S. Weston's "Simbelair" catteries have been producing outstanding Whites that have been "Best in Show" many times. Mr and Mrs Weston bred and showed a fabulous White male, Grand Champion "Simbelair's Aristocrat", that set a new record by winning "Best in Show" forty consecutive times. Each of these breeders can show English blood-lines in their cats' pedigrees.

In praising our present-day breeders and their remarkable achievements, we should also remember the earlier fanciers who did so much to pave the way to success by laying strong foundations and setting high standards. It was their devotion and persistence, coupled with the present-day breeders' genetically controlled programmes, that have made Canada's pure-bred cats sought after by breeders around the world.

PEDIGREE CATS IN FRANCE

Cat shows were held in the Jardin d'Acclimatation in Paris as long ago as the 1890s, and the long-haired cats in particular have always been much admired there. In fact, the first Angoras are said to have made their way to Britain via France nearly three hundred years ago. In spite of this, the numbers of pedigree cats have not multiplied to the same extent as in the British Isles. This may be due to the problem of housing, as many of the people interested in cat-breeding live in town houses without gardens, with the cats being kept indoors as pets. Under these circumstances it is difficult to keep a stud cat, and breeding catteries are rare.

The Cat Club de Paris was founded over forty years ago and the shows run under its auspices, organized by Mme M. Ravel, have done much to make the French public appreciate the beauty of pedigree cats.

The outbreak of war in 1939 practically put an end to pedigree cat breeding with the neutering or putting to sleep of many outstanding cats due to feeding difficulties and the evacuation of the owners. With the end of the War, and things beginning to return to normal, 1946 saw revived interest, and once again cats were imported from Great Britain, with the result that for the most part nearly all the champions today have British ancestry.

There is one variety, however, which up to recently has been entirely French. This is the "Birman" (Burman), also referred to as the "Sacré de Birmanie" (Sacred Cat of Burma) to distinguish it from the Burmese, the short-haired cat of American origin which now appears at French shows.

Birmans have been exported to the United States, Scandinavia, Germany, Holland, and England, and it is said that all the Birmans in the world come from French stock. Legend says that they originated in the Far East and were descendants of the cats that guarded the temples long ago, but it is far more probable that a chance Siamese-Angora cross in 1925 led astute breeders to develop the variety through selective breeding. Even so, there is still a veil of mystery surrounding the true origin of this beautiful breed, with the build and fur of a Persian and the eye colouring and coat pattern of a Siamese, but having white gloves on all four feet. The Cercle du chat Sacré de Birmanie, under its president Mme S. Poirier, has done much to foster interest in this variety.

To mention just a few outstanding cats of this variety, there is International Champion "Fantine", and her daughter, also an International Champion, "Folie de Crespières", "Hamlet de Madalpour", the last survivor of a once very well-known cattery, and International Champion "Gypsie" and her daughter "Iris des Floralies".

International Champion "Nadine de Khlaramour" has been exported to Germany, while Champions "Or de Crespières" and "Narcisse de Crespières" are both doing well in Holland. In the United States "Korrigan de la Regnardière" and "Leslie de Regnardière" are founding this variety in California, and "Nouky de Mon Rêve" and "Orlamonde de Khlaramour" are already well known in Great Britain.

Mr C. Yeates, once president of the Governing Council of the Cat Fancy, and his wife used to travel to France frequently in order to judge. In particular they admired the Whites with orange eyes, and there are still many excellent specimens today, including International Champion "Ondine de la Richardière", three times Best in Show, the outstanding stud International Champion "Iphis de Bois Clary", son of International Champion "Doudou de Padirac", and the world-famous female, International Champion "Jackotte de la Dame Blanche".

The Blue Persian is one of the most popular varieties, and many have been imported from Great Britain, including International Champions "Bayhorne Rebel" and "Daystar of Dunesk".

Colourpoints too are gradually increasing in numbers, those with blue points doing exceedingly well.

Originally there were very few short-haired cats at the shows in France, but over the last twenty years many have been imported, and numbers are increasing all the time, thanks to such imports as International Champion "Rangoon Blue Safir", a magnificent Blue-point Siamese and Champion "Rangoon Earl", a Seal-point Siamese, from Denmark, International Champion "Doneraile Marcella", a Lilac-point Siamese, and International Champion "Elmtower Nut Brown Maid", a Havana, both from Britain.

A short-haired cat which is popular in France is the Chartreux, now basically a cross between a Blue Longhair and a Self-coloured Blue Shorthair. It is believed that originally the Carthusian monks were responsible for bringing these cats to France from South Africa. Certainly it is possible that they did bring blue cats with them, but through selective breeding the Chartreux today are almost the same as the British Blues, having similar standards. International Champions "Jimbo" and "Idole de Bertouget" and Champion "Michou de St Pierre" are excellent examples of this variety.

The Cat Club de Paris and a number of other clubs are affiliated with the Fédération Internationale Féline d'Europe, which looks after the interests of its associated clubs in eleven continental countries.

There is also the independent Union Nationale des Associations Félines with its affiliated clubs all over France holding a number of shows ably organized by the president, Mme M. Lochet. Cats bearing famous prefixes such as "de Saint Witz", "de la Nourrée", "du Bosquet", "de Bois Clary", "de la Vallée Heureuse", and "De Surabaya" are all frequent winners at these shows, and these strains have bred many International Champions.

Further independent clubs are affiliated to the Cercle Félin de France. They too run their own shows, a notable one being that organized by the Baronne de Saint-Palais for the Cercle Félin de Paris. Here again cats with famous prefixes, such as "de la Fortelle", "de Chirvan", "des Princes", and "de Lugh", to mention just a few, are usually among the winners.

Throughout France now the numbers of pedigree cats are slowly but surely increasing, as also is the size of the shows, and the French cat fancy is now becoming famous throughout the world.

THE PIONEERING DAYS OF
GERMAN PEDIGREE-CAT BREEDING

When the first organization dealing with cat breeding was started up in Germany in 1922, under the name of 1. Deutscher Angorakatzen-Schutz- und Zuchtverein (1st German Association for the Protection and Breeding of Angora Cats), the essentials for this new field of breeding were missing. Yet Herr K. Hirschmann organized the first pedigree-cat exhibition as early as 1924 in Nuremberg. The cages contained mostly domestic cats, several Angora cats (still with long noses), and, surprisingly enough, two "Siamese temple-cats" with gold-plated collars. These were the first ever to be shown in Germany and Herr Hirschmann acted as judge, basing his standards on a booklet from England. Exhibitions followed in Frankfurt, Berlin, Dresden, and in Rheims in 1933, Herr Hirschmann having great success with his Red Self Angora cats, whose parents he had imported from England.

As early as 1922 a record book of breeding was kept. The first entry was Herr Hirschmann's "von Brosame", followed by "Puppi Edle von Fipsheim", mother of numerous prize-winning offspring. Then came "Nassak von Frohnau", a Longhair Colourpoint Siamese owned by Frau Hanna Krueger, a breeder from Berlin, then "Michael of Allington", a Blue Persian bred by Miss E. Langston and imported from England in 1933.

During the twenties and thirties Berlin played a leading part in German cat breeding; Frau L. von Werner owned a cream Angora, "Hell von Babelsberg", a beautiful male from Frau von Harbou's breeding. This "Hell" was a direct descendant of the cream tom "Bincie of Bredon", from the Wolfsitz cattery of Baroness von Larisch. "Bredon" was a famous English prefix.

In the thirties Frau von Werner, by selective breeding, succeeded in producing the Colourpoint (Khmer) with all the characteristics of the Siamese; their heads were wide and their eyes blue, but with the long hair of their ancestors; indeed they had reintroduced the genuine Angora hair. One of these was "Fandango", father of today's Birmans.

Frau Hanna Krueger of Berlin took up Birmans; she had an inbred Burmese female, which even had white paws, and was able to introduce new blood by means of such a fine cat as "Fandango". On Frau Krueger's death Mlle Gillet, a Frenchwoman, took over her cats, including the Burmese female. Frau von Werner's female Colourpoints "Fee" and "Flocke" (fourth generation, both registered) were mated with "Fandango" and produced some fine cats, almost all of which were taken to France. "It remains to be seen if this intentionally crossed breed will be successful and stand up before the strict eyes of European judges," was how Frau Liselotte von Werner's records ended. "Thus a breed was formed."

Unfortunately there were no breeders in Germany to follow this breed through. This was left to France, and to Mr B. Stirling-Webb in England, who dedicated himself from 1948 onwards to the forming of the Colourpoint strain.

It was eventually recognized as an official breed by the Governing Council of the Cat Fancy in 1955.

There followed the War and the Deutscher Edelkatzen-Züchter Verband (The German Association of Pedigree-cat Breeders) ceased to exist, while pedigree-cat breeding stopped.

Fräulein E. Eytzinger managed to keep one female Siamese and re-started her cattery after the War. Familiar names appeared again, such as "von Marienhof" with the renowned white Persians, "von Homburg", "von Bellamont", "von Borruta", and so on. With the help of Herr Hirschmann, Deutscher Edelkatzen-Züchter Verband was launched in a modest way a second time in 1949. In 1951 a wish was fulfilled; cordial relations were established with the home of pedigree-cat breeding, England.

In 1950 Fräulein Eytzinger—the first German to do so—visited a foreign exhibition (in Vienna) with her two Siamese. It was the first success. 1952 saw the first exhibition of pedigree cats after an enforced break of twelve years.

The first imports from England were "Philimore Moby Dick of Thornhills", "Halebridge Simon" (a Blue Persian), and "Paragon of Pensford". The number of members and breeders grew. Emphasis must be given to the Longhair cattery "Kohinoor", whose Persian Blues and Blacks won distinction at home and abroad. The following are only some of the imports from England: International Champion "Bayhorne Eager", International Champion "Diamond of Pensford", and International Champion "Georgian Natasha". An outstanding American import was "Silva Wyte TNT of JB".

The English import International Champion "Doneraile Leo", bred by Mrs K. Williams, was one of the greatest importance to the breeding of Siamese; it was named "Best Shorthair" at every exhibition, and was also the "Best in Show" at Paris in 1958. "Doneraile Leo's" aristocratic head with its noble profile, his fine, well-proportioned body, his gentle nature—in short "his outstanding beauty"—caused Prince Sadruddin Aga Khan to go to Germany in 1960 with his female "Saravan Yuk" in order to have them mated. "Doneraile Leo's" name appears in many pedigrees of France, Switzerland, Sweden, Denmark, the United States, and, of course, Germany, being responsible for the prize-winning Siamese strain "von Avalun".

In the course of eighteen years German cat breeding has reached a fine standard by means of selection and importing. German breeders are also the most enthusiastic exhibitors abroad.

THE CAT FANCY IN GREAT BRITAIN

Cats have been popular in Britain since Roman times, as companions, or as working cats on farms, catching vermin, for it was realized how valuable their services were in keeping down the rats and mice which destroyed foodstuffs and were carriers of the fleas responsible for many plagues, such as the Black Death. They were loved or disliked for themselves alone, and no-one thought of them ever occupying a more exalted position, although one or two of the more unusual had been seen as side-shows at county fairs and agricultural shows, but that was all.

With much diffidence, and expecting ridicule, Charles H. Ross wrote *The Book of Cats* in 1867, and was surprised to find it well received.

The book is interesting in itself for the fact that it was written several years before breeding, showing, and keeping records were thought of, but he gives descriptions of definite varieties—for example, "the Cat of Angora, with silvery hair of fine silken texture. Some being yellowish, and others olive, approaching to the colour of the Lion; but they are all delicate creatures, and of gentle dispositions." He mentions the Persian Cat as having hair long and silky, perhaps more so than the Cat of Angora, and being grey in colour. Another variety is the Chinese Cat with glossy fur of black and yellow, with pendulous ears. He refers to Bosman, who apparently wrote about their ears, "It is worthy of observation, that there is in animals evident signs of ancestory of their slavery. Long ears are produced by time and civilization, and all wild animals have straight round ears."

"The Tortoise-shell or Spanish Cat", writes Ross, "is one of the prettiest varieties. The colours are very pure, black, white and reddish orange, and in this country, at least, males thus marked are said to be rare, though they are quite common in Egypt and the south of Europe. Bluish grey is not a common colour: this species are styled 'Chartreux cats' and are esteemed rarities."

The Manx he refers to as a measly looking beast, with staring eyes and a stump of a tail.

Mr Harrison Weir, an artist and naturalist, had for many years noted the large numbers of cats in London alone, and also the various colours and coat patterns, and had given them careful study. His idea was to hold a show to let everyone see "how beautiful a well-cared cat is", and so the first official cat show in Britain was held at the Crystal Palace in 1871, and was a great success. In fact, it has since proved to be the foundation stone of the whole cat fancy throughout the world today. In his book, *Our Cats*, published in 1889, he wrote, "Since then, throughout the length and breadth of the land there have been Cat Shows, and much interest is taken in them by all classes of the community, so much so that large prices have been paid for handsome specimens. It is to be hoped that by these shows the too-often despised cat will meet with the attention and kind treatment that every dumb animal should have and ought to receive at the hands of humanity. Even the few instances of the show generating love for cats that have come before my own notice are a sufficient pleasure to me not to regret having thought out and planned the first Cat Show at the Crystal Palace."

The date at which these words were written should be remembered, and one wonders today what he would have thought if he could have seen how great a hold the pedigree cat would have in the future. In less than a hundred years the number of cat shows held and the number of cats exhibited have increased beyond belief, with the largest, the National, attracting over seventeen hundred cats.

The first cat show in Scotland was held in Edinburgh in 1875. Other shows were held at Birmingham, Brighton, and the Alexandra Palace, the Crystal Palace, and the Botanical Gardens, London.

With the increasing numbers of shows and also the interest shown by the public in the different varieties, Harrison Weir realized that some planned breeding was necessary. Dog shows had started in 1850, and breeding dogs to plan had been fashionable for years, but no-one had really given much thought to cat breeding, or ever thought that to own a pedigree cat would become fashionable. Soon, however, Queen Victoria owned a Blue Persian, and the Princess of Wales (later Queen Alexandra) had a White Persian reputedly bought from Sarah Bernhardt, the famous actress.

In 1876, five years after the first show, Dr Gordon Stables comments in the preface of his book *The Domestic Cat* on the popularity of cat shows and on the breeding of cats "up to as nearly a standard of perfection as possible".

He gives his own classification dividing domestic cats into two classifications:

1. The European—Short-haired or Western cats, and gives the following colours:

Tortoiseshell	Blue and White
Tortoiseshell and White	Tabbies: Red
Black	Brown
Black and White	Blue
White	Silver
Blue or Slate colour	Spotted

He also refers to, but does not give details of, several odd (!) cats, such as the Manx (the tailless cat) and the polydactyl (the six-clawed cat).

2. The long-haired he refers to as Asiatic, which is now confusing as we tend to think of the short-haired Foreign varieties—*i.e.*, the Siamese and Burmese—as Asiatic. He lists the same colour variations as for the European, but the coat, referred to as "the pelage", he says should be long and silky.

He speaks of the long-haired Tabbies and refers to one (no colour mentioned) as being magnificent and says that it "formerly belonged to Troppman, the distinguished [?] French murderer". He also says "longhairs of those days were more delicate in constitution than our European short-hairs, and not so keen on mousing and ratting. They were more expensive to buy as a good kitten at a show would cost at least one pound."

Of course, for the first show in 1871 there were no set standards to judge the cats by, so Harrison Weir prepared his own, allocating 100 points for each variety. He, his brother John Jenner Weir, and the Rev. J. Macdona were the first judges.

Harrison Weir eventually listed these standards in his book *Our Cats*, and, with amendments, they have been very much adhered to to this day. The number of varieties is, of course, much greater, though some listed are now not seen, such as the Blue and White Tabbies, while the Spotted Tabby (one of the oldest varieties known) and the Bi-coloured (not seen for many years) are now being bred and exhibited again, and have received recognition quite recently.

Harrison Weir also realized that it was not sufficient to have standards to breed to, unless some record was kept of the various cats and details of the males—that is the studs—used in the breeding were known. The National Cat Club was founded in 1887, with Harrison Weir as its first president. The club acted as registrar and kept a stud book, as well as running shows annually at the Crystal Palace and another at the Botanical Gardens.

For many years it was the sole authority, but dissension arose, and in 1898 Lady Marcus Beresford founded the Cat Club, with similar interests and similar rules and regulations. Matters soon became rather ludicrous, with cats having to be registered with both clubs to be exhibited at their respective shows. There were many years of trouble and strife, but in 1910 agreement was reached, the National Cat Club giving up its rights to act as registrar, on the understanding that it should always be represented by four delegates from the club on the newly formed "Governing Council of the Cat Fancy" (the equivalent of the Kennel Club in the dog world). Today it is still the same, the Council being composed of delegates of all the affiliated clubs.

The years up to the First World War really saw the heyday of cat breeding as a fashionable hobby, with royalty, such as Princess Victoria of Schleswig-Holstein, owning many cats, and the Prince of Wales, later Edward VII, visiting cat shows.

Large catteries were started, often owned by the nobility of those days, including Lady Decies, Lady Marcus Beresford, the Hon. Mrs McLaren Morrison, and Sir Claude and Lady Alexander, to mention just a few. Staff was plentiful and cheap. It was the thing to be photographed in your cattery, with your uniformed servants who really looked after the cats standing meekly by. It was appreciated that not only the rich had cats, and special classes for the cats belonging to working men and women appeared in show schedules.

More varieties were recognized, but the cat fancy suffered considerably during the First World War. A very bad outbreak of feline infectious enteritis occurred during the years 1919–21, with a deathrate of over one million cats. In fact, when reading about the early cat shows, time and time again one reads of so-and-so losing so many cats after a show, and how someone else has lost all her kittens because of an outbreak. Feline infectious enteritis is still prevalent today, but at least there are now various vaccines available which will give almost 100 per cent immunity, though some losses still occur after shows. By the 1930s nearly thirty varieties had been recognized and exhibited at the various shows. Pedigree-breeding made wonderful progress until 1939 when, with the commencement of the War, it came almost to a complete stop. Many beautiful cats were put to sleep because of the difficulties of feeding, the evacuation of their owners, or their homes being destroyed through enemy bombing. Naturally, very few people had the time or the money to spare for buying pedigree kittens. This state of affairs put the British cat fancy back many years, and indeed it was the same, sad story throughout the whole of Europe. Fortunately, the United States and Canada were able to carry on.

Many outstanding cats were neutered in Britain, so there were few kittens. One or two valiant breeders struggled on, despite rationing, and it is to people like Miss E. Langston of "Allington" fame, Miss D. Collins with the "Kala" prefix, Mrs J. Paddon with the "Trelystan", Mrs A. Aitken and "Bourneside", and Miss M. Sladen and the famous "Stonor" Manx that the British cat fancy is indebted today, for otherwise there would have been no nucleus stock to start the pedigree cat breeding again. Shows restarted in 1946, with a terrific demand for pedigree kittens. Would-be breeders, with little or no experience of cats, bought all varieties, but many soon gave up when they realized that it is not possible to breed kittens to order, and that a cat needs careful attention and, above all, affection. It has been proved over and over again that cats crave affection; this is probably one of the chief reasons why there are so very few large catteries, as it has been found that they thrive and breed better in smaller units where they get individual attention.

In a very few years Britain began once again to be looked on as the top country for pedigree cats, and a flood of exports followed. Blue Persians bred by Mrs J. Thompson of the "Pensford" prefix and Mrs M. Brunton of the "Dunesk" were, and still are, in much demand. The "Allington" (Miss E. Langston) and the "Bonavia" Chinchillas (Mrs M. Turney) became world-famous, while the "Widdington" Creams of Mrs M. and Miss E. Sheppard have won many championships both

89–90   RED-POINT SIAMESE

91   LILAC-POINT SIAMESE

92-93   LILAC-POINT SIAMESE

94   TORTOISESHELL-POINT SIAMESE

95–96   TABBY-POINT SIAMESE

in this country and abroad. With so many varieties it is not possible to mention more than a few, but in the Siamese world Mrs Duncan Hindley and her "Prestwick" cats have made Siamese of British origin internationally famous.

CATS IN JAPAN

There was once a time in history when cats were worshipped like gods, then alas when they were detested, humiliated, and tortured. But today, according to Mrs Bess Higuchi, a well-known cat fancier in Tokyo, these fragile little felines are doing a marvellous job serving as ambassadors of goodwill, and providing a common interest between the people of Japan and other parts of the world.

Ancient writings indicate that pure white cats were dominant, with a minority of black cats and very few tri-coloured cats. Subsequent to the arrival of cats from Korea and China, cats were imported from South-East Asian countries, and cross-breeding among these brought about the so-called "mike" (pronounced "me-kay"). This word in Japanese means "three colours" and thus was applied to the tri-coloured cats. These tri-coloured cats are regarded as lucky, and particularly a tri-coloured tom cat, which is extremely unusual. They are especially worshipped by fishermen, who take them on their voyages, believing that they will help prevent accidents and bring them good luck while at sea. In some parts of the Western world a black cat is considered unlucky, while in Japan black cats are considered good luck charms, and they are also believed to cure various diseases.

The native cats have very short tails, many Japanese not liking cats with long tails, believing that they will take a human form and bewitch people. Cats are also the subjects of Ukiyo painting, a particular Japanese style of painting, which normally portrays only beautiful women and classical Kabuki actors. They also appear in legends and classic novels.

Then there is the charm cat known as the "Maneki-Neko", meaning "beckoning cat". This is a tri-coloured cat figurine sitting in an upright position with the left paw raised up to his ears and beckoning as if to welcome your appearance. This beckoning cat is usually seen in shops and, particularly, in restaurants and other places serving food. It comes from the superstition and popular tradition that with the beckoning of a cat comes the beckoning of prosperity.

With the advent of economic stability and abundance of leisure in Japan today, the Japanese are turning to pedigree animals as pets to occupy their leisure, for companionship, and as a fascinating hobby to breed from and to exhibit at shows.

CATS IN THE NETHERLANDS

Notwithstanding the fact that the official cat fancy in the Netherlands is only thirty-five years old, cats of particular breeds have been kept and bred since the early years of this century. This does not refer to the "ordinary" European Shorthair, of course, because these have multiplied themselves without any human interference and this can hardly be called breeding.

In the years 1900–20 long-haired cats, which were called "Angoras" in those days, were few in number, and the two Orange-eyed White Longhairs, whose favourite seat was in the window of a schoolmaster's house in the centre of Rotterdam, were for the passers-by merely a symptom of extravagance. This was in 1910, a year in which the pedigree cat was the exception rather than the rule.

Apart from the long-haired Angoras, Siamese were occasionally seen. Although not traceable in the official records cat fanciers remember having seen as many as ten to twenty Siamese cats at an exhibition in Rotterdam in 1914. It was, however, not until 1920–30 that one could speak of a developing cat fancy. Cat breeders showed their cats in poultry and rabbit shows, and they travelled with their cats to Antwerp. It was here from 1920 onwards that cat shows were organized at regular intervals by Les Amis du Chat, founded in 1917, the first cat club on the continent of Europe. The Dutch cat breeders did not yet have an organization of their own, but there was an exchange of pedigrees with the Belgian club. The showing of cats in Holland continued, and about thirty cats, the majority of which were Longhairs, were shown at the exhibition of the Rotterdam Poultry and Rabbit Association in 1928. The judge was Mr R. Hagedoorn, who bred Longhairs and kept a hundred or more in his house in Scheveningen. Hagedoorn was one of the promoters of the Dutch cat fancy, a man who also taught the exhibitors what to look for in a good specimen, and who explained the faults of the cats. There were only one or two Siamese breeders at that time and it is remarkable to note that no European Shorthairs were shown. It was not until thirty years later that, reluctantly, specimens of this breed were admitted to the show hall.

After the cat fancy had flourished to some extent for a dozen or so years, the first cat club, the Dutch Association of Cat Breeders and Cat-lovers Felikat, was founded in 1934, and the first international championship show was held on December 16th of that year in Haarlem. Here the well-known English judge Miss E. Langston officiated. There were over a hundred cats, again mostly Longhairs, now called Persians, and some Siamese, and at that time a cat obtained his championship on one single show. The first Siamese champion was a cat called "Ossiamo of Bordeaux", imported from France.

Felikat founded its own stud-book in which, during the years 1934–40, over seven hundred cats were registered. The majority were Persians and included the following varieties: Black, Blue, Cream, Tortoiseshell, Blue-Cream, Chinchilla, Silver, Brown and Silver Tabby, Smoke, and White. Even odd-eyed cats were registered and judged as such!

The Seal-point Siamese were the minority, and they were registered either as "long-tailed", or as "kink-tailed" or "short-tailed". The long-tailed affix was probably due to the introduction of imported Siamese of better type than the hitherto-bred "old-fashioned" type of Siamese. Although the Persian cats were of outstanding quality, the Siamese were rather poor in type compared with today's standard. It is remarkable that the Dutch cat fancy during the first twenty years of its official existence was only really made possible by the longhair breeders, and a pedigree cat was nearly always supposed to be an Angora, or later Persian. It was not until the late fifties that the breeding of short-haired cats was given a new impetus.

The Second World War interrupted the activities of Felikat, as the German occupants showed a vivid interest in the properties of so called "non-commercial organizations".

After the War the Dutch cat breeders had to start again, as only relatively few good pedigree cats had survived the years of food shortage and of starvation. The first post-War exhibition was held in 1947, and in the years after that the cat fancy began to flourish again. The quality of the Persian cats was high. Excellent Blues were seen in relatively large classes. One of the specialities of the Dutch cat fancy became the breeding of Blacks and Smokes.

A very high standard was developed in the Chinchillas, partly due to some excellent imports from Britain. An example of a Chinchilla cat that year after year became "Best in Show" Longhair was International Champion "Jolyon of Allington", a male that contributed much towards the high quality of the Chinchillas for which the Netherlands was famous on the continent of Europe.

About five years ago the Chinchilla breed in the Netherlands was enhanced by the import of some excellent cats from the United States. They and their descendants often 'steal' the European shows and many champions have been bred from them.

As mentioned above, many excellent Blue Persians have been bred and shown and a number of them are worthwhile mentioning, but space does not permit. An exception must be made, however, for one of the very best Blues ever seen in European shows—International Champion

122

"Bentveld Pagliaccio". He was a dream: big, round, copper eyes, a really even blue coat, and of a type nearly better than the standard, if that were possible. This magnificent cat was "Best in Show" on many occasions, and not only as a young male!

All other colours in long-haired cats have been bred and shown in the Netherlands. The first Colourpoint owned by a Dutch breeder was introduced on the Dutch show bench in 1961. This breed has rapidly gained popularity and is now seen at every show.

A typically French breeding product is the Sacred Cat of Burma, a long-haired cat with Siamese markings and four white feet. This cat is occasionally bred in the Netherlands and some specimens are shown from time to time.

After 1945 it was the Seal-point Siamese that gained in popularity. Was it the blue eyes, or the kink, or even the knot in its tail that made the Siamese a somewhat mysterious but attractive cat? As compared to the standard the Siamese cats on the show bench were not of top quality in the first years after the War. Imports from Britain during the years 1950–57 improved the breed, and mention must be made here of International Champion "Lancy King Khan".

As has been said before, the Longhairs have long been the most popular pedigree cats, and up till 1960 amounted to over 70 per cent of the entries at Dutch cat shows, while the Seal-point Siamese was second with some 20 per cent. This scene, however, has changed completely since then.

In 1960 some enthusiastic Shorthair breeders imported not only top quality Siamese but also other foreign breeds: Abyssinians, Havanas (Chestnut Browns), Burmese, and so on, thus extending the variety and breeding possibilities of the Shorthair cat.

These imports were also indirectly a stimulus to experimental breeding: already by 1962 Tabby-point Siamese were bred, and nowadays Foreign Whites of high standard are bred and shown.

The Abyssinians are extremely popular, and both the normal and the red variety have been bred in great numbers. Their quality in general is excellent and Dutch-bred champions are to be seen in shows all over Europe.

The Havanas, or Chestnut Browns as they are sometimes called, are of outstanding quality, thanks to the English imports in the years 1962–63. The Burmese, both brown and blue, are increasing, while the Russian Blue, of which a Dutch strain has existed since 1959, is developing very well.

The most popular Shorthair is still the Siamese, now as Seal-points, Blue-points, Chocolate-points, Lilac-points, Tabby-points, Tortie-points, Red-points, and even Cream-points and Blue-Cream points! They are shown in great numbers and in big classes, amounting now to 30 to 35 per cent of the exhibits.

Of the newer breeds like the Rex and the Bi-coloured cats, a number of specimens are being kept and are now being bred from.

The Manx appeared at shows in 1964 but are few in number, although an almost perfect red-and-white male, International Champion "Red Robber Knight", has done well at European shows. The European Shorthair, popular as a pet in the Netherlands, has never received much interest from breeders. A few people are breeding them, but on the whole they are still looked on as "just an ordinary cat". A magnificent orange-eyed white alley-cat of unknown ancestry made history a few years ago by winning his championship at three successive exhibitions, in one of which he became "Best in Show". Nevertheless, the European Shorthair does not seem to have a future as a pedigree cat.

As outlined above, the interest in pedigree cats in the Netherlands has increased tremendously in recent years. In 1962 a second cat club, the Dutch Society of Cat Friends, and in 1966 a third, the Dutch Association of Cat Breeders, were formed.

The total number of cats registered since 1934 is now well over ten thousand, the rate at this moment being approximately two thousand a year. The interest in the pedigree cat is greater in the Netherlands than ever before, and this can, to a great extent, be attributed to that country's superb champion cats.

THE CAT FANCY IN SCANDINAVIA

The first cats are said to have arrived in Scandinavia about A.D. 1000, and they have always been very much connected with folk lore and early legends.

In spite of the many tales concerning cats, interest in pedigree ones had a very slow start. This was possibly due to the fact that cats cannot live outside in Norway and Sweden because of the very cold winters, with temperatures of $-15°C$ to $-30°C$, with the earth frozen and more than eight feet of snow. The majority of pedigree cats live in houses as pets, with perhaps one room set aside for them. Under these circumstances it is very difficult to keep a full male, and so there are very few stud cats. For this reason, Denmark with its milder winter has more catteries.

Pedigree cats were imported from England, with the first cat shows being held in the late 1920s. The first cat club formed was the Dansk Race Katte Klub in 1931. Others followed, all being associated with the Fédération Internationale Féline d'Europe. The Kattevennes Klubb started in Norway in 1934, and there are now three clubs associated with FIFE. There are also the independent clubs, the Norwegian Rasekattclubben and the Drammen Rasekattclubb. In 1946 the first Swedish cat club was started under the auspices of FIFE, and there are now several others, in addition to the independent Sveriges Nye Raskattklubb and the Gastriklands nya Raskattclubb. All the cat clubs are flourishing, and the number of cat shows held are increasing annually.

In Finland the Suomen Rotukissayhoistys r.y. (Surok), founded over ten years ago, holds well-attended shows under the jurisdiction of FIFE. Shorthairs are popular, the Brown Tabbies and Abyssinians being very good, while Chocolate-point and Lilac-point Siamese are excellent. A well-known and beautiful Lilac-point is International Champion "Ronnvikens Frosted Candy", the first one actually bred in Scandinavia. Colourpoints, Chinchillas, and Blue and Silver Tabby Longhairs are also of an extremely high standard.

CHAMPION CATS OF SWITZERLAND

Switzerland began relatively late with the breeding of pedigree cats. Shortly before 1930 there were a few breeders, mostly in the French part of Switzerland. They had been encouraged to take up this interesting hobby by the French, who had already been breeding pedigree cats for some time.

The first international exhibition took place in Geneva in 1933, and many German-speaking Swiss came to admire these magnificent creatures, most of which were Longhairs. It was a great success, and acted as a stimulus to the formation of an association in Zürich, in German-speaking Switzerland, called the Verein der Zürcher Katzenliebhaber (Association of the Cat-lovers of Zürich).

A year later the association organized a show in Zürich where a number of extremely dark Red Tabbies from Germany were exhibited, including Champion "Astor Aki von Brosame". There was also Champion "Mick of Bredon", a Cream male imported from England. These were the only champions in Switzerland at that time.

There was little interest shown in Siamese, but Persians were very popular, and various cat fanciers imported cats from abroad—for example, from France or Germany. But the serious breeders knew that if they wanted to buy really good stock, England was the only possible source. Cat breeding originated there and has been thoroughly developed over a hundred years. Their winners faced a lot of competition and were therefore select cats, purely bred through many generations and producing good pedigree kittens. From this crop of the best-bred animals the Swiss now tried to buy up material for future breeding.

There are five cat clubs in Switzerland, affiliated to the FIFE (Fédération Internationale Féline d'Europe) and abiding by the rules of the English Governing Council of the Cat Fancy. These are the Cat Club Vaudois of Lausanne; Verein der Katzenfreunde Zürich (Zürich Association of Cat-lovers); Der Katzen- und Edelkatzenklub Bern (Berne Cat and Pedigree-cat Club); Gesellschaft der Katzenfreunde Luzern (Lucerne Society of Cat-lovers); and Societé Suisse du Chat Persan et Siamois (Swiss Society of the Persian and Siamese Cat), which was founded last. Founded by Frau G. Bridgett, it is the only specialist club, and covers the whole of Switzerland. The Cat Club Vaudois was founded by Fräulein Perrin, and was very active before the War, organizing many international exhibitions.

We now come to the pioneers of the pre-War period. By far the most successful breeder at that time was Fräulein Perrin of Lausanne. She specialized in White Persians with blue and orange eyes, and bred, owned, and exhibited a number of champions. Her Blue-eyed Whites were outstanding in that they were just as good a type as the Orange-eyed Whites, and the blue of the eyes was a deep sapphire blue. The name of her cattery was "du Léman". Herr Gruber of the "de Sabba" cattery was breeding in Berne.

In Zürich there was the cattery "du Château de Goldbach", which belonged to Frau Professor Bürgin. Herr Gruber and Frau Bürgin were mainly interested in Chinchillas at the time, and Frau Bürgin's English import of this variety was "Dreamland Kathi". She was not a champion, for there were very few exhibitions in Switzerland and scarcely anybody travelled abroad. It was for this reason that there was scarcely a cat with one or more challenge certificates. The winners were mostly English imports or the offspring of these imports.

During the War there were no exhibitions. Of great importance to the Swiss cat fancy was the fact that Frau L. Gibbons and her sister Frau G. Bridgett left France in 1941 in order to take up residence in Switzerland, which was free from war. They chose to live in Lausanne and brought with them all their wonderful cats, which, being then of a unique type, helped to make Swiss breeding better. Every breeder counted himself lucky if he got the chance to have his queen mated with their famous studs, and there were soon offspring from "Farquhars", the name of Frau Gibbons's cattery, and from "de Valescure", Frau Bridgett's cattery.

With the end of the War several new breeders started, including Frau Pia Hollenstein-Mertens who began to breed in German-speaking Switzerland, specializing in cream-coloured Persians. The name of her cattery is "de la Viamala", which was entered in the breeding record book as early as 1933. She imported good Creams from England. The first male was International Champion "Glenfield Pius Peterkin". His grandmother, Champion "Parkwood Nerika", came from England later, and from these cats Frau Hollenstein produced a number of international champions.

The Hon. Mrs M. Haden-Guest came to Switzerland somewhat later after the War and lived near Geneva, and is now considered to be the best Chinchilla breeder there. The name of her cattery is "Snowdrift". She imported some English Chinchillas "von den Bonavias", bred by Mrs Turney, one tom being a magnificent champion called International Champion "Bonavia Hanniball".

Another Chinchilla lover is Frau Kuster. She also imported all her winners from England, one of the best of which was International Champion "Laurus of Allington", son of the famous English champion "Fidelio of Allington". One of his daughters, bred by Mrs E. Polden and owned by Frau Kuster, is International Champion "Poldenhills Lady Ingrid".

Switzerland now has many long-haired champions, all varieties being included, mostly descended from English stock.

There may be comparatively few pedigree cats in Switzerland, but the quality is high and successes at European shows have been considerable.

PEDIGREE CATS IN THE
UNITED STATES OF AMERICA

As in Britain the real interest in pedigree or fancy cats began with a cat show. This was held in Madison Square Garden in May 1895 and, organized by Mr J. T. Hyde, an Englishman, attracted an entry of 176 cats by 125 exhibitors. Mr Hyde had visited the Crystal Palace Show in London and surmised correctly that such a show would prove a major attraction in New York. There had been a few private shows held before this, but the Garden Show was the first to make an impact on the general public. The "Best Cat in Show" was a Brown Tabby, named "Cosie", owned by Mrs E. Barker. More shows followed, and Brown Tabbies appeared to have been very popular, as one, "Kind Humbert", imported from England, was "Best in Show" several times. A show held in Chicago in 1899 resulted in the formation of the Chicago Cat Club. This had a very short life, as the Beresford Cat Club formed shortly afterwards soon put the original club out of existence.

The Beresford Cat Club was named in honour of Lady Marcus Beresford, the founder of the Cat Club in England and a leading English breeder. In 1900 this club organized the first of its many championship shows. The entries included Longhairs of all colours, and Shorthairs, including Siamese, Manx, and Russian cats. An English import, "Lockehaven Smerdis", bred by Mrs Trumper and owned by Mrs Clinton Locke was "Best in Show". Mrs Clinton Locke, the first president of the Beresford Cat Club, also had the distinction of being the first woman in the United States to run a cattery, and this was many years before the club was founded.

The Beresford Cat Club began keeping a register and stud-book in 1900. The club ceased being the governing body with the formation of the American Cat Association in 1906.

The club continued to hold shows and in 1908 Mr L. Wain, president of the National Cat Club in England and the well-known cat cartoon artist, was invited to judge in Chicago. Most unexpectedly, and to the surprise of the American breeders, he made his best cat a Siamese Seal-point female, "Lockehaven Elsa". This gave the variety a big boost, which was probably the beginning of the popularity still enjoyed by the Siamese today.

1908 saw arguments starting regarding some of the rules laid down by the American Cat Association. This resulted in the formation of the Cat Fanciers' Association, Inc., which has now become the largest registering body of cats in the world, with nearly three hundred clubs in America, Hawaii, Japan, and even Alaska. In 1967 alone twenty thousand cats were registered at its central office.

In addition to the Cat Fanciers' Association there are at least six other associations with their own registrars and stud-books—The American Cat Association, Inc.; The American Cat Fanciers' Association; Cat Fanciers' Federation, Inc.; Crown Cat Fanciers' Federation; National Cat Fanciers' Association, Inc.; and the United Cat Federation, Inc. They are all associated with clubs holding very many shows each year.

The United States have far more pedigree cats than any other country in the world, with many of their outstanding prize-winning strains having British stock in their pedigrees. Until comparatively recently the long-haired cats outnumbered all other varieties, but now the Shorthairs are ahead. This is not due, as one might think, to the increasing numbers of Siamese, but to more breeders taking up Abyssinians and Brown Burmese.

Now to mention just a little about some of the breeds. The Siamese are numerous and very elegant. There was the outstanding Grand Champion "Makanda Matil" and many other champions bearing the same prefix, while the winning, very typy Blue-point male, Grand Champion "Ko-Ling Symetry", is a grandson of an English import, Champion "Roseway Cinderella".

The Burmese cat, which was developed in America and exported to Britain, is still a very strong contender at all shows. Most American Burmese of any quality are descended in some way from the "Mizpah" line, which is a high tribute. Grand Champion "Mizpah Trotskoy of G(Len)n" and Grand Champion "Shawnee Cases Jones" are said to be two of the most lovable of Shorthair studs, while a top winning female is Grand Champion "Hillhouse Daniella of Shawnee".

While the Manx is enjoying a small revival in Britain, the numbers are increasing even more in the United States. The Black male, Grand Champion "Tra-Mar Sunny", the Brown Tabby, Champion "Truantail Christopher", his son, Grand Champion "Brier Brae Maxie", and the ageless White Grand Champion "Wila-Blite Pola of Silva-Wyte" are all outstanding winners of this variety.

One of the most delightful Abyssinians ever seen was the late Grand Champion "Pharoh Rameses II". His brilliant colouring and flawless ticking won him the supreme award of "1966 Cat of the Year". The Grand Champion female "Chota-Li Russet" was another outstanding Abyssinian, and her prize-winning qualities have been passed on to her daughter, Grand Champion "Chota-Li Flair".

The Rex cats are increasing rapidly, with two females, the Grand Champion "Hi-Fi's Hedwig of Katzenreich", a Tortoiseshell, and Grand Champion "Rodell's Ravenesque", a Black, being so good that it is difficult to believe that they will ever be bettered.

The well-known breeder, the late Miss E. Hydon, often said that her Champion "Lavender Chu Chu", an imported Blue Longhair son of the English Champion "Mischief of Bredon", was the most exciting cat she had ever purchased and that everything good in the American long-haired cats could be traced back to him. From that strain came the outstanding Blue Persians, Grand Champion "Lavender Liberty" and his son, Grand Champion "Lavender Liberty Beau", the "1950 Cat of the Year". "Lavender Liberty Beau" sired a Black son that eventually became world-famous and one of the greatest sires of all time, the Grand Champion "Vel-Vene Voo Doo of Silva-Wyte", the "1959 Cat of the Year". "Voo Doo" was renowned for his almost-perfect type and brilliant eye colour. He was bred by Mr and Mrs R. Green of New Jersey and owned by Mr R. Gebhardt, the well-known international judge and president of the Cat Fanciers' Association. He sired many Champions, Grand Champions, and International Champions, and was responsible for two very beautiful Blacks, Grand Champion "Silva-Wyte Jack-A-Napes of J.B." and his sister, Grand Champion "Silva-Wyte Trafari of J.B.", owned by Mr J. Bannon.

The female, "Trafari", set a new record by winning forty "Best in Shows" in one season. Both "Trafari" and "Jack-a-Napes" have been responsible for many "Best in Show" winners and Grand Champions. An interesting note is that this line of cats goes back to the oldest recorded Blue Persians in England.

One of the greatest show cats of all time in the United States was the orange-eyed White male, Grand Champion "Shawnee Moonflight". He was three times winner of the "Cat of the Year" award, and his early death was a great loss to the cat fancy. Another outstanding White is Grand Champion "Azulita Paleface of Caca Cielo", "1963 Cat of the Year". Other noted Longhairs are the Blue-eyed White Grand Champion "Gallahad Heritage", Grand Champion "Longhills Red Treasure", Grand Champion "Longhills Michael", and his son, Champion "Longhills Michaelangelo", outstanding Creams.

The phenomenal rise in the number of cats in the United States is said to be responsible for a many-million-dollar turnover, with large sums being paid for the cats themselves, for cat food, registrations, transfer, vets' bills, cat boxes, toys, and many other such items, making cats and their owners play a very important part in the country's finances.

CATS ILLUSTRATED AND THEIR OWNERS

1 **Orange-eyed White Longhair.** Ch. J. B. Van Cleef of Silva-Wyte
  (*Mr Richard Gebhardt, U.S.A*)
2 **Orange-eyed White Longhair.** Ch. Snowhite Herald
  (*Mrs J. Hogan, England*)
3 **Blue-eyed White Longhair.** Ch. Nantom's Nymph
  (*Mrs B. Wyant, England*)
4 **Orange-eyed White Longhair.** Ch. Coylum Marcus
  (*Miss E. Sellar, England*)
5 **Orange-eyed White Longhair.** Gr. Ch. Romeo Van Hoog Moersbergen
  (*Mme Maien Svenningsen, Norway*)
6 **Black Longhair.** Gr. Ch. Silva-Wyte Trafari (*Mr John Bannon, U.S.A.*)
7 **Black Longhair.** Ch. Deebank Cassius (*Mrs M. Tapp, England*)
8 **Odd-eyed White Longhair.** Gr. Ch. J. B. Showpiece of Jo-Ni
  (*Mr John Philpot, U.S.A.*)
9 **Blue Longhair.** Ch. Orion of Pensford (*Mrs E. Burrows, England*)
10 **Blue Longhair.** Ch. Sugardaddy of Dunesk (*Mrs M. Brunton, England*)
11 **Blue Longhair.** Int. Ch. Whopee of Great Yarmouth
  (*Mrs Edel Ringsted, Denmark*)
12 **Red Self Longhair.** Ch. Pathfinders Rose Red
  (*Miss N. Woodifield, England*)
13 **Red Tabby Longhair.** Ch. Comari Clover
  (*Miss Diana M. Vine, England*)
14 **Cream Longhair.** Ch. Startops Sans Souci (*Mrs D. M. King, England*)
15 **Blue-Cream Longhair.** Ch. Opal of Pensford
  (*Mrs J. Thompson, England*)
16 **Smoke Longhair.** Ch. Hardendale Nicholas (*Mrs E. D. Hoyle, England*)
17 **Cream Longhair.** Ch. Wildfell Ploughboy (*Mrs E. Tillotson, England*)
18 **Brown Tabby Longhair.** Ch. Karnak Brochfael
  (*Mr R. Chapman, England*)
19 **Brown Tabby Longhair.** Ch. Trelystan Spinel (*Mrs J. Paddon, England*)
20 **Shaded Silver Longhair.** Gr. Ch. Kitza's Silverlove of Summerset
  (*Mrs James B. Lovelace Jr., U.S.A.*)
21 **Silver Tabby Longhair.** Ch. Dorstan Darius
  (*Mrs M. Greenwood, England*)
22 **Tortoiseshell Longhair.** Ch. Bamboo Betula, Ch. Chadhurst June Melody
  (*Mr & Mrs G. R. Britton, England*)
23 **Tortoiseshell Longhair.** Ch. Comari Persian Garden
  (*Mrs M. Robinson, England*)
24 **Tortoiseshell and White Longhair.** Ch. Pathfinders Posy
  (*Miss N. Woodifield, England*)
25 **Chinchilla.** Ch. Bonavia Bella Maria (*Mrs M. Turney, England*)
26 **Chinchilla.** Ch. Shengo Eleiza (*Mrs Aase Nissen, Denmark*)
27 **Chinchilla.** Ch. Bonavia Bella Maria (*Mrs M. Turney, England*)
28 **Bi-coloured Longhair.** Ch. Pathfinders Goldstrike
  (*Miss N. Woodifield, England*)
29 **Blue-pointed and Seal-pointed Colourpoint (Himalayan).** Copplestone
  Maria, Ch. XOX Betula (*Mrs Y. Bentinck, England*)
30 **Blue-pointed Colourpoint (Himalayan).** Ch. Mingchiu Ghunti
  (*Mrs S. Harding, England*)
31 **Blue-pointed Colourpoint (Himalayan).** Ch. Int. Natty des Grandes
  Chapelles (*Mme Robert Delbushaye, Belgium*)
32 **Tortoiseshell-pointed Colourpoint (Himalayan).** Ch. Sheba Van't
  Spinnershonck (*Mrs H. M. Prosé, Holland*)
33 **Seal-pointed Colourpoint (Himalayan).** Ch. Niobe Shere Khan
  (*Mrs Joan Hann, England*)
34 **Turkish.** Ch. Van Alanya (*Miss Laura Lushington, England*)
35 **Shaded Cameo.** Barrose Honey Bear
  (*Mr & Mrs G. R. Britton and Mrs B. D. Ellis, England*)
36 **Blue-pointed Birman.** Ch. Osaka de Lugh (*Mrs Elsie Fisher, England*)
37 **Seal-pointed Birman.** Ch. Int. Sinh-Francis de Mun-Hâ
  (*Mme & M.J. L. Chauvelon de Pindray, France*)
38 **Seal-pointed Birman.** Ch. Praha Shawnee (*Mrs Elsie Fisher, England*)
39 **Shell Cameo.** Gr. Ch. Dorker Clown Princess of Minuet. Photographed by
  Victor Baldwin of 'Cat Fancy Magazine'
  (*Mrs Charles O. Talley Jr. and Lark, U.S.A.*)
40 **Black Shorthair.** Int. Ch. Sweet Sue de Rocawini
  (*Miss E. M. Zegers, Holland*)
41 **Black Shorthair.** Ch. Jezreel Mosstyn (*Mr R. A. Pearson, England*)
42 **Blue-eyed White Shorthair.** Ch. Heartsease White Heather
  (*Mrs E. Wethered, England*)
43 **Orange-eyed White Shorthair.** Ch. Dellswood Saint
  (*Mrs C. Betts, England*)
44 **Blue-Cream Shorthair.** Ch. Pensylva Fantasia (*Mrs J. Richards, England*)
45 **British Blue.** Int. Ch. Kabbarps Belli (*Miss M. Ahrent, Sweden*)
46 **British Blue.** Ch. Jezreel Jomo (*Mrs I. Johnson, England*)
47 **Cream Shorthair.** Ch. Pensylva Flaxen Nymph
  (*Mrs J. Richards, England*)

48 **British Blue.** Ch. Pensylva Mirus (*Mrs J. Richards, England*)
49 **Brown Tabby Shorthair.** Ch. Brynbuboo Brown Peter
  (*Mrs P. Absalom, England*)
50 **Brown Tabby Shorthair.** Ch. Swedish Freydis of Kandahar
  (*Miss Katrine Liaaen, Norway*)
51 **Silver Tabby American Shorthair.** Gr. Ch. Shawnee Blood Brother of
  Jo-Ni (*Mr John Philpot, U.S.A.*)
52 **Silver Tabby Shorthair.** Ch. Lowenhaus Fingal
  (*Mr R. A. Pearson, England*)
53 **Red Tabby Shorthair.** Peerless Red Glint (*Mr Norman Winder, England*)
54 **Red Tabby Shorthair.** Int. Ch. Tommy de Rocawini
  (*Mr Joop Noppen, Holland*)
55 **Tortoiseshell and White Shorthair.** Ch. Pathfinders Rachel
  (*Miss N. Woodifield, England*)
56 **Tortoiseshell Shorthair.** Ch. Kita's Dandelion
  (*Mrs J. Southerland, England*)
57 **Manx.** Int. Ch. Red Robber Knight (*Mr & Mrs A. Damsteeg, Holland*)
58 **Manx.** Ch. Rosental Dishy Dolly (*Mrs C. S. Colville, England*)
59 **Spotted.** Ch. Lowenhaus Ferragus (*Mr R. A. Pearson, England*)
60 **Chartreux.** Ch. Int. Pussy Prince (*Mme L. Letheux, France*)
61 **Spotted.** Ch. Culverden Charlotte and kitten (*Mrs J. Higgins, England*)
62 **Chartreux.** Ch. Int. Puylévêque D'Andeyola (*M. J. Durodié, France*)
63 **Bi-coloured Shorthair.** Ch. Pathfinders Barry
  (*Miss N. Woodifield, England*)
64 **Chinchilla American Shorthair.** Ch. Brandywoods Chinchilita. Photographed by Victor Baldwin of 'Cat Fancy Magazine'
  (*Mrs Ann Kimball, U.S.A.*)
65 **Abyssinian.** Ch. Taishun Leo (*Mrs E. Menezes, England*)
66 **Abyssinian.** Int. Ch. Parkans Tiy (*Helen and Carl Fr. Nordane, Norway*)
67 **Abyssinian.** Gr. Ch. Chota-Li Flair, Chota-Li Rustelle, Gr. Ch. Chota-Li
  Russet (*Mrs Edna Field, Canada*)
68 **Abyssinian.** Int. Ch. Cenicienta van Mariëndaal
  (*Mrs Ans van der Sluys, Holland*)
69 **Red Abyssinian.** Int. Ch. Dockaheems Caresse
  (*Mrs Ans van der Sluys, Holland*)
70 **Russian Blue.** Int. Ch. Dasja Lefine (*Mr Eskild Hejnsen, Denmark*)
71 **Russian Blue.** Ch. Hengist Stroganoff (*Mrs Natasha Fiske, England*)
72 **Russian Blue.** Ch. Int. Leila de Fleurville (*M. J. Durodié, France*)
73 **Brown (Sable) Burmese.** Gr. Ch. Shawnee Casey Jones of Phi Line
  (*Dr Roger W. Sanftner, U.S.A.*)
74 **Blue Burmese.** Ch. Bahkta Pilot (*Miss E. M. J. Jameson, England*)
75 **Brown (Sable) Burmese.** Gr. Ch. Kittrick's Gung Ho of Silkwood
  (*Mrs Sally Bray, Canada*)
76 **Brown (Sable) Burmese.** Ch. Silkeborg's Clarissa
  (*Mr Milo Wilhelmsen, Norway*)
77 **Havana.** Ch. Dandycat Hula Dancer (*Mrs A. Sayer, England*)
78 **Havana.** Ch. Int. Janosz von Asindia (*Mrs Barbara Eleveld, Holland*)
79 **Devon Rex.** Ch. Annelida Icicle (*Mrs A. E. Ashford, England*)
80 **Cornish Rex.** Ch. Cavalien Sugar Tong (*Mr Milo Wilhelmsen, Norway*)
81 **Cornish Rex.** Ch. Lohteyn Golden Peach (*Mrs L. Heath, England*)
82 **Korat.** Dbl. Ch. Cedar Glen's Sipha of Brandywood. Photographed by Victor
  Baldwin of 'Cat Fancy Magazine' (*Mr & Mrs Dennis L. Wood, U.S.A.*)
83 **Seal-point Siamese.** Ch. Thaumasia Amethyst
  (*Mrs M. Hudson, England*)
84 **Seal-point Siamese.** Int. Ch. Brämhult Mycing
  (*Mrs Maj-Britt Ericsson, Sweden*)
85 **Blue-point Siamese.** Int. Ch. Rangoon Blue Zia
  (*Mrs Edith Dunvald, Denmark*)
86 **Chocolate-point Siamese.** Ch. Reoky Shim-Wah and kitten
  (*Mr & Mrs R. A. Burgess, England*)
87 **Blue-point Siamese.** Int. Ch. Selena van Siana
  (*Mrs M. R. Kuipers-Kossen, Holland*)
88 **Blue-point Siamese.** Gr. Ch. Koh-Ling Symmetry
  (*Mrs Raymond Kohl, U.S.A.*)
89 **Red-point Siamese.** Ch. Pitapat Shane (*Mrs A. Sayer, England*)
90 **Red-point Siamese.** Ch. Shere-Khan-Redfa du Fond'Roy
  (*Mlle M. Valentyn, Belgium*)
91 **Lilac-point Siamese.** Int. Ch. Lilac Guy Van Siana
  (*Mrs M. R. Kuipers-Kossen, Holland*)
92 **Lilac-point Siamese.** Int. Ch. Salween Blue's Lilac Flossy and kitten
  (*Mme Maien Svenningsen, Norway*)
93 **Lilac-point Siamese.** Ch. Pi-Den Zeus (*Mrs Julie Farley, England*)
94 **Tortoiseshell-point Siamese.** Ch. Rivendell Apache
  (*Mrs D. Deakin, England*)
95 **Tabby-Point Siamese.** Ch. Reoky Jnala (*Mrs A. Sayer, England*)
96 **Tabby-point Siamese.** Ch. Senty-Twix Frangipani
  (*Mrs D. Deakin, England*)

128